NARRATIVE CON/TEXTS IN *ULYSSES*

Narrative Con/Texts in *Ulysses*

BERNARD BENSTOCK

University of Illinois Press
Urbana and Chicago

© 1991 by Bernard Benstock

Printed in Hong Kong

C 5 4 3 2 1

Library of Congress Cataloging-in-Publication Data
Benstock, Bernard.
   Narrative con/texts in *Ulysses* / Bernard Benstock.
      p.   cm.
   Includes bibliographical references.
   ISBN 0–252–01773–0
   1. Joyce, James, 1882–1941. *Ulysses*.   2. Joyce, James, 1882–1941 —
—Technique.   3. Narration (Rhetoric)
PR6019.09U6255   1991
823′.912 — dc20   90–36458
                                                                    CIP

To Shari

silent partner
secret collaborator
staunch critic
stalwart supporter
specially adored

and with gratitude to
Belinda Ghitis and Zack Bowen

Contents

Acknowledgements

Earlier versions of parts of the following chapters have appeared in *Modern British Literature*, the *James Joyce Quarterly*, the *Journal of Narrative Technique*, *Rivista di Letteratura Moderne e Comparate* and *Les Cahiers de l'Herne*, as well as chapters in *Work in Progress: Joyce Centenary Essays* (Southern Illinois University Press), *Genèse et Métamorphoses du Texte Joycien* (Publications de la Sorbonne), *James Joyce: An International Perspective* (Colin Smythe/Barnes and Noble), and *International Perspectives on James Joyce* (Whitson).

The author and publishers wish to thank the Executors of the James Joyce Estate and The Bodley Head, for permission to reproduce the extracts from the works of James Joyce.

A Note on the Text

The edition cited in the text is the 1986 *Ulysses*, which is commercially available in the United States and Great Britain (published by Random House in New York, and The Bodley Head in London). Designations are by chapter and inclusive line numbers. The chapters are indicated as follows:

Te	Telemachus (1)
Ne	Nestor (2)
Pr	Proteus (3)
Ca	Calypso (4)
Lo	Lotus Eaters (5)
Ha	Hades (6)
Ae	Aeolus (7)
Le	Lestrygonians (8)
SC	Scylla and Charybdis (9)
WR	Wandering Rocks (10)
Si	Sirens (11)
Cy	Cyclops (12)
Na	Nausicaa (13)
OS	Oxen of the Sun (14)
Ci	Circe (15)
Eu	Eumaeus (16)
It	Ithaca (17)
Pe	Penelope (18)

Other works by Joyce cited in the text include *Finnegans Wake* (*FW*) (New York: Viking, 1947), cited by page and inclusive line numbers; *Dubliners* (*D*) (New York: Compass, 1967); *A Portrait of the Artist as a Young Man* (*AP*) (New York: Compass, 1964) and *Stephen Hero* (*SH*) (New York: New Directions, 1963).

Introduction: The Nature of its Narrative

Bluntly: all texts and contexts will be thought of here as tending to lose their separate identities, collapsing purposefully into each other and existing rather as what we might call (con)texts.

Valentine Cunningham

Narrative Con/Texts in 'Ulysses' is composed of seven essays written over the past ten years as separate approaches to the ways in which narrative functions in *Ulysses* in relation to the changing contextual situation in that narrative; some of these essays have appeared in earlier forms in journals and as book chapters. They have been rewritten for the purpose of a book-length study but do not constitute a seamless narrative, nor is there a central thesis that constrains the various investigative avenues of approach, and certainly no attempt is made to track the eighteen chapters of *Ulysses* sequentially. Instead, several individual tracks move through the Ulyssean terrain, criss-crossing each other and opening and reopening the possibilities of analysing the narrational methods in operation and co-operation with each other. Various heightened moments and complex knots that intensify the narrative experience in Joyce's *Ulysses* are returned to more than once to re-examine their function and impact from different perspectives.

Anyone in the late 1980s undertaking still another study of *Ulysses* has the advantages and disadvantages of a polypantheon of authorities to contend with, and someone who has been writing on *Ulysses* for several decades has numerous obligations to predecessors and contemporaries, most of them now impossible to acknowledge accurately. Those who only derive their secondary elements from reading Joyce studies may be able to keep a record of what they have gleaned from whom, but those of us who also function within a very active Joycean community have been inundated with ideas and information and attitudes from a complex reservoir. (I once quoted someone who orally mentioned an idea that seemed appropriate for what I was writing, only to be

1

told later that it had itself been transmitted orally by someone else, who may in turn have received it from some other source – the compound nature of Joyce studies is as complex as Joyce's texts themselves.) In *Narrative Con/Texts in 'Ulysses'* I have intended to avoid all contention with those with whom I (within each particular context) happen to disagree, but even that became impossible in the chapter that sets out the matrix for dealing with the catechistical method in 'Ithaca'. None the less, the basic directional thrust of this study is to carve out wherever possible my own lines of critical approach, indicating along the way some of the places at which I am aware that I have been anticipated, and others where a body of conflicting approaches is available. Any attempt at a pristine critical text, endnote-free, had to be abandoned along the way, but the intention remains at the heart of this study of as few distractions from the critical text as possible. The only authority essential for this study is the *Ulysses* text itself.

The non-linear aspect of *Ulysses* invites such circularity of critical method: the repetition of the initial time-frame, the gaps in the hourly sequences, and the simultaneity of occurrences as well as thought and speech and action contend as anti-linear contextualisations with the steady march of the hours through the single-day blueprint. 'Context' as a narrative device usually serves as an agenda for the events of a novel, a programme of action against which the reader tests the accuracy and authenticity of the responses of the characters to those events, and validates thematic determinants from such responses. Where the contexts become multiple and fluid and contradictory, where no clear distinction is allowed to exist between style and content in the narrative strategy, binocular visualisations need to replace the monocular, and perhaps stereocular visualisations where humanly possible would be preferable. Con/Text in *Ulysses* presents a field of play in which such counters as content, conflict, confluence, contradiction and consistency (as well as inconsistency) are constantly operative. Merely attempting to account for the presence of Shakespeare's herbalist in the Ormond, in a contextual arrangement where Shakespeare's representative, Stephen Dedalus, is not present, is sufficient cause for concern over the singular efficacy of the traditional concept of 'context': the inherent contradiction and the patent inconsistency may depend upon a hitherto unacknowledged confluence.

'MOGUPHONOISED BY THAT PHONEMANON'

The developmental process in *Ulysses* can be articulated in terms that exist in the text, terms that are attached to Leopold Bloom and Tom Kernan, and internally held up for derision by their compeers, but none the less are functionally, albeit comically, operative. Certain base lines are established as 'natural phenomena' (*pace* Bloom) that are presented as recollections in transition (Kernan's 'retrospective arrangement') and acquire the stylistic character generated by their context (Kernan's 'trenchant renditions'). Bloom avails himself of six opportunities to assert his belief in natural phenomena, past which he rarely moves: first when explaining the hanged man's erection (Cy 465–6), resulting in caustic commentary from the barfly-narrator; then in his calming explanation for the thunder that Stephen attributes to Blake's 'Nobodaddy . . . in his cups' (OS 419, 428). 'Every phenomenon has a natural cause', Bloom asserts to Bella Cohen's fan, but undercuts that certainty by crediting his downfall to the absence of his potato talisman (Ci 2794–6), soon after declaring to the Nymph that 'Capillary attraction is a natural phenomenon' (Ci 3354–5) – the transformational magic in 'Circe' results in such convoluted rearrangements. In the cabman's shelter he directly opposes the notion of a 'supernatural God' with that of a 'farreaching natural phenomenon such as electricity' (Eu 768–70), inadvertently pointing to the presence of Gerard the herbalist in the Ormond, of whom he remains quite unaware. And finally in his kitchen he credits Milly with admiring the concept of 'a natural phenomenon' when he had explained such matters to her (It 925). Erections and potato preservatives, capillary attractions and telescopes and electricity, these are the raw materials that are contextualised at baselevel in *Ulysses*, although Stephen may be seen as following 'A star by night' or 'A pillar of the cloud by day' instead, what Lister had termed 'celestial phenomenon' for him (SC 942–4).

Retrospective arrangements, on the other hand, rearrange themselves, dependent only on the passing of time and the new context into which they fall. Just as Bloom will become the subject of conversation by Power and Cunningham and Dedalus once he is outside the funeral carriage, so Tom Kernan is their subject although not present in their carriage. He is quoted from the previous evening for applauding a '*trenchant rendering*' of a song, but also quoted from an unspecified time in the past as referring to a *'retrospective arrangement'* (Ha 147–50). True to form Tom Kernan replays the past as he wanders through the historically significant streets of Dublin several hours later, thinking of 1798 as 'Times of the troubles': 'When you look back on it all now in a kind of retrospective arrangement' (WR 781–3). The scene rearranges itself almost immediately for him as he savours the gin he had just drunk and remembers Dollard's singing of *The Croppy Boy* last evening, also rearranging his own *mot juste* to 'Masterly rendition' (WR 792). Once he has entered the Ormond it is inevitable that he will request the same song from the same singer. His entrance is apparently noticed by Bloom from his oblique vantage-point in the restaurant as he plucks a resonating rubber band, 'while Tom Kernan, harking back in a retrospective sort of arrangement talked to listening Father Cowley' (Si 797–9), Bloom having probably absorbed the 'retrospective arrangement' from the funeral carriage. Also true to form Kernan awards Dollard with the familiar praise, 'Most trenchant rendition of that ballad, upon my soul and honour it is' (Si 1148–9).

Recollected in transit, transitionally rearranged, Tom Kernan's phrase becomes the property of Leopold Bloom. When in his memory he rolls back the years to his own youth it is all done with memory-mirrors, 'as in a retrospective arrangement, a mirror within a mirror' (OS 1044), and the Bloom of 'Circe' can invite Josie Breen to rearrange herself back to Josie Powell: 'Do you remember, harking back in a retrospective rearrangement, Old Christmas night' (Ci 442–3), where the games then were 'the Irving Bishop game, finding the pin blindfold and thoughtreading' (Ci 444–5) – mental telepathy and seeing in the dark are important critical methods for the reader of *Ulysses*. Bloom also plays Irish history through his own perspective in the cabman's shelter, where the Parnell narrative oddly mirrors his own marital situation, although he prefers to keep it sufficiently distanced if possible, commenting to himself that 'Looking back now in a retrospective kind of arrangement all seemed a kind of dream' (Eu 1400–1). The presumably objective narrational process in 'Ithaca' falls prey to Bloom's repossessing of Kernan's ridiculed phrase, and Bloom's father's life is recalled as having been 'narrated to his son' as a 'retrospective arrangement of migrations and settlements' (It 1906–7). The natural property of Tom Kernan in spoken language, mocked by his detractors, it is rescued and given a new status in

Bloom's thought process, until it acquires the dignity of its own existence as part of the narrational stance of the text.

As a phrasemaker Kernan seems to know the importance of revitalising his language on occasion, and although 'retrospective arrangement' suffers a decline into common usage and therefore becomes cliché, his 'trenchant rendition' at first allows for variations at his hands – into 'masterly' rendition (but only in his own thoughts). The narrational strategies in 'Cyclops' call for excessive re-renderings, the gigantisms that track the natural phenomena of pub conversations with exaggerated versions from the styles of pre-existing texts. These in turn improve on Kernan's trenchant and masterly, offering an 'admirably rendering' in one instance (Cy 537) and a 'remarkably noteworthy rendering' in another (Cy 915). Trenchancy, however, does not fare as well. It is true that Bloom attempts to rescue it for proper usage when he considers Mrs Bandmann Palmer a 'Trenchant exponent of Shakespeare' (Ci 496–7), speciously as it happens since he is fabricating an experience for the evening that he has not had, but it deteriorates drastically at the hands of Cunty Kate. Kate is obviously enthralled by Stephen's drunken expostulations when she tries to better Biddy the Clap's verdict of 'marked refinement of phraseology' with 'such apposite trenchancy' (Ci 4443–5). That within the natural-phenomenal world of Biddy and Kate no such refinement exists and no such phraseology is validatable renders their dialogue as stylistically rearranged by the Nighttown/nighttime world of Circean narrative, evidence that the narrational possibilities throughout *Ulysses* are dependent on context and are as a consequence self-determining.

Kernan can have no more awareness of the consequences of his utterances once they have left his possession during the course of ordinary conversation than Bloom has of the fate of the Elijah throwaway that he consigned to the tides of the Liffey. Words have their independent existences as they are being transmitted and appropriated, as witness the effects of rumour and gossip during the course of the narrative in *Finnegans Wake*. Recently the word 'love' has been re-introduced into the text of *Ulysses* and has caused a great deal of controversy. The revised edition of 1984 has Stephen challenging himself during the library discussion with the question, 'Do you know what you are talking about? Love, yes. Word known to all men' (SC 429–30), which should satisfy his earlier indecision on Sandymount Strand: 'What is that word known to all men?' (Pr 435). Is it significant that in the earlier instance he is motivated by sexual desire and in the second by an understanding of family affection? Is it also significant that in the brothel he accosts the ghost of his mother with the plea, 'Tell me the word, mother, if you know now. The word known to all men', occasioned by her reference to '*Love's bitter mystery*,' (Ci 4191–2)? Even if the recuperated portion of 'Scylla and Charybdis' was an accidentally lost rather than a discarded entity, the nature of the question has undergone several changes, and each of the two (or three) instances transforms the concept and the context, and therefore the meaning of the word itself.

Stephen can hardly be aware of how unequivocally Leopold Bloom can deal with the 'word known to all men', if that word is actually expected to be the word 'love'. Under pressure from the unloving Citizen he utters the word that he claims 'everybody knows', and even defines it: 'Love. . . . I mean the opposite of hatred' (Cy 1482–5). No sooner has he made his precipitous departure than the word undergoes immediate transformations. The Citizen, oddly enough, is rather accurate in his interpretation of 'Universal love', while sympathetic John Wyse Nolan domesticates it for application to Bloom himself ('Love your neighbour'), while the sneering barfly purposely misrepresents it as amorous love: 'He's a nice pattern of a Romeo and Juliet' (Cy 1489–92). But the matter does not end there, having engendered (on the mere basis of that universally known word) an excessive response in a comic aside, beginning with 'Love loves to love love', enumerating ten specific 'love affairs' of dubious value, and concluding expansively with 'You love a certain person. And this person loves that other person because everybody loves somebody but God loves everybody' (Cy 1483–1501). What in the privacy of Stephen's innermost being may be mysterious and exalted in the common currency of a bar-room controversy can be demeaned to meaninglessness.

What is operative in *Ulysses* is what every bullfighter learns, that every human element gravitates instinctively toward its own area of comfort and strength. Once he has determined the bull's *querencia*, he manoeuvres him away from that part of the arena in order to impose his own advantage. The Citizen has attempted the same manoeuvres in emphasising the religious terrain where he assumes that Bloom will be most disadvantaged: 'Are you talking about the new Jerusalem?' he asks him pointblank; 'A new apostle to the gentiles', he comments as soon as Bloom has left (Cy 1473, 1489). But he has been drawn unaware into Bloom's *querencia*, and as much as he sneers when he says it, he does announce the existence of 'universal love' in an echo of Bloom's intended meaning.

STEPHEN AWAKES

Less obvious than the love-knot in *Ulysses* is the position of the oft-quoted statement by Stephen about history as a nightmare. Every critic who introduces the subject relies on its presence in Mr Deasy's office, where the subject is the same as that which the Citizen implies, that Jews are outside the pale of salvation: 'They sinned against the light, Mr Deasy said gravely' (Ne 361). 'Who has not?' is Stephen's rejoinder, and when that proves incomprehensible to Deasy, he makes his elliptical manoeuvre: ' – History, Stephen said, is a nightmare from which I am trying to awake' (Ne 373, 377). But he is immediately aware of his weakened position, speculating, 'What if that nightmare gave you a back kick?' (Ne 379). Deasy has been dealing with him as a fellow Christian (Bloom in the cabman's shelter will make the same assumption about Stephen), and Stephen has no intention of either facing the issue of the history of the Jews from a Christian vantage-point or allowing Deasy to see his equivocation on the subject of Christianity. That Deasy is secure in assuming shared Christianity is proven by his definition of history in terms of the 'manifestation of God', almost nullifying Stephen's opposition. His mode of expression, however, allows Stephen his new opening as he turns the cliché against Deasy: in his defensive assertion that 'All human history moves towards one great goal, the manifestation of God' (Ne 380–1), Deasy has accidentally trivialised that manifestation in terms of the goals being scored on the hockey field outside his window. Stephen moves in quickly to define God as a shout, 'A shout in the street' (Ne 386), and the nightmare of history is left in abeyance.

That Stephen is 'trying to awaken' from the self-described nightmare of history has become a fixed concept in dealing with his attitude toward history, and yet Stephen himself proves to be anything but fixed on that particular concept. Only a few hours later, in the newspaper office, he is confronted once again with the issue and reacts rather differently. Myles Crawford is recounting the journalistic coup in the transmitting of the news of the Phoenix Park murders, and refers to the story as 'the whole bloody history'

(Ae 676–7). For him history in this case is narrative rather than either the event itself or a process that includes the event, but although Stephen is essentially outside the conversation – actually it is Crawford's monologue – he reacts internally to 'the whole bloody history', thinking, 'Nightmare from which you will never awake' (Ae 678). That the murders took place the year of Stephen's birth may account for the forcefulness of his reaction and make the definiteness of 'will never awake' so unrelenting, yet in the solitude of his own mind Stephen uses the second-person singular instead of the first-person, addressing himself as such but still distancing himself somewhat from that inevitability. As with the love problem, we are faced with two differing statements about the nightmare of history as it imposes itself on Stephen Dedalus, and only by differentiating between the context in 'Nestor' and the context in 'Aeolus' can we balance the two aspects of the problem and realise its changing possibilities for Stephen.

DEDALUSDAY

Situations in *Ulysses* become complicated as they develop, and only occasionally are they clarified depending on whatever laws govern such natural phenomena. In a linear progression the evidence may accumulate regarding, for example, the problem of the Blooms' sexual relationship as the circumstances of Rudy's birth and deformity are enumerated. Essentially we wait for the longer and more fully developed expositions late in the text, through internalised monologue in 'Oxen of the Sun', through dramatised possibilities in 'Circe', through itemised accounts in 'Ithaca', although in each case we constantly question the authority, provenance, and reliability of sources, and the verifiability of an alternative perspective in 'Penelope'. At various instances, however, the line between two associated points provides a link without necessarily arranging for clarification of the first point, and a third, but often elusive, element seems to be needed in order to create a triangularisation to enclose a tangible possibility. Just accounting for Stephen Dedalus on 16 June 1904 requires answers to such questions as:

1. What determines Stephen's decision not to join Mulligan and Haines at the Ship?

2. How does Stephen manage to rid himself of Mulligan after they walk out of the National Library together?
3. Why does Stephen spend the afternoon and evening drinking to the extent that he does?
4. What causes Stephen to accept Bloom's proffered friendship when he had been so unresponsive for so long?
5. Why does Stephen none the less refuse a night's lodgings at 7 Eccles Street once a rapport seems to have been established?

Because we have always assumed that we understand Stephen's artistic temperament, we may never have been curious enough to question the points of intersection between his modes of behaviour and the determinants that affect that behaviour. Definitive answers may not exist within a configuration of external action and internal thought, when the actions complete the process, and the thoughts that should initiate them are subject to the vagaries of random associations – and time gaps occasionally interrupt.

We assume that somewhere in 'Proteus' is contained the clue to Stephen's decision not to meet Mulligan, yet early on in the chapter he seems intent on keeping the appointment: 'The Ship, half twelve', he reminds himself, and lest it seem anything other than an acknowledged commitment, he adds, 'By the way go easy with that money like a good young imbecile' (Pr 58–9). Thereafter he remembers that Buck has the tower key, that he saved men from drowning, that he was responsible for the shoes Stephen is wearing, and that he threw Stephen's handkerchief to him that Stephen did not retrieve – none of these necessarily contains the germ of a decision not to show up at the Ship at 12.30 p.m. Yet, no sooner had Stephen reprocessed the information about the appointment than he thinks in terms of a visit to the Gouldings, and manages to walk past their house while contemplating the nature of his intended visit, a bypassing that could create in his mind the prospect of bypassing the Ship even more definitively. On the other hand, Stephen may not be totally aware of his sense of disaffection from Mulligan, despite the somewhat unpleasant nature of their morning hour together. He had searched Mulligan's countenance that morning for tell-tale signs, first deciding on 'Chrysostomos' and then 'Usurper' (Te 26, 744), which may have suggested that a third term in the series was still missing, one that falls into place only when Mulligan has hunted him down in the library: 'Catamite' (SC 734). In the interim, given his initial unease at Mulligan's attempts at physical contact with him atop the tower, at Buck's programme to teach him 'the Greeks' (Te 79), Stephen may well have acted on instinctual avoidance.

Not only do we not know why Stephen wanted to rid himself of Buck Mulligan that afternoon, but by what process he managed to do so. Nothing in Stephen's segments of 'Wandering Rocks' includes thoughts about Mulligan, nor does Buck's conversation at the D.B.C. with Haines reveal what happened, although he does pronounce Stephen as destined for failure as a poet, blaming the Jesuits with having driven 'his wits astray' (WR 1072). ('There may be irony in his verdict that Stephen 'will never capture the Attic note' – WR 1072–3.) Yet at the end of 'Scylla and Charybdis' there is every indication that Stephen is determined to break away: 'Part. The moment is now. Where then?' (SC 1199), but he is plagued by the possibility of coincidental confrontations. 'My will: his will that fronts me', he acknowledges (SC 1202), and only when Bloom passes between them, and Stephen finds himself recalling his dream ('A creamfruit melon he held to me' – SC 1208), does the sign for augury present itself. Mulligan's anti-Semitic comment on Bloom, and his suggestion that Bloom has a pederastic interest in Stephen ('The wandering jew. . . . He looked upon you to lust after you' – SC 1209–10), may have decided Stephen against allowing himself to remain in Mulligan's clutches. The careful countering of Deasy's anti-Semitism was restrained by Stephen's awareness of his position as an employee, but no such reticence would now apply to his reaction to Mulligan.

The Stephen observed from early morning to mid-afternoon displays no outward signs of determined serious drinking, although his reputation as a profligate drinker has been well established. Mulligan in particular makes a point in the library about Stephen's drunken escapades, and in the D.B.C. he gloats to Haines, 'You should see him . . . when his body loses its balance' (WR 1066). But, although Stephen had initiated the drinking session with the denizens of the newspaper office, he none the less turned up reasonably sober at the National Library soon after, again calculatingly aware of the money spent on drink so far:

> Three drams of usquebaugh you drank with Dan Deasy's ducats.
> How much did I spend? O, a few shillings.
> For a plump of pressmen. Humour wet and dry. (SC 533–6)

Nor do his thoughts in 'Wandering Rocks' indicate a desire to drink himself into a stupor. He seems introspective, amused, observant, interested in the world around him, the lapidary's stones and the bookseller's wares, until he encounters his sister Dilly. His agonised realisation that 'She will drown me with her, eyes and hair' (WR 875–6) leads to the final 'Misery! Missery!' (WR 880), and Stephen is not seen again until he appears extremely drunk at the lying-in hospital, having spent the day in such pubs as 'Mooney's en ville, Mooney's sur mer, the Moira, Larchet's' (Ci 2518–19), if we can trust the testimony of Philip Sober. The image of Dilly on a bicycle prefaces the ghostly apparition of Stephen's mother in 'Circe', and Mrs Dedalus's suggestion to him, 'Get Dilly to make you that boiled rice every night after your brainwork' (Ci 4202–3) brings Stephen close to collapse. When he has sobered sufficiently at the cabman's shelter, he deflects Bloom's suggestion that he return home to his father's house, but his memories of it are relatively serene, 'Stephen's mind's eye being too busily engaged in repicturing his family hearth the last time he saw it with his sister Dilly sitting by the ingle, *her hair hanging down*' (Eu 269–71, emphasis added).

The newly established relationship of Stephen and Bloom, in its future potential, has divided critics who either view the mismatched acquaintances as permanently separating after relieving themselves in the Blooms' garden or having formed the basis for a future friendship that may well be reaffirmed as early as the next morning. (In which case Molly Bloom may or may not be an operative factor.) An inconvenience for those who anticipate an on-going relationship is the fact that Stephen inexplicably rejects spending the night in the spare room, a thoroughly logical solution to his homelessness so late in the night, whether he intends becoming a lifelong friend or not. Almost as daunting to those who see him departing permanently from 7 Eccles Street is accounting for the sudden degree of intimacy that surfaced at the closing moments of 'Eumaeus'. Until then Stephen had maintained his sour disposition over the undrinkable coffee and uneatable bun, very much the 'displeased and sleepy' (Te 13) Stephen who had been so unresponsive to Mulligan that morning. (In important ways that Stephen–Bloom relationship can be read as a parallel to the Stephen–Mulligan relationship now permanently dissolved, 'Eumaeus' as a complementary text to 'Telemachus' and 'Ithaca' to 'Scylla and Charybdis'.) On leaving the cabman's shelter Stephen allows Bloom to take his arm and becomes quite convivial thereafter, when he had so specifically shrunk from Mulligan's arm around him that morning.

Just prior to the linking of arms, the point at which Stephen says 'Yes' to Bloom's assistance (Eu 1723), the two had made their escape from the shelter and Stephen had made a casual comment that Bloom responded to immediately:

> – One thing I never understood, he said to be original on the spur of the moment. Why they put tables upside down at night, I mean chairs upside down, on the tables in cafés.
>
> To which impromptu the neverfailing Bloom replied without a moment's hesitation, saying straight off:
>
> – To sweep the floor in the morning.   (Eu 1708–13)

The convoluted intelligence and artistic temperament of Stephen Dedalus are somewhat jarred by the common sense and direct response from Bloom, at this first instance in 'Eumaeus' that Bloom has said anything 'straight off'. That Stephen may have come to appreciate an intelligence so different from his own bodes well for a potential writer of Irish life and cuts through the attempts at intellectual conversation that had previously alienated him by its circumlocutions and elliptical assumptions. This 'righting' of the conversational balance carries on into 'Ithaca', where the narrational medium mirrors that balance, and even the (presumed) gaucherie on Stephen's part of introducing the anti-Semitic song fails to disturb that equilibrium, Bloom – perhaps unperturbed by the 'nightmare of history' – accepting 'Hugh of Lincoln' as an historical text.

MR FOX WENT A-COURTIN'

Yet the newly formed friendship seems to end at a standoff under the stars. Our reading of Stephen's personality as a shape that cannot be changed allows us to envision a proud and isolated integrity, cutting all ties and flying by all nets, and therefore alone and friendless and homeless and jobless – and incorruptible. Our reading of the text uncovers numerous blanks, not necessarily in conflict with Stephen's assumed personality, but mysterious blanks none the less. As much as we learn from Molly about her speculative 'acceptance' of Stephen Dedalus, we learn nothing from Stephen's reactions to the existence of a Molly Bloom whose picture he has seen and whose presence he has been made aware of in the room above. When Bloom presents the eight-year-old photograph for viewing, it is as an afterthought to the topic of Kitty O'Shea as a Spanish type that Bloom admires, but Stephen treats the subject as an excuse to recall bits of songs about Spain and Spanish women. There is no evidence that Stephen has any positive reaction to the photo, which Bloom continues to re-examine and 're-read', indicating his appreciation for the 'slightly soiled photo creased by opulent curves' and his predilection for 'linen slightly soiled' (Eu 1465–9). As much as he hopes that Stephen 'could drink in the beauty for himself' (Eu 1458–9), there is no indication that Stephen does, although Bloom reports that 'he said the picture was handsome' (Eu 1479) – evasive enough – and the photo is kept on the table until Bloom suggests that they leave. The pocketing of the photo coincides with Stephen's thoughts on where to sleep that night:

> The best plan clearly being to clear out, the remainder being plain sailing, he beckoned, while prudently pocketing the photo, to the keeper of the shanty who didn't seem to.
> – Yes, that's the best, he assured Stephen to whom for the matter of that Brazen Head or him or anywhere else was all more or less. (Eu 1647–51)

The existence of a Mrs Bloom seems totally irrelevant to Stephen, who apparently has no speculative interest in this particular married woman, akin to the Spanishy woman who, as Deasy informed him, 'brought Parnell low' (Ne 394). For him Molly Bloom may be as remote as the Georgina Johnson whom he declared 'dead and married' (Ci 3620).

If Molly Bloom is the apex of the triangle for which Stephen and Poldy are the base points, then Georgina Johnson may the apex of the triangle for which Molly and Stephen form the base. Georgina Johnson may also play another oblique role – in a triangle that includes Molly and Kitty O'Shea. The Georgina who, according to Stephen, is a 'clergyman's daughter' (SC 195–6), has an analogue in the Kitty that Stephen irrelevantly labels 'The king of Spain's daughter' (Eu 1414), and if she actually married 'Mr Lambe from

London' (Ci 3636), Kitty can be said to have married a 'Mr Fox' (Ci 1762). Leopold Bloom, during a lengthy speculation in 'Eumaeus' on the Parnell affair, seems quite sanguine about that parallel cuckolding, apparently unaffected by his verdict on the husband in that instance as 'not being up to the scratch' (Eu 1380), although readers tend to see Bloom as Captain O'Shea in a French triangle that has Molly as Kitty and Boylan as Parnell. From his own perspective, however, Leopold Bloom may see himself as Charles Stewart Parnell, and perhaps even as the Mr Fox that was Parnell's secret self-perspective.

For a novel so frequently credited with masterly characterisation, particularly a Bloom that the reader presumably gets to know in detail, *Ulysses* evolves into a literary text that makes the notion of finite characterisation problematic. With the coming of night a dissociation of characterisation is in process, anticipating the character-multiplicity aspects of *Finnegans Wake*, and the various facets of Bloom's personality suggest various extensions of character, *multiple* Blooms. In 'Circe', where the process of such transformations is in constant activity, John Howard Parnell places the mantle of Charles Stewart Parnell on Bloom's shoulders: 'Illustrious Bloom! Successor to my famous brother' (Ci 1513–14). It is one thing for Bloom to glory in an undeserved reincarnation, but quite another, once the tide has turned against him, for the new persona to persist among those around him. 'THE MOB', in their execrations, make the ready transition from his identification with Parnell to his identity *as* Parnell: 'Lynch him! Roast him! He's as bad as Parnell was. Mr Fox!' (Ci 1762). Bloom in turn shifts the persona from one shoulder to the other: 'I am guiltless as the unsunned snow! It was my brother Henry. He is my double' (Ci 1769–70). His mirror at home recomposes these vagaries of self with the question regarding the 'composite asymmetrical image' and the apposite 'characterisation' of the 'solitary (ipsorelative) mutable (aliorelative) man':

> *Brothers and sisters had he none.*
> *Yet that man's father was his grandfather's son.*   (It 1348–53)

Whereas Leopold Bloom might wish to think of himself as the 'uncrowned king of Ireland' (as Parnell the statesman), his sense of sexual guilt crowns him as 'Mr Fox'. Bella Cohen is largely responsible for activating that guilt, especially in her guise as the brutal Bello, yet it was as a benign 'Mother Slipperslapper' (Ci 1287–8) that she is advertised by Zoe in luring Bloom into the house. In his departure from the house, after Stephen has run out into the street, Bloom misrepresents himself to Bella sufficiently to awe her momentarily, '(*almost speechless*) Who are. Incog!' (Ci 4308), but she soon recovers to instigate a pursuit ['*Bella from within the hall urges on her whores*' (Ci 4320–1)], which evolves into a fox hunt:

A pack of bloodhounds, led by Hornblower of Trinity brandishing a dogwhip in tallyho cap and an old pair of grey trousers, follow from far, picking up the scent, nearer, baying, panting, at fault, breaking away, throwing their tongues, biting his heels, leaping at his tail.

(Ci 4328–32).

Of the items then thrown at Bloom the Fox are a pair of 'woman's slipperslappers' (Ci 4334), identified with Bella, and the linkage exists in the song known both as 'The Fox' and 'Old Mother Slipperslapper'. It is hardly surprising that among Foxbloom's pursuers is none other than John Howard Parnell.

The subject of Parnell resurfaces then in 'Eumaeus', where change of identity already exists in the character of the keeper of the shelter 'posing' as Skin-the-Goat or Skin-the-Goat 'posing' as the keeper, and seaman Murphy's credentials hardly seem in order. The unidentified cabman, whose actual identity as a cabman may be in question, recycles the theory that Parnell is not dead and buried, but has altered his identity: 'He changed his name to De Wet, the Boer general' (Eu 1305). The notion rather tantalises Bloom, who had not been within earshot when the idea that the coffin was filled with stones was suggested at Glasnevin and summarily dismissed by Joe Hynes ('Parnell will never come again. . . . He's there, all that was mortal of him' – Ha 926–7). Metempsychosis has its influence on Bloom, despite his allegiance to natural phenomena, and his image of himself as a re-incarnation of Parnell allows for a retrospective arrangement: 'You had to come back. The haunting sense kind of drew you. To show the understudy in the title role how to' (Eu 1331–3). His credentials may depend on a moment of physical proximity, on the exchange of a hat, as Bloom recalls the incident in his own thoughts, when he 'handed him his silk hat when it was knocked off and he said *Thank you*' (Eu 1335–6). Moments later, as a result of the discussion on the Parnell adultery, Bloom 'replays' the hat incident for Stephen's edification, and although the narrational method remains in the third person, the kinds of information included indicate that Stephen is the auditor. In this instance Parnell's line reads, *'Thank you, sir'* (Eu 1523). The rearrangement results in a slightly more trenchant rendition, characteristic of many of the narrational strategies throughout *Ulysses*.

Part One
Styles, Structures, Sources

1

Opaque and Transparent Narrative

'TO BEGIN AT THE BEGINNING'

'Stephen closed his eyes to hear his boots crush crackling wrack and shells' (Pr 10–11). In this manner the second paragraph of the 'Proteus' chapter begins, and it would be only partially disingenuous to contend that nothing has quite prepared the reader for a sentence of such clear and open presentation, since many similar sentences in the first two chapters, 'Telemachus' and 'Nestor', are as lucid and direct. The sentences that open those first two chapters have the same quality and capacity for active narration:

Stately, plump Buck Mulligan came from the stairhead, bearing a bowl of lather on which a mirror and a razor lay crossed.

(Te 1–2)

– You, Cochrane, what city sent for him?   (Ne 1)

These chapter openings seem to presume a foreknowledge of that which they would introduce: the language in which Buck Mulligan and Cochrane (as well as Pyrrhus, the referent for 'him' in the second example) are called forth suggests not a *presentation*, an introduction, but rather a *re-presentation*, a seeing (and meeting) again. That in 'Proteus' Stephen is walking along the shore with his eyes closed is readily apprehended, yet facets of that declaration depend on the nature of the internalised narrative of the opening paragraph, itself an oblique initiation: 'Ineluctable modality of the visible: at least that if no more, thought through my eyes' (Pr 1–2).

What serves presumably as 'objective' (or transparent) narration, devoid of inflections and mannerisms that mark the idiom of its subjects – to establish the manner of walk and the condition of the terrain – is dependent upon the subjective (opaque) materials of

19

the internalised precedent: 'thought through my eyes'; 'Limit of the diaphane'; 'Shut your eyes and see' (Pr 1–2, 7, 9) arrange for the slightly tangential concept of 'closed his eyes to hear' (Pr 10). Even more removed from direct narration is the 'product' of Stephen's auditory perceptions. With his eyes open and an alternative form of awareness operative for him, he might not be as exact in defining the 'crush crackling wrack and shells'. Stephen has already determined the density and fragility of the matter under his feet as he evaluates with his eyes still open his immediate environment: 'Signatures of all things I am here to read, seaspawn and seawrack' (Pr 2–3). It is no longer transparent narrative that suggests 'wrack' under his boots but Stephen's own system of classification, and the assonance and alliteration of 'crush crackling wrack' are dependent not on open narration but on Stephen's literary mode of presentation.

Even more oblique are those readily recognised shells that litter the beach: 'unseen' by his eyes, they are conceived for Stephen Dedalus by the collection of shells he saw earlier that morning in Mr Deasy's office, aware that shells were once a medium of currency, so that he can parallel them with Deasy's 'tray of Stuart coins' (Ne 201) – Stephen, after all, is in the office to receive his wages:

> And now his strongroom for the gold. Stephen's embarrassed hand moved over the shells heaped in the cold stone mortar: whelks and money cowries and leopard shells: and this, whorled as an emir's turban, and this, the scallop of saint James. An old pilgrim's hoard, dead treasure, hollow shells.
> A sovereign fell, bright and new, on the soft pile of the tablecloth.   (Ne 212–17)

(The fall of a sovereign, a coin depicting a king's head, fits the allusion to the Stuart monarchs, one of whom – Charles I – was beheaded; Mr Deasy of course remains a staunch monarchist, prelapsarian.) The shells of the opening sentence of the 'Proteus' paragraph bide their time until the end of the paragraph, where Stephen's association of Deasy's ducats falls into place: 'Crush, crack, crick, crick. Wild sea money. Dominie Deasy kens that a'' (Pr 19–20).

'Proteus' is the first chapter of *Ulysses* in which narration is characterised by a certain opaqueness, although the technique itself was often anticipated in the first two chapters. Even a simple declarative sentence can begin transparently and evolve into opaqueness, as can be seen early in 'Telemachus': 'Stephen bent forward and peered at the mirror held out to him, cleft by a crooked crack. Hair on end' (Te 135–6). The opening direction of the sentence is toward an uninflected narration, but even if the preposition 'at' does not immediately signal a warp in the narrative line, 'cleft by a crooked crack' – prefiguring 'crush crackling wrack' – betrays the influence of Stephen Dedalus's idiom. And 'Hair on end' is Stephen's personal view of that crack in the glass, his metamorphic substitution, as he refuses to look into the mirror at his own disgruntled image, foiling Mulligan's aggressive purpose. 'Hair on end' warps the narrative in two directions, darkening its transparency toward opacity: if there is a temptation to read the comment as Stephen's observation of/on his unkempt appearance, it is also his obstinacy in refusing to obey Mulligan's insistence that dominates and determines the narrational direction ('Look at yourself . . . you dreadful bard!' – Te 134). As a syntactic unit the sentence unfolds in three distinct stages: it begins with simple narration generated by the activity in progress ('Stephen bent forward and peered at the mirror held out to him' – Te 135), takes on the tone of the subject's sophisticated method of depiction ('cleft by a crooked crack'), and ends with an internalised observation unexplicated in the subject's consciousness ('Hair on end').

When the technique is altered to accommodate Bloom's intellectual patterns, sentences like 'He pulled the halldoor to after him very quietly, more, till the footleaf dropped gently over the threshold, a limp lid' (Ca 75–7) appear transparent enough – rendering action without commentary on the action – except for the necessity of accounting for 'more' (Bloom's directive to himself), and the suggestive 'limp lid' (suggesting Bloom's own phrasing). Later, such intrusions are more remarkable. When in 'Lestrygonians' 'Mr Bloom smiled O rocks at two windows of the ballastoffice' (Le 114), it is no longer possible to ignore the invasion into the narrative: 'O rocks' marks the irrepressible recollection in Bloom's mind of Molly's expletive, which reappears here to interrupt the narrational movement. Testiculate images abounded in the previous paragraph of Bloom's internal monologue ('troubled eyes', 'Timeball', 'Robert Ball's', 'pike hoses', 'O rocks!' – Le 108–13), and rebound within the next attempt at transparent narration.

That the narrative is warped and coloured by the lexical and syntactic patterns of individual characters is soon a commonplace in *Ulysses* – unremarkable in itself – introduced in 'Telemachus' with the reliance on a single grammatical element: the adverb. From the first word of the text ('Stately') adverbs have a tenacious life of their own throughout the early pages. From the second sentence of *Ulysses* – 'A yellow dressinggown, ungirdled, was sustained gently behind him on the mild morning air' (Te 2–4) – cascades a profusion of adverbs: coarsely, solemnly, gravely, coldly, smartly, sternly, briskly, gravely, quietly, gaily, wearily, and so on throughout the opening pages. Hardly a sentence of descriptive action lacks its adverb, and even a line of Mulligan's speech repeats the tendency: 'That will do nicely', he says (Te 28). Although some readers might attribute this embarrassment of adverbs to a careless and unwitting stylist, and others to an authorial mannerism that exceeded the dictates of decorous taste, most commentators on *Ulysses* would seek more compelling justifications. One becomes aware of just how much Buck Mulligan insists through these early scenes in dominating the action, attempting to enthrall Stephen and bring him into his own sphere of influence, his own *querencia*, and he does so less by persuasive language than through physical gesture and bodily presence. He commands attention by his actions and by the physicality of his pronouncements, a conscious and even compulsive actor determining his manner of delivery at all times. As Mulligan's campaign weakens and Stephen firmly detaches himself, the adverbs begin to fade away, relatively inconspicuous by the end of the chapter.

Nowhere in the first two chapters is there a narrative directive as transparent as 'His pace slackened' (Pr 61) or 'He halted' (Pr 158), perhaps the only two sentences in 'Proteus' not directed by internalised commentary. (And even with these, the choice of verbs – slackened, halted – suggests the influence of a Dedalean vocabulary.) Those narrational indicators in 'Telemachus' and 'Nestor' that advanced action and set the scene invariably contained opaque elements that constantly called attention to themselves, the internalised portions set within the framework of a compact narrative. The crisp dialogue – for the most part the extended effort of Malachi Mulligan's insistence – carries the major burden in the first half of the chapter, and a paragraph like the one intercalated between two of Buck's speeches is typical of the combination of the transparent and the opaque:

He swept the mirror a half circle in the air to flash the tidings abroad in sunlight now radiant on the sea. His curling shaven lips laughed and the edges of his white glittering teeth. Laughter seized all his strong wellknit trunk.   (Te 130–3)

Even in this early moment of narration the uniqueness of Stephen's methods in observing Mulligan are evident; in particular, the 'white glittering teeth' are the focus of Stephen's first commentary on him: 'his even white teeth glistening here and there with gold points. Chrysostomos' (Te 25–6). The hard line that should separate narration proper from internalisation has been effectively softened, so that 'white glittering teeth', like 'strong wellknit trunk', suggests the influence of Stephen's perception and is rendered in his idiom. 'Chrysostomos' detaches Mulligan from the immediate context and separates narrative observation – of the white teeth with gold points – from definition. The gold-pointed teeth provide a metonomy that lodges itself – through a pun on 'goldenmouthed' – in the identity of one of two Greek orators named Chrysostomos. Moreover, the appellation 'Chrysostomos' has a retroactive effect, turning back on the narrative description of Mulligan's 'even white teeth glistening here and there with gold points' – representing that 'golden mouth' – so as to undermine the surety of the transparent and uninflected nature of the narrative. 'Chrysostomos' may sum up a narrative position already traced in the previous sentence. Each may have fallen under Stephen Dedalus's rhetorical powers, making the terms of this description self-reflexive.

READING FROM WITHIN

By the end of 'Nestor' the three aspects of narrative exercise have blended into a balanced amalgam: Mr Deasy carries the dialogue with Stephen; Stephen's thoughts present themselves as stichomythically as Deasy's curt sentences; and the encapsulating narration offers the odd bit of support: 'Stephen raised the sheets in his hand'; 'Mr Deasy shook his head'; 'Stephen rustled the sheets again' (Ne 399, 405, 408). Yet the last sentence of the chapter raises the narrative line to imaginative heights, as Stephen retreats from the laughing words issuing from Deasy's mouth:

– She never let them in, he cried again through his laughter as he stamped on gaitered feet over the gravel of the path. That's why. On his wise shoulders through the checkerwork of leaves the sun flung spangles, dancing coins. (Ne 446–9)

No narration couched in transparent prose and intent on conveying meaning without subjective instrusion could possibly be responsible for the sarcasm of those 'wise shoulders', the poetic viewing of that 'checkerwork of leaves', or the associative significance of the 'dancing coins' whose companions now reside in Stephen's pocket.

At the close of the 'Nestor' chapter a balanced integration of all the methods of narration has been achieved, and the culminating chapter of the 'Telemachia' caps that achievement. Only a single line of 'heard' speech intrudes in 'Proteus' ('Tatters! Outofthat, you mongrel' – Pr 353), in a chapter that specialises in the thoughts and remembered fragments resident in Stephen's consciousness. The active components of narrative that bring Stephen physically along the strand, down toward the shore in the direction of the Kish lightship, back to the road, among the boulders, are minimalist in construction, some of the rarest instances where Joyce's language assiduously avoids calling attention to itself. The barest outlines are offered ('The grainy sand had gone from under his feet'; 'He halted'; 'He had come nearer the edge of the sea and wet sand slapped his boots' – Pr 147, 158, 265–6), so that the slight opacity of such translucence – usually apparent in the verbs and adjectives – is easily overlooked. In an early instance the intrusion of a single word, appropriately foreign, reveals a fleeting fragment of Stephen's silent observation, much as did the 'Chrysostomos' of the first chapter: 'They came down the steps from Leahy's terrace prudently, *Frauenzimmer*: and down the shelving shore flabbily, their splayed feet sinking in the silted sand' (Pr 29–31). *Frauenzimmer* forcefully, even intrusively, suggests Stephen's lexicon. Less noticeable is the way in which the succeeding clause expands beyond the demands of transparent narration, apparent in the tendency toward alliteration ('shelving shore ... splayed ... sinking ... silted sand') introduced by Stephen, who is both an observer to the scene and a self-announced writer. And the prudence that will characterise the two women in Stephen's later fictional representation of them – in The Parable of the Plums – is here registered by the adverb 'prudently', which acts grammatically as a hinge between the terms of the women's location (Leahy's terrace) and their presumed profession (as midwives). The women's movement from one set of these terms to the next – from the terrace to midwifery – is accomplished 'prudently'.

Only a few minutes later Stephen Dedalus will offer an exemplum of just such narrative re-enactment, a literary creation out of almost nothing, as he records his hypothetical, but typical, visit to the Gouldings of Strasburg terrace. The vignette is constructed primarily of short lines of dialogue, mostly between Uncle Richie and himself, with young Walter as a marginal participant. Several segments of active narrative occasion the progress of the scene, and efforts are made by the story-teller to refine himself out of the process by employing a measurable degree of transparency. As such, certain sentences begin quite innocently: 'I pull the wheezy bell of their shuttered cottage: and wait'; 'He lays aside the lapboard whereon he drafts his bills of costs'; 'Walter squints vainly for a chair' (Pr 70, 80, 93). Even the simplest requirements of verisimilitude make a bell sound 'wheezy' and the cottage look 'shuttered', and specify a 'lapboard' for a bedridden clerk; since Walter has been described as 'skeweyed' (Pr 67), his efforts to locate a chair account for his 'squint'. The concluding sentence of Stephen's vignette parallels numerous others in the 'Telemachia' in their tone and structure: 'His tuneful whistle sounds again, finely shaded, with rushes of the air, his fists bigdrumming on his padded knees' (Pr 102–3). Compare, for example, 'Then, catching sight of Stephen Dedalus, he bent towards him and made rapid crosses in the air, gurgling in his throat and shaking his head' (Te 11–13) – from 'Telemachus' – or, 'He peered from under his shaggy brows at the manuscript by his elbow and, muttering, began to prod the stiff buttons of the keyboard slowly, sometimes blowing as he screwed up the drum to erase an error' (Ne 296–8) – from 'Nestor'. These are fragments of external narration that fit exactly Stephen's literary attempt to create the same sort of external narration within his own mind, and are of the same blend of transparency and opaqueness that attest to the primacy of Stephen as the subjective centre of the 'Telemachia'.

As the 'Proteus' chapter moves toward its climax, even so balanced a consistency cannot be depended upon. The vagaries of Stephen's musings, which at first were controlled by a gentle rhythmic movement, as of a shallow tide, are intensified as if by a narrowly constricting inner core of a whirlpool. (Indeed, Stephen's internalised commentary is influenced by his physical surroundings, the sea, sand and water directing word choice and syntactical structures.) The Aristotelian experiment with ineluctable modalities of the visible and audible are carried out with leisure and nonchalance, as are the extended recollections of the Gouldings at home and the Egans in Paris. But once Stephen becomes aware of the aimlessness of his wanderings, and the hypnotic rhythms of the tides have brought him dangerously close to the edge of the bay, he becomes far more alert to his external surroundings, the dangers of dogs and the pursuing floods, the smooth strand suddenly as treacherous as the cliffs of Elsinore. The opening sentences of many of the later paragraphs reflect aspects of Stephen's frightened awareness: 'A bloated carcass of a dog lay lolled on bladderwrack. Before him the gunwale of a boat, sunk in sand' (Pr 286–7). The alliterative pattern dominates (bloated/bladderwrack, lay lolled, sunk in sand), a facet of Stephen's literary method of description. Death by drowning, as well as immersion in quicksand, trouble his thoughts once he senses 'his feet beginning to sink slowly in the quaking soil' (Pr 268). 'A point, live dog, grew into sight running across the sweep of sand' (Pr 294) introduces an observed phenomenon *as observation* – Stephen's most explicitly – as his weak eyes recognise the live dog develop from a mere point on the horizon. 'The dog's bark ran towards him, stopped, ran back' (Pr 310) carries forward the experiment with the modality of the audible – it is the movement of *sound* that Stephen perceives first. And once 'A woman and a man' (Pr 331) come into view and are claimed by their dog, the terrifying animal becomes 'domesticated', and narrative depiction relaxes: 'Their dog ambled about a bank of dwindling sand, trotting, sniffing on all sides' (Pr 332–3). Stephen's fears have abstracted themselves out of the external narration.

The entire paragraph that follows, beginning with the single-word sentence, 'Cocklepickers' (Pr 342), poses effectively as transparent narration, a descriptive essay on the behaviour of man, woman and dog in the shallow waters. The heightened language intensifies the depiction, even to the extent of referring to the dog's tongue as 'a rag of wolf's tongue redpanting from his jaws' (Pr 346–7), so that the displacement of dog for wolf suggests – without actually insinuating – Stephen's mode of perception. The paragraph provides the longest instance of ostensibly uninflected narration in 'Proteus', and is sustained until the final sentences:

'Dogskull, dogsniff, eyes on the ground, moves to one great goal. Ah, poor dogsbody! Here lies poor dogsbody's body' (Pr 350–2). In both subject and style this commentary directs itself toward Stephen, reiterating Deasy's pronouncement that 'All human history moves towards one great goal, the manifestation of God' (Ne 380–1). The dog in the 'Proteus' passage falls heir to Stephen's conception of the Dog/God figure – the 'enemy' – scrutinised in a vignette that the self-proclaimed writer might well entitle 'Cocklepickers', with a concluding epitaph that reads: 'Here lies poor dogsbody's body'.

(An 'identification' of the actual cocklepickers allows for an overlay of transparencies: the man and woman in charge of Tatters are designated as 'Cocklepickers', presumably by Stephen, but the two women he had designated under the title of *Frauenzimmer* prove to be cocklepickers as well, evidence for which surfaces eventually in 'Wandering Rocks': 'Two old women fresh from their whiff of the briny trudged through Irishtown along London bridge road, one with a sanded tired umbrella, one with a midwife's bag in which eleven cockles rolled' – WR 818–20.)

The narrative openings of all 'Proteus' paragraphs consequently become suspect. 'Shouldering their bags they trudged, the red Egyptians' (Pr 370) depends in its coda-word on Stephen's determination that the cocklepickers are gypsies, and the past participle 'trudged' effects a later deployment of what Stephen has seen and heard: 'She trudges, schlepps, trains, drags, trascines her load' (Pr 392–3) – the verb moves through various languages as the Gypsy has moved through various countries. (The so-called *Frauenzimmer* trudge as well, as is apparent in their trek through Irishtown in 'Wandering Rocks'.) 'His lips lipped and mouthed fleshless lips of air' (Pr 401) could not be described as 'transparent' narration, deriving as it does from Stephen's mouthing of his vampire poem ('mouth to her mouth's kiss' – Pr 398). 'His shadow lay over the rocks as he bent, ending' (Pr 408) suggests in itself the shadow of Stephen's modes of perception and expression as they determine the objectifications of his actions. And although the word 'trudged' is later recuperated from Stephen's internalisations, in the case of 'His gaze brooded on his broadtoed boots, a buck's castoffs, *nebeneinander*' (Pr 446–7), the subtext anticipates the verb: '*And no more turn aside and brood*' (Pr 445) – the Yeats line triggered in 'Telemachus' by Buck Mulligan's caution against 'moody brooding' (Te 235–6).

The moody brooding of 'Proteus' dominates the last half of the chapter, often lulling Stephen into somnolence, as in the passage that begins 'In long lassoes from the Cock lake the water flowed full, covering greengoldenly lagoons of sand, rising, flowing' (Pr 453–4). The physical action corresponds to Stephen's lethargic state of mind, resulting in the risk of his ashplant floating away. His *active* participation, however, consists in taking over the means of expression, becoming the narrator of the events occurring around him. Listening to the sound of the waters Stephen decides to 'give' speech to the noises that he hears (as Bloom will do in 'Aeolus'), imposing 'language' upon the natural phenomena: 'Listen: a fourworded wavespeech: seesoo, hrss, rsseeiss, ooos' (Pr 456–7). Stephen has usurped the mechanics of narration, and goes on to complete his sound-study of the protean environment:

> Vehement breath of waters amid seasnakes, rearing horses, rocks. In cups of rocks it slops: flop, slop, slap: bounded in barrels. And, spent, its speech ceases. It flows purling, widely flowing, floating foampool, flower unfurling.   (Pr 458–60)

In effect, Stephen is providing the opaque narration for the event that is occurring concurrently in time in *Ulysses*, Leopold Bloom's languorous indulgence in the baths in Leinster street, an event that follows the 'Lotus Eaters' chapter, but for which no transparent narration is ever provided in the actual text.

'. . . AND TO BEGIN AGAIN'

Some of the paralleling examples from the early sections of the Odyssey proper have already indicated that the skilled fusion of transparent and opaque qualities carry over from the 'Telemachia' into the succeeding segments of *Ulysses*. The opening of 'Calypso' poses certain immediate concerns, although only in retrospect, since it is impossible to determine intentional opaqueness before the nature of narrational transparency is clearly established. That 'Mr Leopold Bloom ate with relish the inner organs of beasts and fowls' (Ca 1–2) is deceptively similar to 'Stately, plump Buck Mulligan came from the stairhead' (Te 1–2), assuming an insistent present action, until one realises that 'beasts and fowls' hardly comprise a single repast in the process of being consumed, existing instead in the hypothetical past, along with Stephen's visits to the Gouldings. The sentence, therefore, is one of descriptive predilection, and 'with relish' intensifies that particular appetite along subject lines. That 'Most of all he liked grilled mutton kidneys which gave to his palate a fine tang of faintly scented urine' (Ca 3–5) is an observation of such personal idiosyncracy as to cause the reader discomfort at having egregiously intruded on Leopold Bloom's privacy. Yet no aspect of the initiating paragraph of 'Calypso' implies actual internalisation, although skirting dangerously close. So much so that the second paragraph informs us that 'Kidneys were in his mind as he moved about the kitchen' (Ca 6), but not until the last sentence does the narration move more than halfway toward total subjectivity: 'Made him feel a bit peckish' (Ca 9) lacks a grammatical element, a direct subject for the sentence, anticipating the manner of presentation of the thoughts of Leopold Bloom. And 'a bit peckish' will prove through later examples of verbal mannerisms very much a characteristic of Bloomian diction: 'Got a short knock' (Ca 62); 'Make a picnic of it' (Ca 80–1); 'Got up wrong side of the bed' (Ca 233–4).

The road into internalised narration in this new portion of the text winds subtly with these several anticipations, especially when past the third paragraph (which consists of a single sentence of unchallengeable transparency, 'The coals were reddening' – Ca 10), the fourth feints in the direction of pure internalisation before outright commitment:

> Another slice of bread and butter: three, four: right. She didn't like her plate full. Right. He turned from the tray, lifted the kettle off the hob and set it sideways on the fire. It sat there, dull and squat, its spout stuck out. Cup of tea soon. Good. Mouth dry. (Ca 11–14)

The opening clause should be sufficient to indicate internalised elements. The lack of subject and verb shortcircuits the act of placing the slices of bread, while the presence of the predication alone implies Bloomian observation: the first slice has escaped classification and remains 'understood', as Bloom places the second on the plate. 'The coals were reddening' as an active observation has displaced the perception of placing the initial slice, and as the sentence exists *in medias res*, so does the thought itself.

The repetition of Bloom's verdict of approval ('Right') calls attention to itself, expressing his satisfaction at the arrangement, but also recovers the rather innocent sentence that initiated the second paragraph: 'Kidneys were in his mind as he moved about the kitchen softly, *righting* her breakfast things on the humpy tray' (Ca 6–7, emphasis added). Once the indicator 'in his mind' is fixed, objective narration becomes suspect: Bloom is unusually aware that his act of balancing is a matter of *righting* the tray. That the tray is 'humpy' might be obvious to any observer of the scene, but it exists as a fixed concept for Bloom: the singlemindedness of that particular adjective returns later, when Bloom 'fitted the teapot on the tray. Its hump bumped as he took it up' (Ca 296–7).

Although the first 'right' clinches the entry into internalisation, the second 'Right', standing alone as a single sentence, duplicates the impact of 'Chrysostomos', that first instance of Stephen Dedalus's internal commentary. The forthrightness of the repeated word establishes the method for the Bloomian cogitations, but later aspects of the same paragraph tend to diminish narrative clarity, determining the ambiguous quality of many internalised statements. 'Cup of tea soon', muses Bloom, adding, 'Good. Mouth dry' (Ca 14). Is it for himself or for Molly that he contemplates the relief for a dry mouth? That 'She didn't like her plate full' (Ca 11–12) seems to indicate that it is Molly's needs that he immediately seeks to serve, but there is no reason to assume that he himself is not undergoing the same sensation of a dry mouth. And the 'removed' sense of the verb 'didn't', rather than a direct 'She *doesn't* like her plate full', places this internal observation slightly outside the precise process, setting up a bridge between objective narration and internalisation. The existence of anything in *Ulysses* that can be certified as 'objective narration', even the simplest forms of the transparent ('On the doorstep he felt in his hip pocket for the latchkey' – Ca 72), becomes progressively more elusive, for this transparent example can be challenged on the basis that only Bloom can know for certain that it is his key that he is feeling for. A statement as innocent in its directness as 'He listened to her licking lap' (Ca 43) has been prepared for by a previous observation of the household cat: 'He watched the bristles shining wirily in the weak light as she tipped three times and licked lightly' (Ca 39–40).

What no aspect of objective, transparent narration can directly disclose in Calypso is the heliotropic, warmth-oriented, sun-worshipping aspect of Bloom's personality, something he himself probably remains unaware of and could not make a direct statement about – as he could easily make about feeling for his latchkey. Yet it is precisely in the opaque nature of the external narration that the evidence persists and accumulates. A factor contributing to Bloom's unexplained peckishness pre-exists the statement of his condition: 'Gelid light and air were in the kitchen but out of doors gentle summer morning everywhere. Made him feel a bit peckish' (Ca 7–8). Bloom gravitates out into that gentle summer morning ('summer' here is a subjective adjective) as soon as he can, and his first recourse once he is out of doors is to cross 'to the bright side' of the street, rather than wait to cross at the corner of Eccles and Dorset streets. 'His eyelids sank quietly often as he walked in happy warmth' (Ca 81), and even the sighting of the bread van reminds him that Molly prefers day-old loaves *reheated*. Sunny thoughts accompany him as far as the pork butcher's, and even when his musings on the exotic East culminate in the fall of night ('Getting on to sundown.... Night sky, moon' – Ca 92–6), he retrieves immediate sunshine: 'in the track of the sun. Sunburst on the titlepage' (99–100). The narration is quick to corroborate the joke about 'a homerule sun rising up in the northwest' (Ca 101–2) when Bloom spots Larry O'Rourke in his pub ('Baldhead over the blind' – Ca 111) – on the *northwest* corner of Eccles and Dorset streets.

The animal aspects of the servant girl making her purchases at the pork butcher's ('her moving hams') stir sensual desires in Bloom – 'Pleasant to see first thing in the morning' – and he is eager to follow her: 'Hurry up, damn it. Make hay while the sun shines' (Ca 172–3). Although she works in the house next to his, the servant girl heads westward, but Bloom must head east to return home, and he contents himself with perusing the Agendath Netaim prospectus instead ('He looked at the cattle, blurred in silver heat' – Ca 201), until a dark cloud overtakes him and he is plunged into dejection, once again feeling decidedly peckish and dry: 'Morning mouth bad images. Got up wrong side of the bed' (Ca 233–4). Desperate to get back home, Bloom's quest now is 'to smell the gentle smoke of tea, fume of the pan, sizzling butter. Be near her ample bedwarmed flesh' (Ca 237–9), to recuperate warmth.

Direct narration in *Ulysses* rarely displays any consciousness of its own, hardly comparable to the omniscience for which narrative sources are often credited in fictional texts. Essentially, Joycean narrative directions depend upon the limited consciousness of the 'centred' character: we are informed about Bloom's gastronomic preferences when Bloom is subject to such preferences; that the coals are reddening displaces notice of the first slice of bread when Bloom is conscious of reddening coals: two thoughts exist simultaneously in time, one of them submerged for the linear spacing of narrative presentation. In 'Lotus Eaters' Bloom moves physically away from Molly's bedwarmed flesh – the news of the Boylan assignation distances him from that source of comfort, but does not as yet fully discomfit him. He can achieve a certain distancing from it by focusing on a more immediate concern, the funeral of Paddy Dignam ('At eleven it is', he realises in 'Lotus Eaters' (Lo 11–12), answering the question asked at the end of 'Calypso', 'What time is the funeral?' – Ca 542–3). The intrusion of a *timed* event for the morning holds at bay the time of Boylan's scheduled arrival for the afternoon: 'At four, she said. Time ever passing' (Si 188). Bloom dawdles away the pre-funeral hour taking elliptical routes and lingering in way-stations, delays that consume so much time as to necessitate a change from the intended baths at Tara street to the nearby baths on Leinster street.

When Bloom stops before the window of the tea company prior to entering the Westland Row post office, he expresses a reaction to the hot weather that the external narrative in no way corroborates. Rather than inform us of 'the bright side of the street' or of 'quick warm sunlight', the narrational indicators are silent, despite Bloom's excessive preoccupations: 'Rather warm', 'Very warm morning', 'So warm' (Lo 19, 22, 27). Bloom's meterological comments are intentionally deceptive: he needs an excuse to remove his hat and mop his brow, surreptitiously transferring his Henry Flower card from headband to waistcoat pocket. Bloom's deceptiveness conditions the bland vagueness of the narrative, which follows his actions but makes no effort to account for them. Whereas directed narrative understood that a latchkey was being sought (an overt intention), that same kind of narrative has to delay until the action is out in the open: 'His fingers found quickly a card behind the headband and transferred it to his waistcoat pocket' (Lo 25–6). When it becomes a matter of returning card from pocket to hat, Bloom varies his deception: having decided on the deserted Cumberland street as a safe place where he can read the letter, and having opened it in his pocket and taken out the letter itself, he folds it into his newspaper, so that if observed at all, it would be assumed that he was reading the paper. The back entrance to All Hallows Church on Cumberland street affords him the opportunity to replace the card: 'Stepping into the porch he doffed his hat, took the card from his pocket and tucked it again behind the leather headband' (Lo 318–20). The narrative line remains totally ingenuous, keyed to Bloom's mind, and his mind remains coyly blank on the subject, but there is good reason to assume that the unexplained visit to the church is part of the deception. Like a good spy (coming in from the heat), Bloom avoids using the same ploy twice.

'Lotus Eaters' provides numerous examples of the subjective sources for the presumably objective narration. At no time is the warm sunshine a subject of narrative description for its own sake; at all times it is Bloom's prerogative, as when he concentrates on the woman about to step into the carriage: 'beneath his vailed eyelids he saw the bright fawn skin shine in the glare'; 'Flicker, flicker: the laceflare of her hat in the sun: flicker, flick' (Lo 111, 139– 40). There is no indication that Bloom is facing eastward, any more than had the narration signalled that Bloom was on the left side facing the altar at All Hallows (he would logically have entered from the door nearest Brunswick street); only his mistaking I. H. S. as I. N. R. I. on the priest's back locates him on the left. When, at the end of the chapter, Bloom thinks, 'Heavenly weather really' (Lo 558), even the assumed observation is deflective. He is rehearsing a possible conversational approach to the Trinity College gatekeeper, which would have begun had Bloom actually said, 'How do you do, Mr Hornblower?' and been answered with 'How do you do, sir?' (Lo 556–7). His actual preoccupation is now with warm water, and there is no time left for a chat, even if Hornblower had been as cordial as Bloom would have liked: 'Enjoy a bath now . . . the gentle tepid stream' (Lo 565–6). Replacing both hot food and bedwarm Molly, the contemplation of a warm bath allows Bloom to write his own narrative: 'He foresaw his pale body reclined in it at full, naked, in a womb of warmth' (Lo 567–8). As such Bloom creates his own time-warp, posits his own, self-determined future, delays the scenario being written by Molly and Boylan for the late afternoon.

Even a minimal narrative statement in this chapter can prove misleading, and a simple declarative sentence that resembles outward narration reveals itself as inner-directed: between Bloom's musings on the pins in women's clothes ('Queer the number of pins they always have. No roses without thorns' – Lo 277–8) and his recall of the ditty about '*Mairy lost the pin of her drawers*' (Lo 281), a simple sentence intrudes: 'Flat Dublin voices bawled in his head' (Lo 280). Like its predecessor early in 'Calypso', it delineates what is 'in his mind', but is neither objective narration nor directly verbalised thought process – more particularly a temporary bridge between. And the next sentence, which in the absence of an operative verb indicates internalisation, arranges for the dramatic transition in the piece of doggerel about *Mairy*: 'Those two sluts that night in the Coombe, linked together in the rain' (Lo 279–80). The language of time-indication is insistently vague, as the commonality of the past-tense verb reveals, and no link between present thought and recollection is particularly necessary. Yet 'Flat Dublin voices bawled in his head' acts once again to undermine the authority of external narration, subverting it actively for the subjective.

Many narrative indicators toward the end of 'Lotus Eaters' are sharp reminders of that subjective function. 'The chemist turned back page after page' (Lo 472) discloses Bloom's unease at causing trouble by not having brought the prescription to the shop ('turned back page after page' implies irritation, whereas 'turned back the pages' would not). 'At his armpit Bantam Lyons' voice and hand said' (Lo 519), a sentence that seems to have placed too heavy a burden on a yoking verb, reveals through its own verbal process Bantam's diminutive size, corroborating his nickname, and also focuses on the manual contact with Bloom's arm – factors not presented as objective narration but as facets of Bloom's immediate perceptions. 'Bantam Lyons's yellow blacknailed fingers unrolled the baton' (Lo 523) contains a Bloomian observation which his mind immediately corroborates with a typical value judgement: 'Wants a wash too. Take off the rough dirt. Good morning, have you used Pears' soap? Dandruff on his shoulders. Scalp wants oiling' (Lo 523–5). From a height of 'five-feet-eight-and-a-half-inches' Bloom looks down at the Bantam's head, and looks forward to a bath, for which he has just purchased a cake of soap. 'He rustled the pleated pages, jerking his chin on his high collar' (Lo 528) seems to lack authoritative substantiation, except in Bloom's judgemental assumption of 'Barber's itch' (Lo 529), once he has noticed that Lyons no longer sports a moustache. And even the innocuous sentence, 'He walked cheerfully towards the mosque of the baths' (Lo 549), contains evidence of Bloom's sighting of the building and the mosque-like architecture that registers itself graphically for him: 'Remind you of a mosque, redbaked bricks, the minarets' (Lo 549–50). Bloom's thoughts tend to pre-determine what thereafter becomes acknowledged as in actual existence. The subjective in these instances precedes physical reality in the narrative method.

A FUNEREAL WHO'S WHO

In the 'Hades' chapter that is parallel in time to 'Proteus', transparent narrative once again suggests itself through many of the early portions, where a balance of dialogue and internalisation carries the narrational burden. The syntax and diction of the opening sentence, for example, are reassuringly familiar by now ('Martin Cunningham, first, poked his silkhatted head into the creaking carriage and, entering deftly, seated himself' – Ha 1–2), and subsequent sentences of this sort take the same responsibility for indicating location, dramatis personae, movement, and direction. Yet, no sooner are the four passengers in the funeral carriage located and identified than the narrative indicators, taking their cue from the lull and slow start of the cortège, begin to echo the tempo in laconic clauses: 'All waited. Nothing was said. . . . All waited. . . . A jolt. . . . At walking pace' (Ha 21–8). It is only with the directive 'Quicker' (Ha 30) that the pace accelerates, as does the development of the narrative sentences: 'The wheels rattled rolling over the cobbled causeway and the crazy glasses shook rattling in the doorframes' (Ha 30–2). As the rhythmic pulsations of the waves in 'Proteus' affected the narrative descriptions, so the jolting and jogging of the carriage in the first half of 'Hades' controls one aspect of the narrative, while the monotony of the journey creates a choreographic counterpoint: 'They went past the bleak pulpit of saint Mark's, under the railway bridge, past the Queen's theatre: in silence' (Ha 183–4). Rarely, however, do these narrative lines call attention to themselves, but remain serviceable in their transparency, subliminally keeping pace with the active ingredients of the on-going process.

Two unusual passages in the later part of the chapter none the less stand out as functioning somewhat beyond their obvious service. It becomes apparent during the funeral ceremony that

Bloom's knowledge of Catholic ritual is marginal at best, and that he lacks the vocabulary necessary to identify the priestly accoutrements and paraphernalia. The presumably objective narration surprisingly reveals the same deficiency: 'The priest took a stick with a knob at the end of it out of the boy's bucket and shook it over the coffin. Then he walked to the other end and shook it again. Then he came back and put it back in the bucket' (Ha 614–16). Not only a lack of functional terminology, but parataxical constructions, blank vocabulary and bland repetitions earn those three sentences low marks. Totally absent are the jaunty verbs (poked, slammed, dragged, rattled), the pointed adverbs and adjectives (silkhatted, creaking, deftly, crazy) and those phrases of heightened descriptions ('curving his height with care', 'covered himself quickly', 'Nose whiteflattened against the pane' – Ha 3, 6, 13). Objective narration now finds itself as limited as the subjective character who is at the centre of the action: Mr Leopold Bloom.

The revealing passage that follows soon after reflects the same dull transparency, until the colouring of its opaqueness becomes apparent:

> The priest closed his book and went off, followed by the server. Corny Kelleher opened the sidedoors and the gravediggers came in, hoisted the coffin again, carried it out and shoved it on their cart. Corny Kelleher gave one wreath to the boy and one to the brother-in-law. All followed them out of the sidedoors into the mild grey air. Mr Bloom came last folding his paper again into his pocket. He gazed gravely at the ground till the coffincart wheeled off to the left. The metal wheels ground the gravel with a sharp grating cry and the pack of blunt boots followed the trundled barrow along a lane of sepulchres.   (Ha 631–9)

Of those seven sentences only the last one returns to the rhythms and diction of opaque style, and the point of departure is a single word in the sixth sentence, Bloom's control word for his behaviour at the funeral: 'gravely'. None of the mourners is particularly aggrieved at the loss of Paddy Dignam – the widow of course is not present at the gravesite – and 'Quarter mourning' (Ha 181) serves well to describe most of those congregated at the Glasnevin cemetery. Bloom makes quite a successful effort to sustain proper decorum, but boredom at the service reduces his observations to mere hackneyed expressions – those that also govern the narra-

tion. Immediately after, when Tom Kernan criticised the reading of
the service, Bloom 'nodded gravely' (Ha 661), and even Martin
Cunningham is described leaving the cemetery, 'talking gravely' to
John Henry Menton (Ha 1006). As far back as 'Lotus Eaters' the
narrative line had indicated that Bloom 'tore the flower gravely
from its pinhold smelt its almost no smell and placed it in his heart
pocket' (Lo 260–1), a sentence that quite explicitly anticipates
Hades and is certainly closer to Bloomian subjectivity than to any
known criterion for objective narration. (Parallel to the key-word
'gravely' in the cemetery service passage is the repeated word
'again' – 'hoisted the coffin again ... folding his paper again',
diagnostic of the hypnotic rhythm of the repetitive actions so
apparently meaningless to Bloom.)

Whereas the other male Dubliners are tempted away from
gravity by their inclinations to exchange witty anecdotes, Bloom is
attempting to control his tendency toward cheerful humming, and
no sooner has he watched the gravediggers follow 'the trundled
barrow along a lane of sepulchres' than he almost gives way: 'The
ree the ra the ree the ra the roo. Lord, I mustn't lilt here' (Ha 640).
At the core of the problem is Corny Kelleher, the primary subject of
that dreary paragraph ('Corny Kelleher opened the sidedoors',
'Corny Kelleher gave one wreath to the boy'), and as far back as
'Lotus Eaters' he is associated in Bloom's mind with just such
lilting:

> Daresay Corny Kelleher bagged the job for O'Neill's. Singing
> with his eyes shut. Corny. Met her once in the park. In the dark.
> What a lark. Police tout. Her name and address she then told
> with my tooraloom torraloom tay. O, surely he bagged it. Bury
> him cheap in a whatyoumaycall. With my tooraloom, tooraloom,
> tooraloom, tooraloom.   (Lo 12–16)

When Bloom is attempting to maintain a grave demeanor with
Tom Kernan after the service, that gravity is once again threatened
by the intrusive presence of the same Corny Kelleher, asking if
'Everything went off A l.... What?'; 'He looked on them from
his drawling eye. Policeman's shoulders. With your tooraloom
tooraloom' (Ha 684–6), even in his natural habitat a spectre of
levity.

The other tell-tale passage at the end of 'Hades' occurs after the
interment of Paddy Dignam:

The boy propped his wreath against a corner: the brother-in-law
his on a lump. The gravediggers put on their caps and carried
their earthy spades towards the barrow. Then knocked the
blades lightly on the turf: clean. One bent to pluck from the haft
a long tuft of grass. One, leaving his mates, walked slowly on
with shouldered weapon, its blade blueglancing. Silently at the
gravehead another coiled the coffinband. His navelcord. The
brother-in-law, turning away, placed something in his free
hand. Thanks in silence.   (Ha 908–15)

This lucidly explicit narration is a *tour de force* of anonymity, and
although there is no reason to attach names to the insignificant
gravediggers, the two persons who are constantly masked as 'the
boy' and 'the brother-in-law' are specifically Master Patrick Dignam and Mr Bernard Corrigan, eldest son and brother-in-law of
the deceased. Here in 'Hades' they are consistently shrouded in
anonymity, but their names will surface later in *Ulysses*, Patsy
Dignam coming into his own in 'Wandering Rocks' and Corrigan
named in 'Eumaeus' in the newspaper account of the funeral. Joe
Hynes, who wrote the account, knows Corrigan by name, but
Leopold Bloom apparently does not, and the narrative depiction of
the grave scene is exclusively determined by Bloom's incomplete
knowledge and bored observations. What masquerades as open
and objective narration is often unmasked as the interplay between
observable phenomena and the limited consciousness of the subjective character, the basic causation of narrative exposition in
these six morning chapters, and with many unusual variations
thereafter in the succeeding chapters of *Ulysses*.

2

Choreographic Narrative

'But ours is the *omphalos*', reports Buck Mulligan expansively (Te 544), in characterising and individualising the Martello Tower in Sandycove that he had rented, where Stephen Dedalus has been staying for at least ten days and Haines for the past three. The three 'residents' have descended from the narrow tower to the open area of Sandycove beach, but Mulligan's allusion to the presumed centre of the world reinforces the tensions of the opening of the Telemachus chapter on the open top of the tower. To that tightly constrained area, enclosed by the parapets but exposed to the sky, Mulligan had summoned Stephen up (and will later call him back down). The verbal sparring that characterises their inter-exchanges in that confined arena sets the stage for the battle for domination that persists between them: 'Parried again', Stephen thinks when Mulligan compliments him egregiously, adding, 'He fears the lancet of my art as I fear that of his' (Te 152) – but the fear may apply more aptly to Stephen than to Mulligan. The vast expanse of open sky around them gives Stephen a certain degree of manoeuvrability; he has the freedom to look past his 'threadbare cuffedge' (Te 106) to the surrounding sea. Mulligan attempts to draw Stephen in, holding up a restrictive mirror for him to view himself, and even in this manoeuvre Stephen manages to remain uncooperative, looking instead at the crack in the glass, like a 'Hair on end' (Te 136). In the tight quarters of the gun emplacement Mulligan 'suddenly linked his arm in Stephen's and walked with him round the tower' (Te 147–8), playing the unusual role of a jovial prison guard. Although they both looked 'towards the blunt cape of Bray Head' (Te 181), that outward objective could only be realised as an ideal, since no one could reasonably be expected to see Bray Head from the Sandycove tower with the naked eye. Mulligan constantly closes in on his prey, but in response to Mulligan's continuous overtures, 'Stephen freed his arm quietly' (Te 182), attempting to remain his own person.

'A LITTLE CLOUD'

Left alone for a few minutes atop the tower Stephen is far from the 'moody brooding' (Te 235–6) that Mulligan attributes to him. His mood is governed by the 'morning peace' (Te 242), now that Mulligan has gone, and he gives himself over to the woodshadows and Yeats's song and the imagined sound of harpstrings. The open freedom, however, proves to be shortlived as an unexpected 'enemy' replaces Mulligan: 'A cloud began to cover the sun slowly' (Te 248). This oppressive presence weighs down upon Stephen, changing his mood and returning his thoughts to his dead mother, so that Buck's call joins with the recurrence of sunlight as welcome relief: 'Stephen, still trembling at his soul's cry, heard warm running sunlight and in the air behind him friendly words' (Te 282–3). At the same moment (although three chapters forward in the text) Leopold Bloom experiences the heavy weight of the same cloud. In the open street, where he has purposely sought the 'bright side' (Ca 77), the darkening cloud catches him unaware: 'A cloud began to cover the sun slowly, wholly' (Ca 218). His morose death thoughts reach their nadir of despair in 'the grey sunken cunt of the world' (Ca 227–8), and he moves quickly toward home and the palliatives of food and Molly: 'To smell the gentle smoke of tea, fume of the pan, sizzling butter. Be near her ample bed-warmed flesh. Yes, yes' (Ca 237–9). Fortunately, 'Quick warm sunlight', a figurative suggestion to Bloom of his daughter Milly, 'came running from Berkeley road, swiftly, in slim sandals' (Ca 240–1), rescuing him while he is still vulnerable in the open space of Eccles Street: 'runs, she runs to meet me, a girl with gold hair on the wind' (Ca 241–2). Bloom and Stephen independently move toward the security of open spaces, find themselves threatened by impinging darkness, seek solace in the drawing near to the comforts offered by others, although potentially endangered by those others.

When Bloom is once again caught in the open by a sudden darkening, he is moving toward lunch as previously he had been moving toward breakfast. He is even smiling at the sun, at the idea of the newspaper banner featuring a 'Home Rule sun rising up in the northwest', when the cloud overtakes him: 'His smile faded as he walked, a heavy cloud hiding the sun slowly, shadowing Trinity's surly front' (Le 473–6). Thoughts of lunacy, painful birth, omnipresent death, urban blight and capitalist exploitation are

blamed on the hour of the day, as previously his dark brooding
had been blamed on getting up on the 'wrong side of the bed' (Ca
233–4). This rationalisation, however, is quickly replaced by
thoughts of food ('Hope they have liver and bacon today' – Le 498),
since after the arrival of Boylan's letter Molly is no longer a
soothing topic of thought. But once the 'sun freed itself slowly and
lit glints of light among the silverware opposite in Walter Sexton's
window' (Le 499–500), Bloom is freed from morbidity, and equilibrium returns.

An interceding moment of cloudiness, equidistant in time between the morning cloud and the midday cloud, occurs in 'Hades',
when Bloom is riding in the funeral carriage with Dedalus,
Cunningham and Power, but there is no significant indication of
Bloom's awareness of the change (although his view of the
gasworks while on the way to Dignam's burial is sufficient to
conjure up thoughts of illness and death), until a 'raindrop spat on
his hat. He drew back and saw an instant shower of spray dots
over the grey flags' (Ha 129–30). From the vantage point of the
enclosed carriage he takes this meterological change in stride ('–
The weather is changing, he said quietly'), and is entertained by
Simon Dedalus's comment that it is 'as uncertain as a child's
bottom' (Ha 132, 138). In this instant Bloom is securely cocooned
among his cohorts (those 'others'), closed off in a snug carriage;
and even if Dedalus, Cunningham and Power are hardly close
friends, they serve for the moment as expediently as Mulligan's
'friendly' voice had served for Stephen marooned atop the tower.

'MAY I TRESPASS ON YOUR SPACE?'

Stephen's descent into the inner confinement of the tower in
'Telemachus' brings him into his most claustrophobic position in
relation to Mulligan and Haines. The bowels of the battlement are a
Dantean inferno, and he has left the 'Warm sunshine merrying
over the sea' for 'the gloomy domed livingroom of the tower',
where 'a cloud of coalsmoke and fumes of fried grease floated' (Te
306, 313, 316–17). Mulligan's exaggerated cry of 'Janey Mack, I'm
choked!' results in Stephen producing the key, of which he is the
temporary keeper, and unlocking the door: 'welcome light and
bright air entered' (Te 323–8). Even the sanctity of Stephen's mind

has been invaded by Mulligan in this chapter of 'close quarters': on top of the tower Stephen had re-created the scene in Clive Kempthorpe's rooms at Oxford on the basis of Mulligan's off-hand mention of the name, a scene that must derive from Mulligan's experiences but subsequently 'rethought' by Stephen, who rescues himself from the dangers of entrapment by moving in his visual recreation outward through the 'open window' (Te 172) to where a deaf gardener moves freely, indifferent to the ragging within. Inside the tower Mulligan's voice rummages about with abandon in Stephen's thoughts, in blatant self-advertisement ('God, we'll simply have to dress the character. I want puce gloves and green boots' – Te 515–16) and in blunt self-aggrandisement ('He wants that key. It is mine. I paid the rent' – Te 630–1). The affluent Mulligan is the obvious renter, as he must often have reminded Stephen, who keeps the recollection of that reminding voice in mind.

Halfway through his wanderings in 'Lotus Eaters' Bloom has taken temporary refuge in All Hallows Church, where he can be 'alone' with his thoughts. Despite his attempts to expunge them, his thoughts are often about Molly, and as he sits in the pew he reads the inscriptions on the officiating priest's 'back' from his vantage place to the side, so that it is the left side of the priest's back that is shown to advantage: 'I. N. R. I.? No: I. H. S.' (Lo 372). Bloom goes on to spell out the acronym for himself: 'Molly told me one time I asked her. I have sinned: or no: I have suffered, it is. And the other one? Iron nails ran in' (Lo 372–4). These classic examples of Bloom's ignorance of Roman Catholicism may be diagnostic (he is innocent of such technical terms as tonsure, alb and chasuble in this context), but he appears to be quoting Molly verbatim on both I. H. S. and I. N. R. I., her voice now echoing precisely within this mind. What cannot be retrieved, however, is the *tone* of Molly's words (she might well have indulged in the standard touches of in-group Catholic wit in these mock-attributions), or the degree to which Bloom – on other occasions appreciative of Molly's witticisms – might not realise the nature of the humour. The spaces occupied by the I. N. R. I. – I. H. S. configuration are several: (1) Molly does not know what the letters stand for and so accepts the absurd explanation; (2) Molly knows quite well what they stand for but perpetuates the 'folk' explanation for its humour; (3) Bloom knows that Molly's explanation is a joke; (4) Bloom is sufficiently ignorant of Catholicism to accept

Molly's explanation at face value; (5) Bloom knows that Molly is being witty, but still may not know what the letters stand for.

Just as the third 'scene' of 'Lotus Eaters' (which brings Bloom back out through the front door of All Hallows to Westland row and on to the baths), the third 'scene' of 'Telemachus' completes Stephen's descent from the tower and out to the bathing area. For Stephen the freedom of the open space is only a foretaste of complete freedom from Mulligan and Haines and the tower-prison ('I will not sleep here tonight', he decides; 'Home also I cannot go' – Te 739–40), and in the open air he is relatively free of Mulligan's taunts and accusations and, perhaps even more threatening, Mulligan's encroaching friendship. No longer 'displeased and sleepy', as he was when Buck first conjured him up (Te 13), Stephen 'expands' sufficiently to become his own master, and he liberally pronounces his maledictions on Haines ('Horn of a bull, hoof of a horse, smile of a Saxon' – Te 732) and on Mulligan ('Usurper' – Te 744). The three-part curse has its obvious Irish 'political' overtones, and is best understood as a response to what Stephen 'reads' as Haines's unspoken 'political' thrust, 'smiling at wild Irish' (Te 731). The three-part malediction exists for Mulligan as well, but carefully spaced in the text and in Stephen's thoughts: at first he had designated Buck as 'Chrysostomos' (Te 26) for his sophistry; *now* he classifies him as a usurper of his privileged space; and he will later brand him as a sexual predator, 'Catamite' (SC 734), each of the three indicative of Stephen's fear of being absorbed, compromised or displaced.

For Bloom the church interior was a sanctuary rather than a confining space, away from the casual intrusions that the streets of Dublin so easily afford. As he was accosted by M'Coy prior to his visit to All Hallows (when he was solely interested in a chance to read Martha's letter in solitude), so is he accosted once he has ventured out of his sanctuary. No sooner has he walked the short distance to the chemist's shop than Bantam Lyons waylays him outside that establishment when Bloom is intent on making his way to the baths. Lyons seems to appear out of nowhere as Bloom emerges from Sweny's, and his interest is immediately directed to the newspaper under Bloom's arm. It might be conjectured that this may not have been an accidental meeting at all, that Lyons had seen Bloom with his *Freeman's Journal* enter the chemist's from his habitual vantage place across the street in Conway's pub, and intentionally crossed the street to apprehend Bloom in order to check the odds on Maximum II ('Hello, Bloom, what's the best news? Is that today's? Show us a minute' – Lo 520). Lyons's directness supports the suspicion that he had spotted his target and moved in on the newspaper, which Bloom is willing to get rid of in order to rid himself of Lyons. M'Coy, on the other hand, had been far more circuitous, but Bloom had no difficulty recognising his ulterior motive, to borrow Molly's valise ('Valise tack again' – Lo 149), which Bloom easily foils since Molly will need it for her tour. M'Coy's sanguine acceptance of failure ('O well. . . . That's good news' – Lo 165) anticipates Lyons's question, 'What's the best news?' With wandering scavengers like M'Coy and Lyons abroad, the open streets are hardly secure for Leopold Bloom, and he navigates through them carefully at all times (on first venturing out this morning of 16 June, he had his antennae alert for danger signals, crossing 'to the bright side, avoiding the loose cellarflap of number seventyfive' – Ca 77).

The second and third chapters of the 'Telemachia' expand the internal/constricting–external/expanding possibilities for Stephen Dedalus. In 'Nestor' he is once again the uncomfortable animal in a cage, and although in a commanding position as an authority figure over his pupils, Stephen lacks real control. A permissive teacher turning a blind eye on the petty dishonesties of his upper-middle-class students, he manages something of a stand-off at best, eventually identifying and commiserating with the pathetic Cyril Sargent, the two of them left behind while the others dash off to the playing field. When even Sargent is liberated and runs off to play hockey, Stephen is ensnared by Mr Deasy, employer and paymaster, for whom he has to wait, uncomfortably cooling his heels within the schoolmaster's controlled domain: 'Stale smoky air hung in the study with the smell of drab abraded leather' (Ne 199–200), a replication of the smoke-filled inner confines of the tower in Sandycove. Their financial transaction (Stephen has periodically been brought into the Deasy lair on pay day) is of course delayed as Deasy holds forth on home economics and foreign policy, while from the vast outdoors the liberated cries of the hockey players offer an obvious contrast: 'Hooray! Ay! Whrrwhee!' (Ne 384). Deasy continues to weave his web around the entrapped school usher, but it is only a matter of time before Stephen will be able to effect his escape. (It is, after all, a Thursday, a half-day at the school and potentially one of relative freedom for Stephen, as all work days apparently are for the 'travelling' canvasser Bloom.) Even after Stephen goes 'out by the open porch and down the gravel path under the trees, hearing the cries of voices and crack of sticks from the playfield' (Ne 427–8), Deasy calls after him, tugging him back with his belated witticism, one final tug on the leash.

It is in 'Proteus' that Stephen achieves a measure of liberation, alone and in the open, footloose and cerebrally fanciful, yet inwardly constricted none the less by the accumulated intellectual debris in his own mind. Externally he is his own man, and even his bodily functions are satisfied *en plein air* – by contrast Bloom holes himself up in his backyard jakes, a 'king' in his 'countinghouse' (Ca 498–9), 'restraining himself' in controlling the movements of his bowels (Ca 506), although he has conveniently left the 'door ajar, amid the stench of mouldy limewash and stale cobwebs' (Ca 496–7). Despite his profession as a wandering agent (Molly would much prefer that he 'chuck that Freeman with the paltry few shillings he knocks out of it and go into an office or something where hed get regular pay or a bank where they could put him up on a throne to count the money all the day' (Pe 504–6), a king in a countinghouse), Bloom tends to gravitate naturally toward enclosed areas, while Stephen seems to thrive best when freed from such enclosures. In his imagination Stephen 'visits' the residence of his maternal uncle, a house under siege by creditors ('They take me for a dun, peer out from a coign of vantage' – Pr 70–1), but when it comes to actually turning into Strasburg terrace he allows the thought instead to serve for the deed: 'He halted. I have passed the way to aunt Sara's. Am I not going there? Seems not' (Pr 158–9). Although he can hypothesise the visit in minute detail from previous experiences there, he chooses to pass the house by (and the chance of a possible night's lodgings) with a conscious decision in favour of remaining out of doors, tangentially concluding that 'This wind is sweeter' (Pr 104).

One can only speculate on what Stephen is doing on Sandymount strand during the final morning hour, and how he managed to get there. The time that has elapsed since the end of the previous chapter is not enough to allow for his having walked all the way from Dalkey, yet if he travelled by train, why not all the way into Dublin, his ultimate destination? The urban centre has been well established as Stephen's natural habitat and his performance stage (in *A Portrait* the move into the city coincides with his coming of age), yet he still has apprehensions: in the newspaper office Stephen will muse: 'Dublin. I have much, much to learn' (Ae 915). If Stephen has intentionally interrupted his venture into the city for a brief respite along the strand (rather than an intentional stop at the Gouldings), he may well have availed himself of the most tranquil hour of his day ('Pan's hour, the faunal noon' – Pr 442), yet not without certain perils. The rhythmic movements of the sea lull his thoughts, determining the rhythms of his thinking as well as the rhythms of his aimless peregrinations. Deprived of an immediate destination (Strasburg terrace) and loath to commit himself to an announced destination determined by the 'enemy' ('– The Ship, Buck Mulligan cried. Half twelve' – Te 733), he is drawn dangerously out toward the sea:

> He had come nearer the edge of the sea and wet sand slapped his boots. . . . Here, I am not walking out to the Kish lightship, am I? He stood suddenly, his feet beginning to sink slowly in the quaking soil. Turn back.
>
> Turning, he scanned the shore south, his feet sinking again slowly in new sockets.   (Pr 265–71)

Movement forward brings the hydrophobic Stephen precariously close to the realm of the drowned man; a cessation of movement causes him to sink downward into the sand. The terrain before him and the terra firma beneath him prove equally treacherous.

The Stephen of 'Proteus', acknowledging his weakness ('I am not a strong swimmer' – Pr 323–4), moves close to the edge of the briny deep, endangering himself as did Hippolytus ('Vehement breath of waters amid seasnakes, rearing horses, rocks' – Pr 457–8), or Lycidus ('Sunk though he be beneath the watery floor' – Pr 474), or even Alonso ('Full fathom five thy father lies' – Pr 470), and is lulled into thinking of his own demise by water as a 'Seadeath, mildest of all deaths known to man' (Pr 482–3). (There is every indication that his cerebral debris contains sufficient resurrection possibilities to offset thoughts of his hypothetical drowning.) Teaching 'Lycidus' in the safe bounds of a schoolhouse in Dalkey is now translated into experiencing Lycidus's seadeath where the drowned man had had his demise and is now a 'Bag of corpsegas sopping in foul brine' (Pr 476). Even the recollection of a simple bowl of still water proves disquieting (as had the 'bowl of white china' (Te 108) in which his dying mother had vomited): 'When I put my face into it in the basin at Clongowes. Can't see! Who's behind me? Out quickly, quickly!' (Pr 324–5). His reflection in the basin draws him close into himself, as he had felt drawn into Mulligan's cracked looking-glass, making him all the more vulnerable from without, but also suggesting the self-destructive lure from within.

The traumatic moment in the sand, unable either to move forward or to retreat, is associated by Stephen with confinement in Mulligan's tower. As he feels himself sinking, he recalls the inner room in which he breakfasted that morning with Mulligan and Haines:

> The cold domed room of the tower waits. Through the barbacans the shafts of light are moving ever, slowly ever as my feet are sinking, creeping duskward over the dial floor. Blue dusk, nightfall, deep blue night. In the darkness of the dome they wait, their pushedback chairs, my obelisk valise, around a board of abandoned platters. Who to clear it? He has the key. I will not sleep there when this night comes. A shut door of a silent tower, entombing their blind bodies, the panthersahib and his pointer. Call: no answer. He lifted his feet up from the suck and turned back by the mole of boulders. Take all, keep all. My soul walks with me, form of forms. So in the moon's midwatches I pace the path above the rocks, in sable silvered, hearing Elsinore's tempting flood. (Pr 271–81)

By creating his own fiction of Mulligan and Haines 'entombed' in their tower – the genesis of a Dedalian Gothic novel continued in 'Oxen of the Sun' (OS 1010–37) – while he, the Hamlet that Haines had evoked by likening the Sandycove structure to Elsinore, survives, Stephen releases himself from the muck that had been drawing him down. The night scene that he conjures up of the 'abandoned' enemies, helpless without him, will be belied by the later events of *Ulysses*, the enemies abandoning Stephen instead, but for the purpose of liberating himself from the dangers at the edge of the sea, the fiction has its miraculous function. Stephen's soul walks confidently with him, escaping the nets flung to keep it down.

The Bloom of 'Lotus Eaters' is equally as unconstrained as he will be at any point during the day, at least until night falls in 'Nausicaa', primarily because he takes elliptical routes in order to avoid contacts with others – despite momentary traps laid by

M'Coy and Lyons. His wanderings will eventually lead him to the lulling baths, the ablutions prior to the Dignam funeral. He meanders (purposely? purposeless?) through the southeastern quadrant of Dublin, perhaps throwing off any mythical spy who might be tailing him, claiming Martha's letter at the Westland Row post office and buying his soap at Sweny's. His thoughts also appear to be aimless, but not particularly troubled as yet: his destination in time is the 11 a.m. funeral, in space the baths on Tara street. That establishment had already connoted for him an element of escape, even before he set out on his mysterious trek: in 'Calypso' he thinks, 'Wonder have I time for a bath this morning. Tara street. Chap in the paybox there got away James Stephens, they say. O'Brien' (Ca 489–91). (That the cashier at the baths may have been involved in the prison break of the Fenian head-centre parallels speculation that the counter man at the cabman's shelter drove the escape cab for the Invincibles after the Phoenix Park murders, complementing Bloom's mood of deflection and deception.) Despite his announced intentions Bloom does not frequent the Tara street baths this morning, but makes his way immediately to Leinster street instead, foiling the plan of anyone attempting to second-guess his intentions. In a chapter that specialises in deflected movements (the longest way to Westland row is through Tara street; in the back door of All Hallows, out the front), any 'shadow' lying in wait for Bloom in the Tara street baths will be frustrated.

As a pedestrian, Bloom takes his tentative stroll in 'Calypso', around the corner to Dorset street for a pork kidney, veering toward the west (bright) side of Eccles street, past the barely friendly sentinel (Larry O'Rourke), and into the temporary haven offered by Dlugacz the pork butcher. There he is tempted by an even friendlier haven, a 'return' to a Palestinean homeland advertised as Agendath Netaim, although a siren in the form of the next-door maid almost leads him off course ('To catch up and walk behind her if she went slowly' – Ca 171–2). Not only does she go off in the opposite direction (she 'sauntered lazily to the right' – Ca 174), but once he is outside the shop Bloom cannot locate her at all ('No sign. Gone. What matter?' – Ca 190), and he returns 'back along Dorset street' (Ca 191), only to encounter the menace of the black cloud. Now neither side of the street is safe. The excursion to the outdoor jakes, a tight enclosure within the outer enclosure of his garden wall – and the door left comfortingly ajar – provides a few moments of particular solace for him at the end of 'Calypso', when neither the home that he does not rule nor the streets that he cannot safely navigate offers sanctuary.

The respite in All Hallows, and presumably the wallowing in the public baths, are Bloom's most secure moments in 'Lotus Eaters', while the encapsulation in the carriage in 'Hades' contrasts sharply with public exposure in the Glasnevin cemetery. Although slighted both on entering and leaving the carriage (the last one in and the last out), he seems to find himself nicely contained, snug: he is in a position to observe Stephen even when Stephen's father cannot (the 'advantage' of Bloom's having been placed with his back to the driver); he can ignore Boylan by gazing down at his nails; he can retreat inside himself when the painful subject of suicide is raised; and although he fails in his effort to narrate the Reuben J. Dodd anecdote, he remains quite unconcerned when it is taken away from him by Cunningham. The Dodd story, after all, had only been a dodge in order to deflect group awareness of his difference from them. At Glasnevin, however, the open terrain leaves Bloom vulnerable: the other three can now actually discuss him behind his back. Even solicitousness proves uncomfortable when Tom Kernan attaches himself to him, Bloom being neither a good enough Catholic nor Protestant to deal readily with the situation. Kernan is unequivocal in stating that 'This cemetery is a treacherous place', and notes the kinship between himself and Bloom as they emerge from the mortuary chapel, 'We are the last' (Ha 657). Bloom echoes the sentiment, acknowledges the kinship, and seems eager for Kernan's continued association: 'Beside him again. We are the last. In the same boat. Hope he'll say something else' (Ha 662–3). The subject of the 'service of the Irish church', however, disadvantages Bloom and he quietly disassociates himself from Kernan, isolated once again, and finally snubbed by John Henry Menton when attempting to perform the act of a Good Samaritan.

'PORTALS OF DISCOVERY'

An aspect of survival for Leopold Bloom is his ability to control the doors that are his means of ingress and egress – not just the 'crazy door of the jakes' (Ca 494), but the front door to his house as well.

Keyless throughout the day, Bloom is deprived of the usual mastery of even his own house door, and must resort to clever substitutes. His first ploy when going out to the butcher's is to manipulate the appearance of his front door: 'He pulled the halldoor to after him very quietly, more, till the footleaf dropped gently over the threshold, a limp lid. Looked shut. All right till I come back anyhow' (Ca 74–6). In 'Aeolus', however, doors operate outside Bloom's volition in a chapter in which movement is governed by cross-current winds ('They always build one door opposite another for the wind to. Way in. Way out' – Ae 50–1), the counter-flow process already embodied in the printing machines that shuttle relentlessly in and out, forward and back: 'The machines clanked in threefour time. Thump, thump, thump. Now if he got paralysed there and no-one knew how to stop them they'd clank on and on the same, print it over and over and up and back' (Ae 101–3). The rhythmic language of 'Aeolus' follows the same self-reflexive/self-retroactive motions inaugurated by the rolling of beer barrels near the beginning of the chapter: 'Grossbooted draymen rolled barrels dullthudding out of Prince's stores and bumped them up on the brewery float. On the brewery float bumped dullthudding barrels rolled by grossbooted draymen out of Prince's stores' (Ae 21–4).

Although Bloom is particularly sensitive to the mechanical movements, he is none the less subject to their laws, and anthropomorphic in his analysis of the printing process that seems to hypnotise him:

Sllt. The nethermost deck of the first machine jogged forward its flyboard with sllt the first batch of quirefolded papers. Sllt. Almost human the way it sllt to call attention. Doing its level best to speak. The door too sllt creaking, asking to be shut. Everything speaks in its own way. Sllt. (Ae 174–7)

Bloom's manipulation of doors in Aeolus, despite his ability to 'speak their language', breaks down, and venturing into the *Evening Telegraph* office to use the telephone places him in a tight box: 'The doorknob hit Mr Bloom in the small of the back as the door was pushed in' (Ae 280–1). This sudden encounter with J. J. O'Molloy is re-enacted soon after when Bloom comes through a door and bumps against Lenehan: '– My fault, Mr Bloom said, suffering his grip. Are you hurt? I'm in a hurry' (Ae 419). A chain of involuntary contact has been established, a falling of dominoes (O'Molloy to Bloom to Lenehan), that takes its pace from the sllt-ing of the presses, so that inevitably 'A COLLISION ENSUES' (Ae 414). Although the newspaper offices are Bloom's familiar working areas, he is none the less buffeted about in a series of closed boxes, rooms in which doors are mysterious and dangerous. For someone who in the streets of Dublin can guide Josie Breen clear of Cashel Boyle O'Connor Fitzmaurice Tisdall Farrell's maniacal stride and help a blind stripling across the street, he finds himself helpless in the hall of the winds, where various transients hustle about ('The inner door was opened violently and a scarlet beaked face, crested by a comb of feathery hair, thrust itself in' – Ae 344–5), and newsboys are unceremoniously pushed through doors: 'It was the big fellow shoved me, sir' (Ae 398). And once Bloom manages his escape, the curses of Myles Crawford echoing after him, the newsboys follow him down the street and mock his walk. Stephen, on the other hand, slithers in and out of the newspaper office with apparent ease: the rhythmic movement operates faultlessly as Dedalus *père* manages to sllt out before Dedalus *fils* sllts in, and the two never making contact with each other. Whether or not Stephen comes to the *Telegraph* office of his own volition (he is, after all, an errand boy for Deasy on this occasion), he adjusts rather comfortably to the situation, having bypassed his appoint-ment with Mulligan at the Ship. Eluding the trap of a pub selected by his enemy, he now recommends adjourning to an alternative pub, although Lenehan usurps the privilege of making the choice ('My casting vote is: Mooney's!' – Ae 892). As guiding spirit Stephen leads the contingent of five into the street, and at this juncture takes it upon himself to begin a disquisition of his 'parable' on the way.

By setting the five prospective listeners (MacHugh, O'Molloy, Crawford, Lenehan and Burke) in motion with the suggestion of a drink, Stephen has severely jeopardised the chances of having his parable heard by his audience: the open-ended possibilities of O'Connell street defeat his purpose. Of the quintet, Professor MacHugh survives as his only consistent auditor; Lenehan and Burke have jumped the gun and are already on their way to Mooney's before Stephen can start, whereas Crawford lingers behind in his inner office, where O'Molloy apprehends him for a possible loan and even Bloom tries to delay him over the Keyes advertisement. The professor proves to be an imperfect recipient of the parable, indulging in editorial comments along the way and even offering a title for it, but at least he stays with the narration. The advance pair never quite connect with the tale, and only Stephen's 'sudden loud young laugh' at his own story causes them to take notice for a fleeting moment: 'Lenehan and Mr O'Madden Burke, hearing, turned, beckoned and led on across towards Mooney's' (Ae 1028–30), their jerky movements temporarily interrupting their purposeful strides. Myles Crawford, coming abreast of Stephen and MacHugh, hears a bit of the parable and assumes that Stephen's laugh indicates closure ('Finished?' – Ae 1031), apparently indifferent to having missed almost all of it. The Parable of the Plums begins *in camera*, continued down the stairs to the disruptive rhythm of a 'bevy of scampering newsboys' who rush 'down the steps, scattering in all directions, yelling' (Ae 955–6), and presumably ends in the middle of tram-crammed O'Connell street, topographically *in medias res*, where MacHugh re-reads the narrative in the landscape: 'He halted on sir John Gray's pavement island and peered aloft at Nelson through the meshes of his wry smile' (Ae 1067–8). Lord Horatio Nelson, an incidental character in Stephen's tale, usurps the limelight, stealing Stephen's thunder by his overpowering presence and Stephen's disproportionate witticism, which MacHugh savours as he comments: 'Onehandled adulterer. . . . That tickles me, I must say' (Ae 1072–3).

Stephen fares somewhat better in Lyster's office at the National Library, where the four walls can cohesively contain the listeners to his Shakespeare disquisition. The office door, however, operates to his disadvantage in allowing for several interruptions: George Russell effects his escape a third of the way through ('The door closed behind the outgoer' – SC 344), and Buck Mulligan invades a third of the way from the end of Stephen's performance ('Hast thou found me, O mine enemy?' – SC 483). In addition, the Quaker librarian, Stephen's most polite and attentive listener, is twice called out by library clients, one of whom is Leopold Bloom, who had already once interrupted the parable in Crawford's office by his intrusion there. It is fitting irony that Stephen should have the opportunity to repeat his parable with Bloom as the sole hearer in the Eccles street kitchen at an hour so late at night that there is no chance of an interruption. Yet no sooner has Stephen offered the title (an afterthought in 'Aeolus', but in 'Ithaca' given in its proper place in advance of the narrative), than Bloom stops listening and wanders off into his own thoughts, the implied subject of Moses determining his tangential speculations:

> Did he see only a second coincidence in the second scene narrated to him, described by the narrator as *A Pisgah Sight of Palestine* or *The Parable of the Plums*?
>
> It, with the preceding scene and with others unnarrated but existent by implication, to which add essays on various subjects or moral apothegms (e.g. *My Favourite Hero* or *Procrastination is the Thief of Time*).   (It 639–44)

MacHugh had created his own narrative on an implied Nelson, Bloom on an implied Moses. Each as a listener invades Stephen's territory and usurps for himself a facet of that space.

'. . . THE DANCERS FROM THE DANCE'

The 'Scylla and Charybdis' chapter is literally the most highly choreographic segment of *Ulysses* (with the possible exception of 'Wandering Rocks', where the entire corps de ballet is in constant motion). On the small stage of the Head Librarian's office, the staff members are on their feet much of the time, moving about while Stephen – at times standing, at times sitting – holds forth on his Shakespeare theory. The stage is lit by a low shaded lamp so that faces move in and out in a choreography of masks: 'Glittereyed his rufous skull close to his greencapped desklamp sought the face bearded amid darkgreener shadow'; 'Anxiously he glanced in the cone of lamplight where three faces, lighted, shone' (SC 29–30, 292–3). Mr Best, who soon is seated and seems to remain seated throughout, none the less manages to indulge in a constant series of gestures with the notebook that he holds, and even from sitting positions he and Eglinton exact a language of bodily motion: 'John Eglinton shifted his spare body, leaning back to judge. / Lifted'; 'Mr Best eagerquietly lifted his book to say' (SC 152–3, 955). Mulligan, once he has intruded, behaves like a puppet on a string, enacting a series of quick, jerky motions: 'Buck Mulligan came forward, then blithe in motley'; 'He lifts his hands. Veils fall'; 'his head wagging, he came near'; 'Quickly, warningfully Buck Mulligan bent down';

'Buck Mulligan gleefully bent back'; 'He jumped up and snatched the card'; 'Buck Mulligan rapped John Eglinton's desk sharply'; 'Monk Mulligan groaned, sinking to a chair' (SC 485–6, 501, 545–6, 568, 573, 606, 655, 773). In the close environs of the office Mulligan's highly animated activity contrasts distinctly with the steady persistent effort being made by Stephen in developing a non-kinetic discourse, and it is to Stephen's credit that he salvages as much of his narrative as he does against the odds.

Stephen's best moments, however, are midway through the scene, once Russell has vacated and the three librarians are *in situ*, as he himself is acutely aware. 'Rest suddenly possessed the discreet vaulted cell, rest of warm and brooding air', so that he is able to luxuriate in his 'Coffined thoughts', drinking in the tranquil atmosphere of the room of books, while his auditors remain momentarily at peace: 'They are still. Once quick in the brains of men' (SC 345–6, 352, 356). Yet the pervading movement of the chapter is that of the Quaker librarian Lyster, a master of Elizabethan dance steps throughout:

He came a step a sinkapace forward on neatsleather creaking and a step backward a sinkapace on the solemn floor.   (SC 5–6)

Twicreakingly analysis he corantoed off.   (SC 12)

Portals of discovery opened to let in the quaker librarian, softcreakfooted.   (SC 230–1)

He creaked to and fro, tiptoing up nearer heaven by the altitude of a chopine.   (SC 329–30)

Brisk in a galliard he was off, out.   (SC 592)

The quaker librarian, quaking, tiptoed in, quake, his mask, quake, with haste, quake, quack.   (SC 887–8)

Lyster's feet obey the laws of dance in sinkapace, chopine, galliard, but his thoughts are affected by the dance of words that he hears about him (analysis, portals of discovery), and although Stephen's narrative describes a straight line of progression ('– It is this hour of a day in mid June, Stephen said, begging with a swift glance their hearing. The flag is up on the playhouse by the bankside' – SC 154–5), his thought patterns are determined by Lyster's dance steps, a series of fragmentary interjections, crisp and sparse, intrusive but apologetic. Shakespeare himself walks a straight line through Stephen's mind ('In a rosery of Fetter lane of Gerard, herbalist, he walks, greyedauburn. . . . He walks' – SC 651–3), while Stephen acknowledges an expanding–contracting momentum (not unlike the perpetual motion of Bloom's printing presses) that provides the counterpoint to the linear progression:

– As we, or mother Dana, weave and unweave our bodies, Stephen said, from day to day their molecules shuttled to and fro, so does the artist weave and unweave his image. (SC 376–7)

Stephen's performance in the National Library can be accepted as having been fairly successful, yet the scene ends when Mulligan brings down the curtain and escorts Stephen offstage, addressing him in tones reminiscent of the opening scene in 'Telemachus': 'Come, Kinch. Come, wandering Aengus of the birds' (SC 1093). The warder has reclaimed the prisoner, unaware that this 'Aengus of the birds' has his aerial means of escape. Once outside on the library steps Stephen retreats into thoughts of the past and aspects of his dream of the previous night: 'Here I watched the birds for augury. Aengus of the birds. They go, they come. Last night I flew. Easily flew. Men wondered' (SC 1206–7). In the short distance between Kildare street and College Green, in less than half an hour, Stephen has somehow succeeded in ridding himself of Buck Mulligan, and in the roiling seas of the 'Wandering Rocks' he is claimed once again, if only temporarily. This time it is his singing teacher, Almidano Artifoni, whose 'heavy hand took Stephen's firmly' (WR 356), but within a matter of a minute or so Stephen is released and he finds himself alone ('his hand was freed' – WR 360–1), so that before the chapter is over he assumes that he actually is free. But the path that takes him to Clohissey's bookshop brings him into direct confrontation with his sister Dilly, there because Stephen's influence has led her to a desire to learn French, and she has bought herself a primer. The briny vortex again makes its presence felt, the hawklike man facing the threat of a watery death: 'She will drown me with her, eyes and hair. Lank coils of seaweed hair around me, my heart, my soul. Salt green death' (WR 875–7). For Stephen Dedalus this threat represents that of a real, rather than a literary, death, without promise of reversal or resurrection, and thereafter Stephen disappears from the scene until the late evening, presumably having spent the interceding hours drinking in such pubs as the Moira and Larchet's, drowning himself in drink. His encounter with his sister may well have changed the pattern of his 'free' day.

The afternoon for Bloom is fully detailed: once he has returned from the cemetery, his morning goal, he immerses himself in his work (the newspaper offices), an object that hardly claims his full attention. He avoids as much as possible troublesome thoughts of Molly and Boylan, which none the less prove unavoidable, and as he walks down Westmoreland and Grafton streets he concentrates on his desire for lunch. Hot food is scheduled to supplant the remembrance of bedwarmed flesh that had been his previous haven, now in the form of cooked flesh: 'Hope they have liver and bacon today. Nature abhors a vacuum' (Le 498). Just as everything he sees and everyone he meets somehow reverts the subject to Molly, so the hot lunch eludes him when the Burton proves to be too disgusting, and he settles for a cold sandwich at Davy Burne's, a lunch of cheese, which he had already related to meat: 'A corpse is meat gone bad. Well and what's cheese? Corpse of milk' (Ha 981–2). Bracketed between the publican and Nosey Flynn, an old acquaintance, he is relatively secure within the pub, although pubs are not his natural habitat, until Flynn mentions Blazes Boylan: 'A warm shock of air heat of mustard hanched on Mr Bloom's heart. He raised his eyes and met the stare of a bilious clock. Two. Pub clock five minutes fast. Time going on. Hands moving. Two. Not yet' (Le 789–91). From this moment on, the relentless movement of time will bring him toward the instance of the Molly–Boylan assignation, which becomes a marker for him until four o'clock: 'Afternoon she said' (Le 1187); 'At four she. . . . Ternoon' (Si 309–10). Despite Flynn's reference to Boylan, Bloom attempts to hold on to his equilibrium, retain his security in the pub ('Nice quiet bar. Nice piece of wood in that counter. Nicely planed'; 'Nice wine it is' – Le 822, 851), but disquieting reality intrudes and his haven becomes a trap: 'Stuck on the pane two flies buzzed, stuck'; 'Stuck, the flies buzzed' (Le 896, 918). His lunch eaten, Bloom drains his glass of burgundy and quickly departs. The real danger, however, awaits him in the Dublin streets.

IN THE TRACK OF BLOOM

Once Bloom leaves the moral pub he finds himself in masterful control of Molesworth street, totally unaware of impending danger, although at first he is somewhat cautious ('Mr Bloom coasted warily' – Le 1033–4). He relies on the residual effects of his light lunch for ballast: 'Feel better. Burgundy. Good pick me up' (Le 1042). His particular triumph at this interval is spatially strategic, the guiding of the blind piano tuner across Dawson street to Molesworth street, a gesture somewhat marred by a recollection of Boylan based on the sighting of Drago's barber shop: 'Where I saw his brillantined hair just when I was' (Le 1083–4). This intimation is immediately diverted as Bloom concerns himself with the blind boy, and he is tempted to stop at the stationer's and then send Martha Clifford a postal order. Had he stopped to do so, instead of deciding to wait and 'Think over it' (Le 1134), Bloom might well have missed the near-confrontation with Boylan on Kildare street. Or had he not dawdled along Molesworth street to experiment with the sense of touch, trying to identify with what a blind person can feel (the stripling is already well ahead of him: 'There he goes into Frederick street' – Le 1138), he might have passed well in front of Boylan. Instead, all the navigational interstices conspire for the inevitable collision, a potential convergence of the twain, as Bloom walks east and Boylan south toward the intersecting co-ordinates. From the sanctuary of the funeral coach Bloom had had no difficulty avoiding eye contact ('Mr Bloom reviewed the nails of his left hand, then those of his right hand' – Ha 200–1), but now in the open street his only tactic is to rush across Kildare street, trusting that the sun is in Boylan's eyes, and dash through the museum gate, all the while pretending to be preoccupied in searching for something in his pockets, until he can declare himself 'Safe!' (Le 1193).

The third time proves a fatal charm. At four o'clock, from the south side of the Liffey, Bloom notices Boylan's jaunting car heading toward the Ormond Hotel, when Boylan should logically be at the door of 7 Eccles street: 'He eyed and saw afar on Essex bridge a gay hat riding on a jaunting car. It is. Again. Third time. Coincidence' (Si 302–3). Unable to resist temptation, consumed by curiosity, Bloom crosses the river and follows Blazes Boylan, stationing himself in the dining room of the Ormond, a coign of vantage from which he can observe Boylan at the bar. Spatial relationships provide Bloom with a strategic position in the closed complex of restaurant, bar and saloon, where sound waves carry the songs sung by Simon Dedalus and Ben Dollard to Bloom's ears, and imagined transmittal of 'sound' the jingle of Boylan's departing car long after it is out of earshot: 'Jingle a tinkle jaunted'; 'Jiggedy jingle jaunty jaunty'; 'Jingle jaunty'; 'Jingle by monuments of sir John Gray, Horatio onehandled Nelson, reverend father Theobald Mathew, jaunted, as said before just now. Atrot, in heat, heatseated' (Si 456, 579, 640, 762–4). The imagined visible accompanies the imagined auditory, Boylan 'seen' in the jaunting car, and the residual presence of Stephen's parable narrated on the pavement island repeats the onehandledness of Horatio Nelson, just as the residual presence of Blazes Boylan persists in the bar of the Ormond: 'Blazes Boylan's smart tan shoes creaked on the barfloor, said before' (Si 761). Bloom was not yet present to hear when 'Blazes Boylan's smart tan shoes creaked on the barfloor where he strode', since he is still outside on Ormond Quay inspecting the parked jaunting car: 'The seat he sat on: warm' (Si 337, 342). And he has not actually seen the tan shoes since the scare on Kildare street: 'Straw hat in sunlight. Tan shoes' (Le 1168).

Wavelengths pulsate unseen throughout the Sirens chapter, characterised by the soundless sounding of the blind stripling's tuningfork, abandoned unintentionally on the Ormond bar piano:

> From the saloon a call came, long in dying. That was a tuning-fork the tuner had that he forgot that he now struck. A call again. That he now poised that it now throbbed. You hear? It throbbed, pure, purer, softly and softlier, its buzzing prongs. Longer in dying call.   (Si 313–16).

And the wavelengths extend beyond immediate hearing; thought waves violate all physical boundaries, the walls of the National Library and the walls of Stephen Dedalus's head, as his musings on 'a rosery of Fetter lane of Gerard, herbalist' (SC 651–2) are wafted (slightly transmuted, distorted) into the Sirenic atmosphere of the Ormond: 'In Gerard's rosery of Fetter lane' (Si 907). Bloom continues to 'hear' the sound of Boylan's car 'Jingle into Dorset street' (Si 812) until it 'Jog jig jogged stopped' and 'Dandy tan shoe of dandy Boylan socks skyblue clocks came light to earth' (Si 977–8), and Blazes is 'heard' knocking at the door of 7 Eccles Street: 'One rapped on a door, one tapped with a knock, did he knock

Paul de Kock with a loud proud knocker with a cock carracarracarra cock. Cockcock' (Si 986–8).

Bloom's concept, formulated when listening to the printing machines in 'Aeolus', that 'Everything speaks in its own way' (Ae 177), is carried forward into 'Sirens', where it has its major reverberancy: 'Understand animals too that way. Solomon did. Gift of nature. / Ventriloquise. My lips closed. Think in my stom. What?' (Si 1093–5). Just as the jaunting car has been speaking in retreat, and the cane of the returning piano tuner speaks as it approaches ['Tap' (Si 1037); 'Tap. Tap' (Si 1084); 'Tap. Tap. Tap' (Si 1119); 'Tap. Tap. Tap. Tap' (Si 1186); 'Tap. Tap. Tap. Tap. Tap' (Si 1218); 'Tap. Tap. Tap. Tap. Tap. Tap. Tap. Tap' (Si 1223)], so too does Bloom's stomach express itself eloquently in thought as he walks away from the Ormond ('Think in my stom'). Flatulence competes with Bloom's silent reading of Robert Emmet's last speech to the Court, as 'Tap. A youth entered a lonely Ormond Hall' (Si 1273), a flatulence silenced by a timed coincidence with the passing of a noisy tram:

> Seabloom, greasebloom viewed last words. Softly. *When my country takes her place among.*
> Prrprr.
> Must be the bur.
> Fff! Oo. Rrpr.
> *Nations of the earth.* No-one behind. She's passed. *Then and not till then.* Tram kran kran kran. Good oppor. Coming. Krandl-krankran. I'm sure it's the burgundy. Yes. One, two. *Let my epitaph be.* Kraaaaaa. *Written. I have.*
> Pprrpffrrppffff.
> *Done.*   (Si 1284–94)

The encounter with the pathetic Dilly may have sent the wandering Stephen into hiding in the pubs until dark, but in various ways Leopold Bloom is a more adventurous Odysseus, and like his prototype takes some unnecessary risks. Pubs are congenially accessible to young Dedalus, whose only danger might be to find himself rubbing shoulders with Dedalus senior in one of them. Bloom, however, has no natural affinity for the public house, and the cool relationship that exists between Larry O'Rourke and himself may be due to his infrequent visits to his neighbourhood local. But he hopes to smoothe over any coolness as he passes the corner pub, yet there is an odd discrepancy between the 'intended' conversation and the eventual version:

> Stop and say a word: about the funeral perhaps. Sad thing about poor Dignam, Mr O'Rourke.
> Turning into Dorset street he said freshly in greeting through the doorway:
> – Good day, Mr O'Rourke.
> – Good day to you.
> – Lovely weather, sir.
> – 'Tis all that.   (Ca 118–25)

The polite Bloom is hardly repaid in kind: no 'sir' or 'Mr Bloom' from the likes of O'Rourke. Molly, however, is far more perceptive and candid about pubkeeper O'Rourke, as she considers their interaction with the local vendor, and seems that much more comfortable with the world of beer and wine:

> Ill have to knock off the stout at dinner or am I getting too fond of it the last they sent from ORourkes was as flat as a pancake he makes his money easy Larry they call him the old mangy parcel he sent at Xmas a cottage cake and a bottle of hogwash he tried to palm off as claret that he couldnt get anyone to drink God spare his spit for fear hed die of the drouth.   (Pe 450–5)

Lunch in a 'moral pub' and an early dinner of sorts in the dining area of the Ormond Hotel are relatively safe for Bloom, but venturing into the hostile arena of Barney Kiernan's (when he should have prudently waited outside for Power and Cunningham) proves to be a mistake, yet Bloom never 'corrects' the error in his afterthoughts. He does start out by waiting in the street, and is noticed by the wary Citizen from his pub stool perch: '– What's that bloody freemason doing, says the citizen, prowling up and down outside?' (Cy 300–1). The pub customers, however, ignore the question and the subject of the observation: they have their own interests in Breen's postcard and Dignam's death to keep them occupied. But the Citizen continues his focus on Bloom, and the second time manages to ignite the interest of the collector of bad debts – although not the others:

> – There he is again, says the citizen, staring out.

– Who? says I.

– Bloom, says he. He's on point duty up and down there for the last ten minutes.

And, begob, I saw his physog do a peep in and then slidder off again.   (Cy 377–81)

Although the expansive narration deriving from parodic gigantism exalts Bloom's bravery ('Impervious to fear is Rory's son: he of the prudent soul' – Cy 216–17), the counterpart narration of the collector of bad debts characterises Bloom's entrance as anything but audacious: 'Bloom that was skeezing round the door'; 'So Bloom slopes in with his cod's eye on the dog and he asks Terry was Martin Cunningham there' (Cy 407–8, 410–11).

Once the atmosphere in Barney Kiernan's intensifies, provoked by the Citizen's particular hostility, Bloom is prodded into taking his stand against injustice, insult and hatred, only to have to make a hasty retreat. Whatever the appointed time for meeting Cunningham and Power had been, there is little doubt that they are late and Bloom on time or even early (a strict consciousness of time in time-casual Dublin does not operate in Bloom's favour). His departure is as abrupt as it is obvious:

–... I must go now, says he to John Wyse. Just round to the court a moment to see if Martin is there. If he comes just say I'll be back in a second. Just a moment.

Who's hindering you? And off he pops like greased lightning. (Cy 1485–8)

Bloom on foot must have been bypassed by Cunningham and Power in the Castle car, and his absence is sufficient for the development of ugly speculation that even his defenders have no way of countermanding: 'The courthouse is a blind. He had a few bob on *Throwaway* and he's gone to gather in the shekels' (Cy 1550–1). When he returns, the hostility has solidified, so that even his innocent statement of the truth acts against him within that environment ('– I was just round at the courthouse, says he, looking for you' – Cy 1756), and the Citizen now mounts his full attack from his position of power within his proper domain. The attempt to rescue Bloom brings him out of the pub and into the street, where an escape car is waiting, but even the streets by now are no longer safe. Aroused onlookers ('all the ragamuffins and sluts of the nation round the door' – Cy 1796) are inexplicably infected by the animosity visited on Bloom, and no area of Dublin seems safe for him. The parodic narration indicates that only the heavens are safe for Bloom, so that he is seen to 'ascend to the glory of the brightness at an angle of fortyfive degrees over Donohoe's in Little Green street like a shot off a shovel' (Cy 1916–18). His departure in great haste will be duplicated by Stephen when he rushes out of Bella Cohen's some seven hours later, but earthbound Stephen lacks a celestial escape mechanism and is humiliatedly knocked senseless on Beaver street.

'DANCING IN THE DARK'

The coming of darkness late on this mid-June night changes the spatial relationships and enforces its own pervasive rhythms. In 'Nausicaa' Bloom and Gerty MacDowell find themselves arranged at a safe distance that also allows for adequate visual proximity to each other, a territorial separation violated (accidentally) by the children's ball and (purposely) by the insensitive Cissy Caffrey intent on asking the time: 'So over she went and when he saw her coming she could see him take his hand out of his pocket, getting nervous, and beginning to play with his watchchain, looking up at the church' (Na 537–9). At the established distance Bloom is a handsome and tragic stranger ('Didn't let her see me in profile', Bloom acknowledges – Na 836), and Gerty a delicate and demure damsel – a relationship that is expected to endure, protected by night falling. Gerty obviously hopes to effect her escape under the cover of darkness, but again Cissy Caffrey violates the timing as she had the spatial ground rules ('Gerty! Gerty! We're going. Come on. We can see from farther up' – Na 756). The night is not yet dark enough to cover Gerty's tell-tale limp, so that Bloom has no difficulty discovering her secret – and she had presumably been aware of Bloom's secretive masturbation under the protective covering of his clothes and the failing light: 'That was their secret, only theirs, alone in the hiding twilight' (Na 750–1). Acutely sensitive probably that the 'distance' between them had been transgressed upon, Gerty moves off in pursuit of the others, 'Slowly, without looking back' (Na 766).

The rain that falls later in the evening inundates Mulligan and

Bannon as they make their way from George Moore's to the lying-in hospital ('overtaken by the rain and for all their mending their pace had taken water, as might be observed by Mr Mulligan's smallclothes of a hodden grey which was now somewhat piebald' – OS 699–701), but leaves Bloom and Stephen unscathed in the warm womb of the hospital commonroom, where both remain relatively protected from abuse. The medical students and hangers-on (Costello, Crotthers, Dr Dixon, Madden, Lenehan, Lynch, along with Stephen and Bloom) are fixed in proximate relationship around the table, joined by the two rainsoaked newcomers, although Dixon is temporarily called away to deal with the Purefoy birth. Whatever tensions exist are diffused among the ten partici-pants and contained easily within the room, but at Stephen's instigation ('outflings my lord Stephen, giving the cry, and a tag and bobtail of all them after' – OS 1391–2) they quickly depart for the last drinks at the nearest pub, and space immediately becomes fluid. The ten of them are 'All off for a buster, armstrong, hollering down the street' (OS 1440), attempting to maintain a military formation: 'March! Tramp, tramp, tramp, the boys are (atitudes!) [*sic*] parching' (OS 1458–9). But Dixon is feeling ill and lagging behind ('Hurrah there, Dix!'), probably accompanied by a solici-tous Costello ('Where's Punch?'). Stephen drunkenly stands out alone from the group, apparently in advance and attracting the unwanted attention of the local street urchins ('Jay, look at the drunken minister coming out of the maternity hospal!'), and it is Bloom who moves them aside and as such earns an invitation to the pub: 'Righto, Isaacs, shove em out of the bleeding limelight. Yous join uz, dear sir?' (OS 1443–8). The doorway of Burke's pub, however, frustrates any attempt by a phalanx to gain simultaneous entrance, so that what began as a military line six abreast disinte-grates into a rugby scrimmage: 'Heave to. Rugger. Scrum in. No touch kicking. Wow, my tootsies! You hurt? Most amazingly sorry!' (OS 1463–4). The transgressor may be Lenehan, who had been bumped into by Bloom in the newspaper office, and may now be echoing Bloom's apology of 'Are you hurt? . . . Sorry' (Ae 419–23).

The Burke's enclosure swallows the ten new customers, that loose-knit entity distributing itself strategically along the counter for drinks. The narrative medium approximates radio transmission, sound without vision, and only the disembodied 'voices' of the ten can be heard in clusters along the bar, the groupings only guessed at through narrative interaction. Stephen, buying the drinks, is very much in his element, and Bloom, for whom a pub had previously been near-disaster, remains calmly secure, despite his choice of a non-alcoholic ginger cordial, which elicits someone's caustic comment, 'Chase me, the cabby's caudle' (OS 1468). Although probably unaware of his triumph, Bloom dominates the unfamiliar terrain sufficiently to frighten Alec Bannon into a hasty exit, when he guesses at his identity: 'Bloo? Cadges ads? Photo's papli, by all that's gorgeous! Play low, pardner. Slide. *Bonsoir la compagnie*' (OS 1535–6). Mulligan slips away with Bannon as well ('Where's the buck and Namby Amby? Skunked?' – OS 1537–8), abandoning Stephen in order to join Haines at Westland Row terminus, while Lenehan had previously made a hasty retreat rather than face the drunken ire of Bantam Lyons: 'Decamping. Must you go? Off to mammy. Stand by. Hide my blushes someone. All in if he spots me' (OS 1520–1). The *'compagnie'* disintegrates as the pub closes, and in the streets they disperse, some to chase the fire engines and some headed for Nighttown.

EXERCISES IN TIGHT PLACES

A similar audio/non-visual transmittal operates on a lesser scale in 'Eumaeus', where the denizens of the cabman's shelter are rather shadowy customers, confined in cramped quarters: 'Let me cross your bows mate', says Murphy the sailor, as he tries to slip past the person sitting next to him (Eu 920). The number of occupants of the shelter remains vague, and their specific identities equally vague: Bloom and Stephen are the only characters in the scene who have a previous existence in *Ulysses*, and the only two other named persons may be sailing under false colours. The sailor displays his papers ('There's my discharge. See? D. B. Murphy. A. B. S.' – Eu 452), but he also shows a postcard, of which he is assumed to be the named recipient, yet the addressee is a *'Señor A Boudin'* (Eu 489), so that Bloom conjectures that 'Our mutual friend's stories are like himself. . . . Do you think they are genuine?' (Eu 821–2). The keeper of the shelter is also of dubious nomenclature, rumoured (by Bloom) 'to be the once famous Skin-the-Goat, Fitzharris, the invincible, though he could not vouch for the actual facts which quite possibly there was not one vestige of truth in' (Eu

323–5). Despite the disclaimer, the putative attribution tends to stick to the keeper, so that the narrative undertakes to refer to 'Skin-the-Goat, assuming he was he' (Eu 985). Of the tertiary characters, an undefined trio begin to emerge in shadowy forms, as 'one longshoreman', 'loafer number two', and 'a third' (Eu 694–6), but advance no further in the establishing of individual identities. One of them, however, undergoes rather dim transformations: at first 'seen from the side' he bears 'a distant resemblance to Henry Campbell, the townclerk' (Eu 661); next he is 'the jarvey who had really quite a look of Henry Campbell' (Eu 908); then he is 'the cabby like Campbell, facial blemishes apart' (Eu 1019–20); and eventually he is unequivocally 'the *soi disant* townclerk Henry Campbell' (Eu 1354–5) – at which point the shelter keeper is unequivocally 'Skin-the-Goat' (Eu 1357). In a chapter in which Stephen asserts that 'Sounds are impostures ... like names.... What's in a name?' (Eu 362–4), the distance in the dark between the speculative and the verifiable narrows appreciably, conjecture doing yeoman service for that which cannot conceivably be verified. In the narrowing of physical distances, the constricture of anonymous and anomalous space, Bloom senses the tension in the cabman's shelter and manoeuvres the way out for himself and Stephen, having observed that 'it's rather stuffy here' (Eu 1644).

As their tenure in the shelter draws to a close, Bloom for the third time that day contemplates turning life into literature, capturing the 'fiction' of existence around him: 'suppose he were to pen something out of the common groove (as he fully intended doing) at the rate of one guinea per column, *My Experiences*, let us say, *in a Cabman's Shelter*' (Eu 1229–31). Whereas in the two previous encounters with literary inspiration he had been quite liberal with his acknowledgement of authorship ('By Mr and Mrs L. M. Bloom' and 'by Mr Leopold Bloom' – Ca 518; Na 1060), in this instance he imposes no auctorial name, succumbing to the enforced anonymity of his surroundings. Yet, immediately after, he sees his 'name' in the *Evening Telegraph*, in a piece of journalistic fiction for which no author receives credit, although Bloom 'understands' the implied authorship ('Hynes put it in of course' – Eu 1248), and finds himself as a misnamed 'L. Boom' (Eu 1260) in someone else's experiences.

Stephen's 'expressed desire for some beverage to drink' and Bloom's suggestion of 'the propriety of the cabman's shelter, as it was called' (Eu 5, 8–9) bring them into the domain of the ex-

Invincible. There the common-named Murphy apparently cut close to the bone in narrating his account of a knifing ('I seen a man killed in Trieste by an Italian chap. Knife in his back. Knife like that' – Eu 576–7), so that even something as common as 'a blunt hornhandled ordinary knife' bothers Stephen: 'oblige me by taking away that knife. I can't look at the point of it. It reminds me of Roman history' (Eu 815–18). Even the insensitive Murphy is aware of the confining closeness of the shelter as he excuses himself with the usual pretext in order to slip outside the temperance shanty (the domain of the 'cabby's caudle') to avail himself of a swallow of rum from his pocket flask, and puts himself in danger of being accosted so that he declares himself off-limits to the local 'street-walker' who 'glazed and haggard under a black straw hat peered askew round the door of the shelter' (Eu 704–5).

The experiences of Bloom and Stephen in the cabman's shelter are bracketed in 'Eumaeus' by the walk out of Nighttown and the walk to Eccles street, the experiences of the open streets late at night. A 'bit unsteady' (Eu 5), Stephen is also relatively uncommunicative at the first instance until the encounter with Corley, when he is suddenly expansive in handing over half-a-crown, and even more expansive in suggesting that Corley might replace him at Deasy's school. Bloom, on the other hand, is momentarily unresponsive when Stephen reports that Corley 'asked me to ask you to ask somebody named Boylan, a billsticker, to give him a job as a sandwichman' (Eu 233–4). In the shelter Bloom does try to take advantage of their being at close quarters to sound Stephen out, but most of their conversation is at cross-purposes, and Stephen becomes somewhat withdrawn. Although they are 'safely seated in a discreet corner', they are immediately 'greeted by stares from the decidedly miscellaneous collection of waifs and strays and other nondescript specimens of the genus *homo* ... for whom they seemingly formed an object of marked curiosity' (Eu 326–30). This large group soon sorts itself out into a mere handful, the initial assertion having been the product of a first glance and a sensing of unfriendliness.

The voyage out of the shelter effects a significant change in the relationship between Stephen Dedalus and Leopold Bloom. Bloom arranges for their escape, signalling for the bill and surreptitiously paying it, but Stephen, less aware of danger than Bloom delays their departure:

– Come, he counselled to close the *séance*.

Seeing that the ruse worked and the coast was clear they left the shelter or shanty together and the *élite* society of oilskin and company whom nothing short of an earthquake would move out of their *dolce far niente*. Stephen, who confessed to still feeling poorly and fagged out, paused at the, for a moment, the door.

– One thing I never understood, he said to be original on the spur of the moment. Why they put tables upside down at night, I mean chairs upside down, on the tables in cafés.

To which impromptu the neverfailing Bloom replied without a moment's hesitation, saying straight off:

– To sweep the floor in the morning.   (Eu 1702–13)

From that moment on Stephen allows himself to be drawn toward Bloom, to narrow the space between them, as if the instance of very ordinary intelligence supplied the necessary balance: 'Lean on me', Bloom suggests, and 'Accordingly he passed his left arm in Stephen's right and led him on accordingly' (Eu 1720–2). The accord achieved allows them to face the dangers on the silent streets, where a horse and sweeper are noticed by the perceptive Bloom,

who was keeping a sharp lookout as usual, [and] plucked the other's sleeve gently, jocosely remarking:
– Our lives are in peril tonight. Beware of the steamroller.
(Eu 1778–80)

Their conversation is now animated and continuous, and their navigation sure-footed. To the driver of the sweeper they suggest a married couple, as 'Side by side Bloom ... with Stephen passed through the gap of chains, divided by the upright, and, stepping over a strand of mire, went across towards Gardiner street lower, Stephen singing more boldly, but not loudly' (Eu 1880–3).

OUTER-DIRECTED

The intervening experiences in Nighttown had been controlled by a transformational magic outside the powers of either Bloom or

Stephen, the pulsating rhythm of which '*jerks on*' like the Idiot, or marches '*unsteadily rightaboutface*' like Privates Carr and Compton, or '*climbs in spasms*' like Tommy Caffrey, or '*lurches*' and '*staggers*' like the navvy (Ci 25, 49, 132, 133, 136) – no respecter of fixed locations or marked distances. Bloom and Stephen had arrived separately, the latter having been shaken loose by Mulligan and Haines at Westland Row terminus and the former having taken the wrong train and gone beyond the intended station: trains, like printing presses, shuttle back and forth, seemingly self-propelled and interminable. In the streets Stephen has the arrogant confidence of the drunk, Bloom the prudent wariness of the sober. 'So that gesture,' Stephen insists, 'not music not odour, would be a universal language, the gift of tongues rendering visible not the lay sense but the first entelechy, the structural rhythm' (Ci 105–7), and his own wild gestures conform to the jerks and spasms and lurches of the dramatic choreography of 'Circe'. Bloom, on the other hand, tries to pursue a straight path through the undulations of Nighttown, and runs straight ahead, contracting a stitch in his side, being grazed by cyclists, and narrowly escaping an oncoming sandstrewer by a 'trickleap' to the curb: 'No thoroughfare', he notes; 'Close shave that but cured the stitch' (Ci 199).

During the day, in the known territory of his native city, Bloom had inadvertently encountered a finite number of acquaintances (Larry O'Rourke, Josie Breen, C. P. M'Coy, Bantam Lyons, Richie Goulding), but in the terra incognita of Nighttown the possibility of infinite numbers of encounters is immediately apparent. Challenged by 'THE FIGURE' for the 'Password', he still attempts to maintain direct and continuous movement ('*He steps forward*'), insisting on the logic of 'Keep to the right, right, right', when a ragman bars his way, causing him to execute a series of complicated movements: '*He steps left. . . . He swerves, sidles, stepaside, slips past and on*' (Ci 218, 222, 231, 222–3, 229). Bloom weaves past and through a host of encounters and arrives mysteriously at the very doorstep he seeks ('Perhaps here' – Ci 1278), and even before entering Bella Cohen's, on the steps he undergoes still another series of visitations, so that the house in which he actually finds Stephen gives the impression of being a safe haven. Yet the demonic *Todentanz* goes on inside as well as out, and both Stephen and Bloom are menaced by the enemies that they carry with them: Bloom's reduction to the 'person' of Bello's Miss Ruby results in his ultimate humiliation, while Stephen's vision of his mother's ghost causes his violent reaction and ultimate eruption into the dangerous streets of the red-light district. Although Bloom '*hurries out*' to follow and protect the fleeing Stephen, he himself becomes the object of a prolonged pursuit, the victim of a foxhunt that includes scores of his 'acquaintances': '*He walks, runs, zigzags, gallops, lugs laid back*' (Ci 4314, 4332–3), metamorphosed into an animal. The Stephen who had so confidently entered Nighttown becomes its real victim; rushing out to the safety of the streets he encounters the irrepressible wrath of the British soldier, and risks being run in by the Night Watch. Only the final transformations (Bloom as Yeats's Fergus, Stephen as Bloom's Rudy) offer a fleeting instance for Stephen of equilibrium, the enduring stasis to be negotiated later in the kitchen and back garden of 7 Eccles Street.

The road to Eccles Street is paved with hazards ('Beware of the steamroller' – Eu 1780), but once Stephen and Bloom have circumvented the horse turds and stepped over the chain, they manage to survive quite easily by following 'parallel courses': 'Starting united both at normal walking pace'; 'then, at reduced pace'; 'then, at reduced pace with interruptions of halt'; 'Approaching, disparate, at relaxed walking pace' (It 1–8). The communion that brings them together in Bloom's kitchen, after the keyless Citizen gains access to his violated citadel, retains the constant shifts of united and disparate contact. The low ebb of their disparateness in the close and intimate privacy of the small room takes place when Stephen – perhaps discomfited by too close a personal contact – sings the Ballad of Little Harry Hughes, seemingly with Bloom's relaxed connivance:

> Did the host encourage his guest to chant in a modulated voice a strange legend on an allied theme?

> Reassuringly, their place, where none could hear them talk, being secluded, reassured, and decocted beverages, allowing for subsolid residual sediment of a mechanical mixture, water plus sugar plus cream plus cocoa, having been consumed. (It 795–800)

United but disparate they also venture out for communal urination in the back garden, not in any enclosed jakes but under the stars, 'the infinite lattiginous scintillating uncondensed milky way, discernible by daylight by an observer placed at the lower end of a cylindrical vertical shaft 5000 ft deep sunk from the surface towards the centre of the earth' (It 1043–6), firmly anchored by gravity.

Stephen goes off homeless into infinite space; Bloom goes in homebound into finite and cramped quarters. The biscuit tin hurled by the Citizen outside Barney Kiernan's flew by Bloom's head without injuring him, but inside his safe house in the late-night serenity the navigator of Dublin's dangerous streets has the 'right temporal lobe of the hollow sphere of his cranium' come 'into contact with a solid timber angle' (It 1275–6) – the furnishings of his familiar terrain have been moved in his absence, although he had only been gone since morning. None the less, all roads that had led to home lead Sinbad's companion into that closed space of sleep, positioned in a circle with Molly head to foot in Cohen's (a.k.a. Lord Napier's) old bed, that round black filled circle that is the element of closure in 'Ithaca'. In a parallel course, but separated by a lapsed hour of time, Molly makes the same progression within the enclosed area that she had barely left during the course of the day, and more specifically in the closed realm of her infinite and intricately choreographed thoughts, where the Rock of Gibraltar with Mulvey ('I was a Flower of the mountain yes' – Pe 1602) occupies the same locus as the Hill of Howth with Poldy ('he said I was a flower of the mountain yes' – Pe 1576). Molly Bloom in her night thoughts, bound in a nutshell, is a queen of infinite space, as she enters the world of dreams.

3

Parallax as Structure

From where she sits at her window Eveline Hill can watch 'the evening invade the avenue', hear 'footsteps clacking along the concrete pavement', and inhale the 'odour of dusty cretonne' (D, p. 36). Leaning on the gunrest of the Martello tower in Sandycove, Stephen Dedalus sees 'the fraying edge of his shiny black coat-sleeve' (Te 101), and when he makes the effort of refocusing his viewpoint, he can glance across 'the threadbare cuffedge' (Te 106) to take in the sea that swells around him. No one has ever suspected Eveline of having impaired vision, although for a while some readers of *Ulysses* experimented with the idea that Stephen had broken his glasses quite recently and could not see much beyond that threadbare cuff. The sea that he sees, that 'ring of bay and skyline', has a greater inner reality for him, on one hand elevated by Mulligan to the realm of 'great sweet mother', and on the other hand redefined by Stephen's memories to 'a dull green mass of liquid' that reminds him of the bowl which once contained 'the green sluggish bile' (Te 80, 107–9) his dying mother had vomited. Eveline's thoughts at the window are also inner-directed: to the various recollections of her past life in the neighbourhood, in her family dwelling, and in the numerous instances of her life lived among the persistent smell of dusty cretonne.

Despite suggested differences of intellect, or even of defects of vision, Eveline and Stephen share the human capacities and limitations of individual perspective, seeing themselves as they think themselves to be and the world around them from their own coigns of vantage, present and past. Without changing position or focus, they can with near-simultaneity both see and visualise – within the context of their own selves. Eveline can easily apprehend Frank as 'very kind, manly, open-hearted' (D p. 38); Stephen can as easily apprehend Buck Mulligan as 'Chrysostomos' (Te 26), 'Usurper' (Te 744), and 'Catamite' (SC 734). To see one's self as a 'helpless animal' (D, p. 41) or an 'impossible person' (Te 222) requires the perspective (accurate or inaccurate) of another, and Joyce's 'Eveline' succinctly concludes with the observation that

'Her eyes gave him no sign of love or farewell or *recognition*' (*D*, p. 41, emphasis added).

Aesop's fable of the blind men and the elephant makes its cogent comment on the committee system of observation, but leaves no doubt that each individual 'observer' was severely limited in his observations. There seems to be nothing as yet that can shake Eveline's trust in Frank or redeem Buck Mulligan in the eyes of Stephen Dedalus, although Frank is under great suspicion from Eveline's father and Mulligan the darling of many, including George Moore. Mr Hill's prejudices against sailors may be as irrational as his prejudice against Italians, but there is always the possibility that a prejudiced observer may also (however accidentally) be accurate. Whereas Frank's judges within the confines of the story are limited and finite, an almost infinite number of observers exists in the readers of 'Eveline', and some among them have few doubts that Frank is a blackguard of the seduce-and-abandon school. Joyce himself had assumed that Mulligan would pale in the reader's estimation as the *Ulysses* narrative progressed, but most readers over the years have continued to be delighted with the quick-witted and sharp-tongued Buck. The Farrington of 'Counterparts', by contrast, has on occasion been singled out by critics as the only villain that Joyce ever created, yet Joyce himself was on record defending Farrington as a pathetic man sorely put upon. The judgement of the world has never been secure as long as reading is a process of re-creation.

Such re-creation – or interpretation – allows for a parallactic perspective based on intelligent speculation, and since the economically honed fictions of *Dubliners* offer few involved observers, even the possibilities provided by its readers are naturally limited. *Ulysses* by comparison contains a much more expansive Dublin, and by the very nature of the enormous canvas there are far more opportunities for lacunae, for blind spots, for places in which to hide. As often as we repeated the commonplace that Bloom is the character in literature about whom we have the most information, it becomes apparent that there are numerous pieces of important information about Bloom that are unavailable in the text. The tight time-frame of the 'single day' format makes the collection of expository facts difficult, yet the proliferation of such exposition accelerates as the later chapters develop: 'Circe' inundates us with 'possible' facts, while the 'Nostos' provides a wealth of possibly more reliable information. None the less, the more we know about

Bloom and the others, the greater the number of questions arise
that seem to remain unanswered.

A MOTHER

Efforts have frequently been made to chart the factual universe of
Joyce's epic, nail down the facts conclusively and concretise the
firm ground on which the narrative stands, a process that insists
on the existence of a single truth wherever conflicting truths
present themselves. Under such determining conditions the critic
must make definitive decisions, yet contradictions persist throughout *Ulysses*. The 'facts' regarding Bloom's mother, for example,
would seem to be easier to assess than the thousands of similar
'facts' about Bloom himself – references to her number a mere ten
in the entire text. In 'Hades' we learn that she is already dead and
buried (the first *fact* about her); in 'Oxen of the Sun' that Bloom
remembers her from adolescence as a thoughtful mother; in 'Circe'
she 'appears' as a worried and solicitous mother, while her potato
panacea is even more important as the talisman Bloom carries in
his pocket; in 'Ithaca' her immediate lineage is uncovered, her
son's resemblance to her is mentioned, and her husband's reference to her in his suicide note quoted; in 'Penelope' she is
momentarily in Molly's thoughts concerning the suicide: 'his father
must have been a bit queer to go and poison himself after her' (Pe
1061–2). The language of Molly's reflective processes is magnificently haphazard, and one can only wonder on the precise
construction of that 'after her' that sounds so correctly idiomatic
Irish but is none the less worrisome. The unreliability of language
is Joyce's forte in *Ulysses*, the reader's quicksand.

There are two salient pieces of evidence among these scant
references to Ellen Bloom that point toward her having been
Catholic. The first comes from the most unreliable of quagmires,
the 'Circe' chapter, where we are led to believe that we actually
hear her voice saying, 'O blessed Redeemer, what have they done
to him! My smelling salts! . . . Sacred Heart of Mary, where were
you at all at all?' (Ci 287–90). Coupled with her possession of 'an
Agnus Dei', these expletives are sufficient proof of a demonstrably
Irish Catholic mother, and it seems arbitrary to ask such a question
as: If this isn't really Mrs Bloom's voice, how is it that Bloom 'hears'

her in this way? Only the assumption that 'Circe' is somehow a drama of psychological realism allows for the concept that Bloom is hallucinating the remembered voice of his mother, following the remembered voice of his father in a Yiddish/German dialect of English. Outside the frame of 'psychological realism', however, these 'experiences' in 'Circe' are dramatically *beyond* hallucination: the ethnic variables of Leopold Bloom's culture determine voices deriving from the situations engendered by a series of happenings, perhaps most importantly his recent purchase of unkosher meats, and whatever vestigal guilt that might be attached to that purchase.

The implication in 'Hades' is that Ellen Bloom is buried in Prospect Cemetery, Glasnevin, the predominantly Catholic burial ground in Dublin, a cemetery open to non-Catholics as well, although primarily including such Protestants as Parnell. At Dignam's funeral in Glasnevin Bloom muses on his own grave: 'Mine over there towards Finglas, the plot I bought. Mamma, poor mamma, and little Rudy' (Ha 862–3). It seems possible, then, that Bloom's mother as well as his son are indeed buried there (rather than in the Protestant cemetery at Mount Jerome), and it is certainly logical that Bloom's conversion to Catholicism when he married Molly qualifies Rudy's burial in Glasnevin. But Ellen Bloom's death must have predated that conversion, and her son's last recollection of her dates from his days as a student in the High School when she provided him with 'a goodly hunk of wheaten loaf, a mother's thought' (OS 1048). Is Bloom in 'Hades' actually confirming her resting place as there in Glasnevin – or only that she is dead? And does her mother's maiden name of Hegarty in any way indicate whether she was Catholic or Protestant? (Her own maiden name of Higgins was apparently changed by deedpoll from Karoly and is consequently of no use in any speculation on her religion – or religions.)

There would be little reason to challenge Ellen Bloom's Catholicism were we not confronted with her husband's conversion from Judaism to the Protestant faith just prior to his marriage to her, and the assumption that has gained ground among commentators on *Ulysses* that he might have done so in order to marry a Protestant. The alternate suggestion is that he converted in order to succeed in business in a society dominated by the Protestant Ascendancy, in which case his marriage to a Catholic would seem counterproductive. And to add to our anxieties about Rudolph Virag

Bloom are the suggestions that he killed himself either because he was despondent over the loss of his beloved wife or because his business venture with the ownership of the Queen's Hotel in Ennis was doomed to bankruptcy.

As every such annoying question seems to lead to alternative possibilities, and each of the conflicting possibilities poses new questions of its own, the intimation that two different plotlines co-exist within the same contextual space in *Ulysses* becomes pervasive. We have learned to accept Joyce's novel – since it is so unlike other novels in so many ways – as containing an open-ended universe constructed to remain inconclusive despite all efforts to impose solutions, resolutions and even happy endings, and it is consequently possible to view *Ulysses* as a parallactic universe in which a Catholic Ellen Bloom has one existence and a Protestant Ellen Bloom another. In either case, she is the daughter of a convert from Judaism – and if we knew as a fact to what religion Julius Karoly Higgins had converted we might have a chance to locate that particular Ellen Bloom in the pattern. But the mystery is far more complex than even a two-track plotline would indicate.

For parallactic purposes Ellen-A is a Protestant, and her husband converted primarily to marry her; she died prematurely and is buried somewhere (but not necessarily in Glasnevin), and some time after her death her doting husband took his own life in order to be, as his suicide letter implies, 'with your dear mother' (It 1884) in heaven. Ellen-B is Catholic and is buried in Glasnevin, and whereas we may assume that Rudolph-A achieved a modicum of business success as a hotel proprietor, Rudolph-B alternatively killed himself when the hotel business failed (the suicidal assertion that 'Tomorrow will be a week that I received' (It 1883) sounds ominously like a notice of financial disaster). By laying down two sets of tracks *Ulysses* offers several diversive tales, each of which is understandably a facet of life in the Dublin being depicted. If Leopold Bloom's father died a bankrupt, then cautious Bloom has himself, on his own initiative, acquired the insurance policy, Canadian government stock, etc., in order to assure Milly's financial future; but if not, Bloom's investments may reflect the proceeds from the sale of his father's hotel holdings. That important second drawer provides irrefutable evidence of his assets, but is silent on the subject of their origin.

TAKING UP TIME

Characteristically, parallax makes its appearance out of synchron-
isation with its exact placement in space in *Ulysses*. The parallactic
universe existed before Bloom was born into it and he finds himself
dealing with parallax long before it occurs to him to worry about
what the word means (knowing the word and yet not knowing its
meaning is in itself a parallactic condition). On Westmoreland
street Bloom consciously undertakes to shift his thoughts away
from the Molly–Blazes afternoon assignation, and the attendant
possibility that suddenly presents itself of his wife contracting a
venereal disease from Boylan:

If he. . . .?
O!
Eh?
No . . . . . No.
No, no. I don't believe it. He wouldn't surely?
No, no.   (Le 102–7)

He quickly satisfies the need to think of something else, something
that requires determined concentration, by focusing his eyes and
his mind on the 'Timeball on the ballastoffice' (Le 109), focusing on
the discrepancy between Dunsink time and Greenwich time, and
by association he remembers Sir Robert Ball's book on astronomy.
The book itself, Bloom's own copy, is on his bookshelf – '*The Story
of the Heavens* by Sir Robert Ball (blue cloth)' (It 1373) – but he will
not actually see the book again until he returns home in the early
hours. If it is now some time after 1 p.m. on 16 June, it will then be
after 1 a.m. on 17 June when he returns to Eccles Street, both the
same day for Bloom and a new day on the calendar. That 'Timeball'
and 'Sir Robert Ball' should so neatly parallel each other does not
occur to Bloom, but the origin of the word parallax does: 'Parallax. I
never exactly understood. There's a priest. Could ask him. Par it's
Greek: parallel, parallax' (Le 110–12). Etymology of course provides one avenue of approach to words, but knowing that 'it's
Greek' does not provide the definition that Bloom seeks. He does
not avail himself of the opportunity to ask the priest anything, nor
does he take the parallel course that later occurs to him of
confronting Professor Joly at the Dunsink Observatory, where he
assumes that the answer to 'what's parallax?' will be 'Show this

gentleman the door' (Le 578). Never very comfortable with religion, and unsure of himself with science, Bloom avoids direct confrontation with both – and with the meaning of parallax.

A subsequent recurrence of parallax in Bloom's thoughts takes place about fifteen minutes later and only a few streets away. The optical concern of Yeates and Son intrudes itself on Bloom's consciousness as the Ballastoffice had previously, and his succession of thought associations includes vision, optical instruments, solar eclipses, timeballs and observatories, until he imagines himself making the mistake of blurting out to Professor Joly, 'what's parallax?' The haughty response that he anticipates darkens his mood considerably, although if he had taken it quite literally, seeing the door from more than one vantage-point would have defined parallax for him. Yet Bloom knows that metaphoric language is non-literal and that one interprets beyond the unimaginative directional signals. His despondent thoughts, consequently, fluctuate within the fields of astronomy, as he despairs of the universe rather than endure the pain of an (imagined) personal slight:

> Never know anything about it. Waste of time. Gasballs spinning about, crossing each other, passing. Same old dingdong always. Gas: then solid: then world: then cold: then dead shell drifting around, frozen rock, like that pineapple rock. The moon. Must be a new moon out, she said. I believe there is.
> He went on by la maison Claire.
> Wait. The full moon was the night we were Sunday fortnight exactly there is a new moon. Walking down by the Tolka. Not bad for a Fairview moon. She was humming. The young May moon she's beaming, love. He other side of her.   (Le 581–90)

Astronomy, the lofty science that served to transport Bloom's thoughts away from Molly and Boylan, has by a parallactic movement brought them back to Molly and Boylan, and Bloom must focus his eyes and thoughts on the mundane reality of 'this is the street here middle of the day of Bob Doran's bottle shoulders' (Le 594–5); in space, Bloom has moved several feet down Grafton street from Yeates' corner to Adam Court, the Empire Bar.

Many light years separate the astronomical significance of the lunar phenomenon from the romantic metamorphoricisation of the moon, and yet the same disc in the sky can be apprehended in a variety of ways, even simultaneously as Professor Joly's moon and Molly's moon. We can assume that Bloom's thinking on the origins, development and destiny of the universe has precise finite limits for him, and that the visible orb in its monthly changes has more immediate meaning. It is as understandable, therefore, that he would gravitate soon enough from the 'dead shell drifting around' to the prosaic 'moon', as it is that he would in his noontime hunger shift from that 'frozen rock' to the more accessible 'pineapple rock'. The next shift then romanticises the moon in traditional sentimental fashion, as the gastronomic appetite finds its parallel in the amorous. The transitional device may well have been the sighting of 'la maison Claire', the dressmaker's shop on Grafton street. Clothes and the female body have their intimate associations for Bloom, and perhaps so obvious an association as the lush 'Claire de Lune' would bring Molly and the moon back as he remembers the riverside stroll together – in the company of Blazes Boylan.

Molly Bloom exists for her husband in a dual capacity: whereas Molly-A is the potential adultress and obviously associated as such with Blazes, Molly-B is the wife he continues to love, the Molly for whom the bedwarmed flesh is reserved for himself alone, and she in turn is associated with young Milly: 'Sitting there after till near two taking out her hairpins. Milly tucked up in beddyhouse. Happy. Happy. That was the night. . . .' (Le 199–201). It is Molly's surrogate, Josie Powell Breen, however, who intrudes on these pleasant memories and takes up most of Bloom's time between the Ballastoffice and Yeates and Son. No effort of will could keep him from thinking about Molly, so that even 'Par it's Greek: parallel, parallax' (Le 111–12) immediately evolved into 'Met him pike hoses she called it till I told her about the transmigration. O rocks!' (Le 112–13) – Molly's Greek 'metempsychosis' produces Bloom's Latin parallel, 'transmigration'. Pleased with Molly's rude wit he can keep his attention riveted to Molly's past accomplishments rather than on her future infidelity. Just as the demented Farrell weaves his way down Westmoreland Street manoeuvring outside lamp posts (in his twisted mind he undoubtedly sees himself walking a straight line), Bloom's thoughts as he walks down the same street weave toward and away from thoughts of Molly, preferring the warm past to the cold future.

When Bloom crossed Westmoreland Street, an act that put him

on a parallel track with the one he would have continued (and inadvertently resulted in his encounter with Mrs Breen), his casual observation of the 'Rover cycleshop' (Le 156) began an associative process back to Molly in happier days ('Happy. Happier then' – Le 170), and although four or possibly five of the men whose names appear on the 'Ithaca' list of Molly's putative lovers are included in his thoughts, Bloom remains quite sanguine. He has developed a weapon that 'defeats' them easily enough by deprecation: Alderman O'Reilly is remembered 'emptying the port into his soup' (Le 160–1; Penrose (as a misnamed 'Pendennis') is devalued as a 'priestylooking chap' (Le 176); Bartell d'Arcy denounced as a 'Conceited fellow with his waxedup moustache' (Le 182); Professor Goodwin dismissed as a 'poor old sot' (Le 189). (Stephen Dedalus has already shown himself to be a master of the destroying of enemies, as he levels such silent invectives against Haines and Mulligan, and Molly, in her midnight thoughts, will also decimate the O'Reillys and Goodwins just as easily.) At the height of Bloom's blissful thoughts, when he and Molly had come home on a cold, windy night to an abode of bliss, Mrs Been intrudes:

> Remember when we got home raking up the fire and frying up those pieces of lap of mutton for her supper with the Chutney sauce she liked. And the mulled rum. Could see her in the bedroom from the hearth unclamping the busk of her stays: white.
>
> Swish and soft flop her stays made on the bed. Always warm from her. Always liked to let herself out. Sitting there after till near two taking out her hairpins. Milly tucked up in beddyhouse. Happy. Happy. That was the night . . . . .
> – O, Mr Bloom, how do you do?
> – O, how do you do, Mrs Breen?   (Le 194–203)

Had heliotropic Bloom crossed over to the bright side again in order to savour happy thoughts of Molly, it is Josie Breen that he encounters instead, but he at least receives the polite greeting of 'how do you do?' (Le 202) that he would have liked to have had from Larry O'Rourke and Hornblower, quite unlike the 'Hello, Bloom' that proves to be standard fare – from M'Coy (Lo 84), Lyons (Lo 520), and soon forthcoming from Nosey Flynn (Le 737).

The journey down Westmoreland street, once he has disengaged himself from Mrs Breen (whose enquiry about Molly he quickly deflected), Bloom has a storehouse of subjects to think about and numerous distractions along the street, and his thoughts steer clear of Molly and Boylan until the new moon/full moon association disturbs them. Fixed on the sight of Bob Doran's 'bottle shoulders' Bloom experiences a parallax of time, transforming the present Empire Bar into the Harp Theatre that once stood in its place, and returning mentally to the prelapsarian days of Lombard street west before Rudy's unfortunate birth and death: 'I was happier then. Or was that I? Or am I now I?' (Le 608). That these questions parallel Stephen's metaphysical thoughts in 'Proteus' provide the potential link between the two along more basic lines of comparison than their black clothes and keylessness, but the questioning itself raises the question of what is affecting Bloom's mood. Previous assumptions of happiness in Lombard street west were unqualified, but now the inner sense of 'Could never like it again after Rudy' (Le 610) intrudes, and he plunges deeper into unstructured introspection, allowing the Grafton street shop windows to provide the fripperies of casual association. Whereas la maison Claire slipped by relatively unnoticed, or at least uncommented upon when Bloom's thoughts were inner-directed, the windows of Brown, Thomas provide 'Cascades of ribbons' and 'Flimsy China silks' (Le 621), speaking to the inner man and inevitably returning him to the present-day Molly: 'Useless to go back. Had to be' (Le 633). That uselessness of return lingers disembodied in his thoughts, a decision that has lost sight of the original assumption (back to the past? or back to Eccles street to ward off the Boylan intrusion?), and there is a gap between the decisiveness of 'Must go back for that lotion' (Le 628) and the uselessness of return.

The demise of Lombard street west is somehow compensated for by a projection into the future, with Molly's next birthday, 'Nearly three months off' (Le 629), for which gifts of lingerie are intended. The sighting of 'Sunwarm silk' (Bloom synaesthetically 'feels' the warmth of the silk he 'sees') invokes a concomitant bodily warmth:

A warm human plumpness settled down on his brain. His brain yielded. Perfume of embraces all him assailed. With hungered flesh obscurely, he mutely craved to adore.
Duke street. Here we are. Must eat. The Burton. Feel better then. (Le 637–40)

Parallel hungers conspire against Bloom, one of which can be easily assuaged (the other might then perhaps fall into line and be quieted). Before breakfast, as now before lunch, he experienced dual discomforts and sublimated the spiritual one by satisfying the physical. As he carried his breakfast kidney home he was over-taken by a dark cloud that precipitously plunged his thoughts into an abyss: 'the dead sea ... the cities of the plain. ... The oldest people ... the grey sunken cunt of the world' (Ca 219–28). There is no relief from the 'Grey horror' that 'seared his flesh' (Ca 230) in the world around him: even the 'Blotchy brown brick houses' (Ca 235) offer no comfort, but Bloom's panacea exists for him only in what he immediately anticipates. Food and Molly, both warm and awaiting him at home, are his consolations, yet five hours later, Boylan's letter having interceded, it is only a hot meal at the Burton that offers salvation. He settles, however, for a cold meal at Davy Byrne's; no 'smell' of 'gentle smoke of tea' (Ca 237–8) but a 'Stink' of 'pungent meatjuice' (Le 650–1) had assailed him at the Burton.

Parallax of mood afflicts Bloom whenever the cloud eclipses the sun, and it happens again on the trek down Westmoreland street. Anticipation of food and the bright quip about the 'Homerule sun rising up in the northwest' (Le 473–4) had somehow succeeded in causing him to smile, but 'His smile faded as he walked, a heavy cloud hiding the sun slowly, shadowing Trinity's surly front' (Le 475–6). We might assume that the eclipse of the sun had caused Bloom's smile to fade, but there is a gap in awareness as the effect anticipates the cause and Trinity *becomes* surly as a result of the shadow. Noise, useless activity, insanity, death, pain in childbirth, exploitation, dishonesty, futility, slavery, ruins and insubstantiality are all in Bloom's mind for the short duration of the cloud's transition across the face of the sun, yet he seems unaware of the subliminal influence on his mood. Whereas that morning he had blamed waking up on the wrong side of the bed and lack of physical exercise for his malaise, now he assumes that it is merely the particular time of day: 'This is the very worst hour of the day. Vitality. Dull, gloomy: hate this hour. Feel as if I had been eaten and spewed' (Le 494–5). It is only when 'the sun freed itself slowly' (Le 499) that Bloom's mood shifts back to equanimity, his place in the sun, a vantage-point from which to view the world from a 'proper' perspective.

'NOW YOU SEE ME, NOW YOU...'

Approximately two-and-a-half inches separate the right eye from the left, a factor that accounts for parallax of vision and allows for depth of field and perspective, disadvantaging those who have lost the sight in one eye. The one-eyed in *Ulysses* range from Admiral Horatio Nelson (literal), valiant defender of the British Empire and occupier of a perch atop a Sackville street pillar, to the Citizen (figurative), staunch opponent of that Empire and occupier of a perch atop a barstool at Barney Kiernan's pub. When the Citizen hurls the biscuit tin, Bloom is spared serious injury because 'the sun was in his eyes or he'd have left him for dead' (Cy 1854) – sun-loving Bloom had previously been spared a confrontation with Boylan when the sun was apparently in Blazes' eyes (Le 1175). The Citizen's role as the 'Cyclops' is complementarily augmented by the presence at the *contretemps* of 'a loafer with a patch over his eye' – a literal One-Eye (Cy 1800). That in the land of the blind the one-eyed is king was parodically demonstrated by Nelson holding his telescope to his blind eye, resisting a view of what he did not want to see: his consequent victory proved his superiority over those who advised him against confronting an overwhelming force. In *Ulysses* the flawed perspective of Cashel Boyle O'Connor Fitzmaurice Tisdall Farrell is apparent when he 'sees' the Metropolitan Hall where the Merrion Hall actually stands, and it is not without justification that the blind piano tuner whom Farrell walks into should denounce him as 'blinder nor I am' (WR 1119–20).

Perspective then is obviously in the eyes of the beholder, and readers of *Ulysses* who fail to allow for that perspective among the characters of the novel find themselves involved in controversies like the 'beef to the heel' dispute that raged for a time through the letters column of the *Times Literary Supplement*. Since Milly Bloom is never 'seen' in *Ulysses*, we intuit Milly from the parallactic overlaps of certain observations. To her father she assumes mythic proportions as a personification of sunlight, an antidote (along with hot food and bedwarm Molly) to cloud-darkened desolation: 'Quick warm sunlight came running from Berkeley road, swiftly, in slim sandals, along the brightening footpaths. Runs, she runs to meet me, a girl with gold hair on the wind' (Ca 240–2). This harbinger of Milly, nymph-like and perhaps evocative of the Homeric Nausicaa (her swift-footedness ironically paralleled by Gerty MacDowell's lameness), is soon corroborated as Bloom arrives home to find her letter, and her card to her mother: he then offers to pull up the blind so Molly can read it – letting in the sunshine (Ca 256). That Milly has been apprenticed to a photographer strengthens the association, since photographs are created by a process that lets sunlight into a *camera obscura*.

Beauty is also on occasion in the eye of the beholder, and the standards for young girls may be different from those for cows. 'Beef to the heel' obviously derives from a cattleman's praise for his livestock, but has devolved into an urban, though hardly urbane, sneer at beefy country women. Milly, transplanted from Dublin to Mullingar, apparently applies it to the women who come into town for the fair ('Fair day and all the beef to the heels were in' – Ca 402–3), and it is in this context that Bloom understands it: 'Thick feet that woman has. . . . Countrybred chawbacon. All the beef to the heels were in. Always gives a woman clumsy feet' (Le 616–18). His own (possibly prejudiced) image of Milly is hardly in keeping with such anatomical features: when he observes Gerty's limp, he contrasts her with Milly, who is 'Straight on her pins anyway not like the other' (Na 928), also remembering the woman with thick feet, 'the one in Grafton street. . . . Beef to the heel' (Na 931–2). It comes as a surprise, therefore, that Alec Bannon, Milly's admirer and probable seducer, should traduce her in the same terms (in the style of a Pepys or Evelyn) as 'a skittish heifer, big of her age and beef to the heel' (Na 502–3). As a Dubliner, Bannon may be suffering from idiomatic parallax as he bandies country terminology about to show off his recent rustification – and sexual conquest – and seems to mistake the expression to mean sexually voluptuous, although we may be required here to negotiate the distance between woman-and-cow and girl-and-heifer. (In *A Portrait* Stephen and Lynch 'followed a sizeable hospital nurse. . . . Two lean hungry greyhounds walking after a heifer' – AP, p. 348.) Except for this solecism Alec Bannon is lavish in his praise of Milly (as stylised in the language of Laurence Sterne, 'so amiable a creature' – OS 763–4), displaying the photograph of her that he carries in his locket.

Bannon and Bloom maintain discrete recollections of Milly Bloom in the hospital scene, Bannon's as eloquent as Bloom's is silent. It is presumably for Bloom that Thomas de Quincey serves as a narrative spokesman when despondency over the loss of Rudy creates a 'clouded silence' (OS 1078), paralleling the two instances of nebulous eclipses suffered in the morning and early afternoon.

Bloom is again concerned with 'cycles of generations that have lived' (OS 1080) as even in the House of the Sun the murder of the Oxen of the Sun results in the darker death-thoughts, modified finally by thoughts of Milly and Molly:

> A region where grey twilight ever descends, never falls on wide sagegreen pasturefields, shedding her dusk, scattering a perennial dew of stars. She follows her mother with ungainly steps, a mare leading her fillyfoal. Twilight phantoms are they, yet moulded in prophetic grace of structure, slim shapely haunches, a supple tendonous neck, the meek apprehensive skull.   (OS 1080–5)

Bloom has modulated Bannon's heifer into his own fillyfoal, improving on the image of Milly Bloom in his eyes, yet the ameliorisation of his morose mood cannot withstand the onslaught of the 'murderers of the sun' (OS 1095). From where he is positioned Bloom is made aware that 'Parallax stalks behind and goads them on' (OS 1089), and the conflict ensues between cattle and horses, until the 'equine portent grows again, magnified in the deserted heavens, nay to heaven's own magnitude, till it looms, vast, over the house of Virgo' (OS 1097–9).

Bloom's unconscious has mysteriously conjured up a mystic realm, possibly influenced by a residual Freemasonry (in celebrating Bridie Kelly he 'chants' in imitation of the masonic oath, 'He will never forget the name, ever remember the night' – OS 1068 – and soon after he envisions a 'region where grey twilight ever descends, never falls' – OS 1080–1), where animal imagery abounds in a zodiacal zoo of 'scorpions', 'bulls of Bashan', 'capricorned', 'lionmaned' (OS 1090, 1093, 1094), an 'Omnivorous revengeful zodiacal host!' (OS 1092). Astronomy and its parallel 'art' of astrology vie for prominence in the constellation of his nebulous thoughts, which reach their culmination in Molly's birth under the sign of the Virgin and travel on to resolution in Bloom's birth under the sign of the bull; and just as sunlight relieves diurnal despair, so starlight (by 'wonder of metempsychosis') suddenly triumphs over nocturnal gloom. In a conflation of Martha and Milly as well as the Blessed Virgin and Bridie Kelly, the new star is celebrated:

> it is she, the everlasting bride, harbinger of the daystar, the bride, ever virgin. It is she, Martha, thou lost one, Millicent, the young, the dear, the radiant. How serene does she now arise, a

queen among the Pleiades, in the penultimate antelucan hour,
shod in sandals of bright gold, coifed with a veil of what do you
call it gossamer. It floats, it flows about her starborn flesh and
loose it streams, emerald, sapphire, mauve and heliotrope,
sustained on currents of the cold interstellar wind, winding,
coiling, simply swirling, writhing in the skies a mysterious
writing till, after a myriad metamorphoses of symbol, it blazes,
Alpha, a ruby and triangled sign upon the forehead of Taurus.
(OS 1100–9)

Mariology is obviously the opiate of this dream, with Milly in gold
sandals as the primary Virgin, her letter providing phrases ('simply
swirling') along with Bloom's own turn of phrase ('what do you
call it'). The precise individuation of characters, a commonplace
and fixed certainty in the real world, no longer pertains in the flux
of intersellar metamorphoses, as Martha and Molly merge as lost,
Martha and Milly as letter-writers, Bridie and Milly as young virgins
at the brink of sexuality. The one individuated self that still remains,
that of Leopold Bloom *as* self, is reconstituted as his focus returns
to the here-and-now, the bottle of Bass's ale and its red-triangle label.

In her 'appearance' in 'Circe', a chapter in which individuated
identity is constantly in question, Milly Bloom is mistaken by her
father for Molly, in a green dress with hair dyed gold: '*Milly Bloom,
fairhaired, greenvested, slimsandalled, her blue scarf in the seawind simply
swirling*' (Ci 3167–8). All emphases on the slimsandalled Milly are
derived from Bloom's singular view of his daughter, but her
mother's eyes provide the authenticating parallax. Although
Molly, at least in her night-thoughts, is often harsh on the
daughter who is replacing her, and resents her impudence and
defiance, she is none the less outspoken in her pride over nubile
Milly, remembering her especially as she recently grew into
comeliness. And it is her legs in particular that Molly acknowledges: 'I had to tell her not to cock her legs up like that on show on
the windowsill before all the people passing they all look at her like
me when I was her age' (Pe 1034–6). There is no indication here
that Milly's mother, any more than her doting father, considers the
girl's legs as 'beef to the heel', and Molly is very much aware of the
contours of her daughter's body, as well as her own. Although she
sets up the parallel between Milly and herself when young, she is
uncomparative when praising herself: 'I bet he never saw a better
pair of thighs than that look how white they are' (Pe 1144–5).

The excessive wealth of detail, what we have come to acknowledge as the 'naturalistic' phenomena of *Ulysses*, occasioned readers – especially during the early years of investigation into the text – to assume that Joyce's was in some way a naturalistic novel, one which offered *une tranche de vie* of Dublin life, despite the experimental patina that clung to it. The stock-in-trade of the devoted naturalist was the assumption that a random slice discovers the typical common denominator of the social condition, but *Ulysses* as a text seems to defy such compartmentalisation, and unselected segments apparently lack validity as firm representatives of a monocular viewpoint. *Ulysses* deals almost exclusively with the Dublin bourgeoisie *as it sees itself*, using that selected microcosm for general representation. The potential arbitrariness of the fictional text, especially when it expands into so many facets and formations, allows for the tentative suggestion of life-and-death decisions on the fate of the characters, a freedom that carries the responsibility of accuracy in an area where so many possibilities remain open. Just as the sanctity of individual characterisation no longer remains definite as the multiple interaction of people continues deeper into the narrative process, so does the single resolution to any particular situation become problematic.

DUBLINERS UNBOUND

The burden of an unfortunate marriage could destroy Bod Doran in various ways; the precarious life of exploitation might eventually trip up a John Corley; the salvation by his friends may restore Tom Kernan to his dignity – but for how long? Kernan's hat is back in shape (as is his tongue), his Protestant scepticism intact, and his taste for gin unchanged, and *Ulysses* attests to a certain permanence to his delicate balance. Corley has hardly fared as well, although his less-fortunate friend Lenehan has enjoyed a limited reversal of fortune which may now prove short-lived. Doran on 16 June is woefully drunk, the predictable result of marriage to the 'little sleepwalking bitch', as the collector of bad debts calls her, 'that used to be stravaging about the landings ... at two in the morning without a stitch on her, exposing her person, open to all comers, fair field and no favour' (Cy 398–402). This jaundiced narrator is endowed with parallactic sight, however, since his alternative view of her is 'wagging her tail up the aisle of the chapel with her patent boots on her, no less, and her violets, nice as pie, doing the little lady' (Cy 812–14) – he seems equally disdainful of Polly whether she has her clothes on or not.

Basically, we accept the 'afterlife' of Mr and Mrs Doran as extending the existing *Dubliners* narrative; we read one text as sequential to the other. Yet the unsurprising condition of that marriage – and of Doran as a drunk – has its own narrative construct in *Ulysses*, and as a consequence 'The Boarding House' is being rewritten – unwoven and rewoven. The collector of bad debts becomes the new narrative voice of time present, who also invokes the perspective of an eyewitness of time past in Bantam Lyons. It is Lyons whom he credits with the information of the naked 'sleepwalker', a designation that can be assumed as metaphoric, and probably attributable to Lyons himself. The Polly of the previous text was neither naked nor walking in her sleep, with the perspective in the short story consistently that of Bob Doran, and despite his nervous realisation of disaster, Doran none the less retains in his mind a rather romantic recollection of Polly in her 'loose open combing-jacket of printed flannel' and 'her furry slippers' (*D*, p. 67), a visualised tableau reminiscent of *La Bohème*, to which the Lyons recall (of this or some similar incident at the boarding house) adds a tableau from *La Somnambule*. That unusual narrator in 'Cyclops' provides a rare instance of a Dubliner's 'reading' of *Dubliners*, a parallactic précis of 'The Boarding House' from a superior perspective in time.

Doran's drunken condition is universally attested to, as if every slice into the narrative turns him up drunk. C. P. M'Coy reports having seen him in that familiar condition the night before at Conway's pub; Bloom sees him going into the Empire; Boylan stops him on the way to the Liberties, and even young Patsy Dignam can recognise the circumstances of Boylan making sport of 'the drunk . . . grinning all the time' (WR 1151–2). With all the self-righteousness of the confirmed tippler, the collector comments on Doran being 'Boosed at five o'clock' (Cy 800–1), but that is only his limited view, fixed at a particular time from his present position: others, like Bloom, Boylan and young Dignam, saw him 'boosed' at an even earlier hour. Yet all of the corroborative evidence is far from diagnostic. If we wonder about just how complete Doran's disintegration has been, we must also weigh the same authority's word that a sober Doran takes his wife to church on Sunday, and that his brother-in-law has made him 'toe the line. Told him if he didn't patch up the pot, Jesus, he'd kick the shite out of him' (Cy 815–16). Another self-appointed biographer of Bob Doran, C. P. M'Coy, tells Bloom that Doran is 'on one of his periodical bends' (Lo 107), but when Bloom sees him some time later, easily reading the 'bottle' in the slope of the drunk's shoulder, he slightly misquotes his source: 'On his annual bend, M'Coy said' (Le 595–6). The frequency rate has suffered a parallactic change from period-ical (vague) to annual (precise) in Bloom's mind, leaving imprecise the exact nature of Doran's alcoholic condition.

The functional limits of naturalism became apparent as *Dubliners* evolved from ten epicleti to twelve and then fourteen, the later stories longer than the earlier ones, and a fifteenth eventually added, with the suggestion of a 'Ulysses' story yet to follow. As we track the Joycean creative process we are invited to speculate on how many slices of life theoretically constitute a proportional representation, and how many variants allow for a democratic cross-section of probabilities? Only by incorporating into each component the possibilities of several permutations can the *tranches de vie* assume dimensionality, especially when the concept of a fourth dimension already exists for experimental augmenta-tion. Bloom in the funeral carriage is a married man whose wife is slated to be unfaithful that afternoon for the first time; Bloom at home after midnight is a married man whose wife has been unfaithful for the twenty-fifth time. With him in the carriage is Simon Dedalus, widower, and Martin Cunningham, husband of a drunkard, as well as Jack Power, who has both a wife and a mistress – at least according to local rumour. Gossip is a fictional force both inside and outside the narrative, and when it remains neither corroborated nor refuted, scepticism tends to fill the vacuum and provides the parallactic alternative. *Ulysses* as a self-contained narrative begins to suggest the start of demographic affairs that obtains in *Finnegans Wake*, that of a 'gossipocracy' (*FW*, p. 476, l. 4).

'THE OLD FORM OF FORMS'

The narrational stance adopted for *Dubliners* fixed many of the characters in those stories with shapes that could not be changed:

Cunningham, for example, 'had married an unpresentable woman who was an incurable drunkard. He had set up house for her six times; and each time she had pawned the furniture on him' (*D*, p. 157). The flat tone of this pointedly objective narration has all the characteristics of codified hearsay, especially with focus on so exact number as 'six', the very specificity of which marks it as transmitted rumour rather than verifiable fact. The report on Mrs Cunningham survives the translation to *Ulysses*, where it exists essentially intact. Bloom takes his turn as subjective narrator of the Cunningham tale, embellishing somewhat on received information, and whereas the collector of bad debts had Bantam Lyons as an eyewitness, Bloom enlists Simon Dedalus for that function:

> And that awful drunkard of a wife of his. Setting up house for her time after time and then pawning the furniture on him every Saturday almost. . . . Lord, she must have looked a sight that night Dedalus told me he was in there. Drunk about the place and capering with Martin's umbrella.   (Ha 349–54)

Dedalus provides an interesting focus of his own, although himself hardly the soul of sobriety, while the perennially sober Bloom combines the adjacent attitudes of sympathy and disapproval, tempered by a sense of humour, in capturing the scene and delineating the character. He is wonderfully inexact in his designation of 'every Saturday almost', a subjective improvement on the suspiciously overdetermined 'six'.

Jack Power fares somewhat better, primarily because the fixed shape that carries over from 'Grace' is relatively minimal: 'His inexplicable debts were a byword in his circle; he was a debonair young man' (*D*, p. 154). In the interim between the story and the novel Power has aged a bit and an 'explanation' for his inexplicable debts has been arrived at. Bloom views him as 'Greyish over the ears', and finds him sympathetic:

> Nice fellow. Who knows is that true about the woman he keeps? Not pleasant for the wife. Yet they say, who was it told me, there is no carnal. You would imagine that would get played out pretty quick. Yes, it was Crofton met him one evening bringing her a pound of rumpsteak. What is this she was? Barmaid in Jury's. Or the Moira, was it?   (Ha 242–8)

Bloom now employs Crofton as his delegated observer as previously he had employed Dedalus, since he is not an intimate in these circles and needs someone who can provide an on-site report. For someone whose wife could become an immediate embarrassment to him, he oddly enough identifies with the victimised wife in this situation. Moreover, it is Molly herself who will eventually testify to this fine bundle of speculation, which never finds any sort of corroboration anywhere in *Ulysses* until the final moments of her soliloquy: 'Jack Power keeping that barmaid he does of course his wife is always sick or going to be sick or just getting better of it and hes a goodlooking man still though hes getting a bit grey over the ears' (Pe 1272–5). Her information could likely come from her husband, although we might assume independent verdicts on his good looks. Bloom actually observed 'Mr Power's goodlooking face' (Ha 242), and whereas Molly might take Bloom's word for the greying hair, she would base her consideration of his good looks on the evidence of her own eyes. Her evaluation seems to derive from direct and fairly recent contact with Power, and the new information about the sick wife rings true. As with Milly's slim legs, this parallel instance of Molly's seconding Bloom offers the dual perspective of parallax, as two pairs of eyes evaluate the same phenomenon.

In that funeral carriage in 'Hades' a quartet of separate and individual men are soon easily identified as husbands, playing out a variety of marital possibilities within the prospects of middle-aging members of the Dublin community. Simon Dedalus as widower becomes distinct from the other three, while the varied 'roles' of the three wives become distinguishing characteristics within Bloom's speculations on the others. Further extensions of their marital possibilities would include the married lives of Bob Doran, Theodore Purefoy, Paddy Dignam, C. P. M'Coy and Tom Kernan, with Ned Lambert for one having the honour of representing bachelorhood, along with the likes of Blazes Boylan. Set apart from the other middle-class husbands in Dublin, Leopold Bloom may still not have the most enviable marriage imaginable, but surveyed within the context of the represented grouping his situation clarifies as decidedly better than when viewed through a non-parallactic focus. From where he stands Bloom would certainly not choose to trade places with any of these other husbands.

Ulysses holds a prismatic mirror up to Dublin, much like the cracked mirror that Mulligan holds up to Stephen ('Stephen bent forward and peered at the mirror held out to him, cleft by a crooked crack. Hair on end. As he and others see me. Who chose this face for me?' – Te 135–7). The face he sees is his own, since he is looking not at the mirror but at the reflection it returns to him. When he observes 'Hair on end' he might be looking at the tousled hair on his head, still uncombed early in the morning, but it is more likely that he is observing the 'crack' that looks like a 'hair on end', in which case he has either made a conscious decision to avoid looking at himself despite Mulligan's insistence or has been distracted away from his face to the peculiar quality of the mirror. The shifts in vision that take place between the short-ranged glimpse of the cracked mirror and the later inspection of his face parallel the views of his cuff and the sea, the microscopic world and the macrocosm beyond, the reality that frames a centre that is the self. Stephen Dedalus has presumably undertaken for himself the responsibility of setting down his views on the Dublin about which he has a lot to learn, a process that is both intensified and impeded by the introspective viewing that inevitably intercedes.

4

Determining the Re-Sources

In the 'Yawn' chapter of *Finnegans Wake*, a heroic effort is under way to obtain some factual information. The method employed is recognisably catechistic, a series of interviews undertaken by the Four Old Men ('Those four claymen clomb together to hold their sworn starchamber quiry' – *FW*, p. 475, ll. 18–19) of the buried body of Shaun/Yawn, resulting in a sequence of various voices responding to their questions. This quartet of 'Shanators' conducts its seance on a hill in County Meath under frustrating circumstances, especially when the Yawn voice is inexplicably replaced by that of Anna Livia Plurabelle, followed by an anonymous witness, then another, and then (in rapid succession) Issy, Kate and Earwicker himself. The claymen prove to be ineffectual and they too are supplanted – by 'bright young chaps of the brandnew braintrust' (*FW*, p. 529, l. 5). Even when the reader feels confident in identifying the sources of the question asked and the answer given, the multiplicity of voices remains confusing and does little to clarify the 'information' obtained.

In the 'Ithaca' chapter of *Ulysses* a parallel situation exists, further complicated by an absence of linear progression of 'sources' to complement the linear progression of plot development. Joyce's schematas designate the 'Technic' of 'Ithaca' as 'Catechism (impersonal)' and as 'Dialogo/Stile Pacato/Fusione' – descriptions that would serve as well for the 'Yawn Under Inquest' chapter of the *Wake*. There are 309 questions asked in 'Ithaca' and, when we are fortunate enough to have an edition of the text that has not discarded the round black dot with which the chapter ends (It 2332), the same number of replies. In various ways the questions-and-answers are a mixed lot. Some are extremely terse: 'As?' (It 892, and again at 1562) and 'No' (It 986) are the briefest examples of query and response, but fortunately not to each other; some considerably longer – various answers range over more than a page and one unusual question itself almost a third of a page long.

Nearly half of the questions begin with 'What', and more than half incorporate the word in their interrogative construction, making it apparent that there is a demand in most cases for some specific kinds of information. These questions demand the substantial, a something, a truth, rather than a description, a process, or an explanation. A handful of the 'questions' are not actually interrogatively phrased at all, but instead make definite demands: Recite, Condense, Describe, Catalogue, Compile, Prove, Quote, Reduce (It 801, 832, 1279, 1361, 1455, 1634, 1868, 1933). These imperative variations appear fairly late in the chapter, the interrogative mode already having taken firm hold on the process.

CATALOGUING THE CATECHISTICS

Rather than imposing a strict uniformity on the materials of this long section of *Ulysses*, the strait-jacketing of questions asked and answered provides an unusual degree of diversity. Commentators have often remarked on the pronounced humour of the chapter (and Joyce claimed this ugly duckling to be his favourite), and it becomes a matter of fascination to observe Joyce's apparent delight in achieving comic variety despite the self-imposed handicap of a highly limiting stylistic device. Even if we conclude that there is a certain randomness to the sequence and types of questions, there is none the less an obvious time-frame and plot-determinant as in any other chapter of *Ulysses*. As A. Walton Litz has found, Joyce 'conceived of "Ithaca" as a series of scenes or tableaux ... and on the early typescripts he blocked out these scenes under the titles "street", "kitchen", "garden", "parlour", "bedroom"'.[1] This five-act structure at first seems disporportionate, as can be seen by the number of questions framed in each:

Street:	1– 18
Kitchen:	19–147
Garden:	148–180
Parlour:	181–272
Bedroom:	273–309

The proportions are actually well balanced: the two magor scenes are of Bloom and Stephen in the kitchen, and Bloom alone in the parlour, with the street scene as a prelude, the garden as an *entr'acte*, and the bedroom as an epilogue. Mood and tone, multi-faceted throughout, are brought to an apex of lyricism at the central point of the chapter, the parting of Bloom and Stephen under the starry sky, returning thereafter to the overly prosaic 'realities'.

Numerous attempts have been made, with the aid of Joyce's own capsulisations in his correspondence and conversations and in his schemata, to 'classify' the technique of the 'Ithaca' chapter. Joyce's key word, Catechism, has set off the major reverberations: Anthony Burgess refers to the 'inhuman catechist' and comments on the 'comic impertinence of the catechism'; Kenneth Grose refers to the 'impersonal catechism of the scientific enquirer'; Matthew Hodgart asks the overwhelming question, 'But who is the cate-chiser?'; more recently, Karen Lawrence notes that 'instead of the human voice of a narrative persona, it offers a catalogue of cold, hard facts'.[2] The emphasis on the cold and inhuman, and especially Grose's stress on the scientism of the entire project (he adds, 'the searching questions, even when probing into personal foibles or secrets, demand factual, statistical, quantifiable answers'[3]) is heard frequently, deriving apparently from the most quoted exchange in 'Ithaca':

What two temperaments did they individually represent?
The scientific. The artistic.   (It 559–60)

The authoritative impact of the answers makes them seem objec-tive and incontrovertible, and seems to lend further authority to the monolithic nature of all authority in 'Ithaca', unless we chal-lenge Bloom as reliably scientific and Stephen as verifiably artistic. Many investigators of the chapter tend to view it in its entirety as reflective of the tension between the scientific and the artistic, although few of them seem to accept the scientism as seriously presented. Robert M. Adams assumes that 'Ithaca' is a 'parody of the scientific, rational mind', while David Hayman considers the 'speaker' of the chapter to be 'after all a projection of Bloom's scientific mentality'.[4] Assuming that science insists on verifiable evidence, it would seem inconsistent to approach 'Ithaca' as a 'load of abstract facts', as Burgess insists on, and more appropriate to classify its 'relevant and irrelevant information and misinforma-tion', as does Adams.[5] The superabundance of 'data' leads C. H. Peake to talk in terms of its 'flat encyclopaedism', although he carefully qualifies it by insisting that 'the flatness is largely on the surface' and that the 'encyclopaedic method seems to exist for its own sake'.[6]

Every commentator finds it necessary to *define* the Ithacan format uniquely, indulging in the use of colourful tag-phrases: 'the garbage of indiscriminate thought' (Adams), 'like some eternal Gradgrind, the voice of the god of statistics' (Burgess), and 'the arduous particularization of data' (Richard Ellmann).[7] The most explicit device called into service has been the computer, an anachronism of course, but none the less of immediate recognition for contemporary readers of *Ulysses*. First coined by Clive Hart (for the Ithacan context), it has been cashed in on by many others, but Hart's usage had an important specificity not often echoed:

> The chapter is written in what appears at first to be the most dehumanized style possible: a sort of *reductio ad absurdum* of scientific question and answer. The apparent dehumanization arises in the first place from the total lack of proportion in the answers given to the questions. They seem to be the answers of a computer which has not been programmed to distinguish between what is important and what is not.[8]

Ellmann, on the other hand, has a great deal more faith in this particular computer. In contrasting 'Ithaca' with 'Eumaeus' he asserts, 'Instead of subjective distortion there is objective distortion. *Trompe l'oeil* gives way to the computer, unreliability to excessive reliability.'[9] These descriptive phrases have been applied to the chapter as a whole, but certain segments have been pinpointed as particularly offending or excessive or characteristic of the technique. Matthew Hodgart, for example, notes that 'the conversation between Stephen and Bloom is summarised like the minutes of a committee meeting', while C. H. Peake regards the material presented about Bloom's dream house to be conceived in a style 'borrowed from houseagents' advertisements and home-and-garden magazines'.[10] Where Hodgart is concerned with a descriptive process that suggests analogous styles, Peake approaches an area of source materials for stylistic innovations.

Accounting for the catechistic technique itself has never been particularly difficult. Stuart Gilbert immediately pointed in the most obvious direction when he categorised 'the ruthlessness of a theological inquisition', but Litz has augmented that indication by noting its parallel possibility: 'It is customary to think of "Ithaca" as deriving from the form of the Christian catechism and Joyce's early Jesuit training, but the parallels with the catechistical methods of the nineteenth-century schoolroom are equally convincing.'[11] Litz goes on to cite as a convincing model a text mentioned in *A Portrait of the Artist*: Richal Mangnall's *Historical and Miscellaneous Questions*. Since then Hodgart has fused the religious and educational precedents in his attempt to answer the questions, 'who is the catechist? And whose is the voice of the answers?':

> In a Catholic catechism it is the priest as instructor who asks the questions, the person under instruction who replies; and that is also true of formal and informal examinations. But throughout most of the process of education it is the pupil who asks, the teacher who answers, and that would seem to be the case in 'Ithaca', although sometimes the questioner seems to be setting problems. Another way of putting it is that the questioner is man the scientist, the answerer is the universe itself, which will usually give correct replies if asked the right questions by experimenters.[12]

Hodgart has undoubtedly compounded the problem in his synthesis, moving from an attempt at a universal solution to what appears to be his own dynamic response, but certainly within the frame of the 'mathematico-astronomico-physico-mechano-geometrico-chemico sublimation of Bloom and Stephen' announced by Joyce himself.[13]

Significant and often abrupt changes take place within the otherwise placid confines of 'Ithaca', although the 'events' are smoothly and evenly advanced toward the eventual, but incomplete, fusion. The dialogue operative within the chapter, between Bloom and Stephen and later between Bloom and Molly, is augmented by a constant implied dialogue between Bloom and the furniture, the stars, the universe, his possessions and his obsessions, as well as commentaries that spin off from the orbital dialogues. Despite the implications of speech and thought, the *dialogo* of the structural format evolves in its own directions and according to its own self-reflexive rules.

The changes that are immediately apparent take place at certain intervals, often unexpectedly: Litz notices that early on the 'plain questions-and-answers are ... followed by two elaborate exchanges on Dublin's water supply'; Adams comments that toward the close the 'catechism fades off into nonsense gabble'; and Hayman summarises, 'The questions and responses range from the most objective to the most personal, the language from the least to the most expressive.'[14] These externals are easily understood as satisfying various needs: the overall pattern requires changes of pace, verisimilitude allows for the drowsiness toward sleep, and comic inventiveness is served by the unexpected inundation of 'facts' when the tap is innocently and logically turned on. The long water-supply passage (It 163–228) is one of the three most frequently quoted sections of 'Ithaca' and has managed to disarrange many a reader, those who often object that it is out of proportion to the logical sense of the exposition. Like the sudden intrusion of the word 'Chrysostomos' on the opening page of *Ulysses* (Te 26), the waterlogged sequence of 'Ithaca' elicits that most nagging of all responses, that even an awareness of its 'meaning' allows for no easy justification for its existence in the text. Such 'anomalies' are part of the greater difficulty in accepting the conceptual structuring of the 'Ithaca' chapter, and it is valuable in undertaking an analysis of 'Ithaca' to bear in mind Hugh Kenner's admonition: 'The questions and answers are designed for separate contemplation; they do not constitute simply an indefensibly circumlocutory way of telling a story.' [15]

WHO SPEAKS WHEN SPOKEN TO?

The traditional assumption allows that an author has a certain reservoir of information accessible for inclusion in a narrative, and that most of what is chosen has narrational applicability to the confines of the text – although readers have long since become inured to elliptical and tangential sorts of information, and even to didactic motives for digressive material. The 'transmission' of information, pertinent or intrusive, has passed from the auctorial presence to the narrational presence in the history of the development of the novel, and the positing of a narrator for 'Ithaca' has for decades had its critical legitimacy. Marilyn French asserts that in 'Ithaca' we are being 'taken by the narrator further and further from the earth', and that at certain instances in the chapter 'the narrator is mocking the reader for his desire to find significances and convergences'. Taking her direction from the 'impersonal' aspect of the catechism, French posits an 'impersonal narrator' who 'assumes that all phenomena except emotion are equally significant'.[16] Other postulators of an Ithacan narrator follow suit: Michael Groden hears the 'voices of the narrators of "Eumaeus" ... and "Ithaca"'; Wolfgang Iser finds 'an anonymous narrator, who more or less asks himself what Bloom and Stephen think, do, feel, intend, communicate, mean etc., and then proceeds, himself, to give answers that are as wide-ranging as they are detailed'; Hayman is concerned that at least at one instance in 'Ithaca' we are being offered the 'product of a narrator's unreliability'; Michael Mason concludes that 'for once the book approached [in "Ithaca"] a conventional third-person omniscient narration (fired by a relish for the vocabulary of physical objects that is very much the author's)'; while, quite differently, Stanley Sultan claims that the 'varieties of narrative' in *Ulysses* 'work to remove the author's voice from their respective chapters', but 'Ithaca' 'avoids even the identifiable narrator, as distinct from author'.[17]

Positing the existence of a narrator under these extraordinary circumstances is usually nothing more than a convention, and allowing 'him' his masculine gender is merely a convenience. If 'he' is not a character in the action nor a 'licensed' story-teller, this body-less body takes up space reserved for someone else, a dog in the manger acknowledged and tolerated because the rightful heir seems to be mysteriously missing. For the purposes of the 'Cyclops' chapter, after eleven chapters of third-person narration, Joyce introduces the 'Collector of bad and doubtful debts' (Cy 24–5), or rather allows him to introduce himself with an immediate implosion of first-person narration: 'I was just passing the time of day with old Troy of the D.M.P. at the corner of Arbour hill there and be damned but a bloody sweep came along and he near drove his gear into my eye' (Cy 1–3). Despite the persistence of his anonymity the collector remains consistently identifiable, in character, resplendent with his own 'voice', and transparent in his prejudices. Yet even in his own domain in 'Cyclops' he is ousted from narrational privilege at some twenty-two instances by a mode of presentation that derives its parodic tone and information from overly elaborate 'literary' forms suggested by the exaggerations inherent in the blather of the customers in Barney Kiernan's pub. The two strains of narration parallel and supplement each other as 'Cylops' progresses, the one consistent because locked within the personality of the collector, the other invariably new because dependent on modulations of the general conversation, generating the formulaic style appropriate to the specific instances. They exist independent of each other and unaware of each other throughout, companion texts and complementing tones, until a fusion occurs in the final moments, when parallel lines eventually meet:

> And they beheld Him even Him, ben Bloom Elijah, amid clouds of angels ascend to the glory of the brightness at an angle of fortyfive degrees over Donohoe's in Little Green street like a shot off a shovel. (Cy 1915–18)

Those who find themselves uncomfortable with the term narrator when contemplating the narrational presentation in *Ulysses* posit instead the existence of a 'voice' (even further disembodied). Adams, who wonders aloud about the identities of the 'questioner and answerer (whoever they are)', none the less refers to an '"answering" voice'; Peake talks about the 'mind of the catechising voice'; and Hayman establishes a definite speaker: 'despite his elaborate pose, the speaker is not completely reliable and his point of view is not always clear'.[18] The author of *Joyce's Voices* offers the muse as answerer to the questions posed:

> she has geometry to impart, and metrical poetry, information about the characters' pasts and about their innermost thoughts; and she can deluge us with information we never thought to want. . . .
> And she is also androgenous Bloom, and the questioner is also Molly, the catechism dictated by the catechetical interrogation that has recently become a habit of Molly's and is barely sketched at the episode's close. . . .
> Then 'Ithaca', the ceremonious exchange between narrator and Muse, formal, the two sharing an idiom that they have under thorough command and permits no voices to be heard but theirs.[19]

Hugh Kenner's arrangement of roles in this context is magnificently metaphorical, but neither defines nor delimits the source of data dredged up in 'Ithaca', and depends as well on a belief in a muse (in addition to a narrator) that is in itself a leap of faith.

Kenner's invocation of the muse indicates the nature of the difficulty in determining the locus of information/misinformation in 'Ithaca'. The convenient assumption has usually been held that somehow Bloom's mind is responsible for what is being transmitted, and again a chorus of critical voices can be heard echoing the concept. Michael Mason phrases it rather carefully: 'The prevailing style, in which actions and objects are seen in their most material, measurable aspect, seems basically to express an aspect of Bloom's mind'; French deals with it somewhat equivocally: 'Bloom's (or the narrator's) memory of person, place and date is ... minutely precise'; Groden accepts it casually, referring to 'Bloom's mind in "Ithaca"'; and Peake, confronting the flow of Dublin's water supply, negates the patent absurdity altogether: 'The detailing of water's attributes ... is certainly not an account of what is passing through Bloom's mind as he carries the kettle.'[20] Peake insists that there are 'other answers which do not relate to Bloom or Stephen at all' – and Mason concurs: 'But the answers in the catechism do often go beyond what could be the content of Bloom's thought or speech.'[21] If the water supply statistics militate against Bloom as the source of direct communication – even 'the borough surveyor and waterworks engineer, Mr Spencer Harty, C. E.' (It 172–3) could hardly be expected to keep such facts in his head – and although it is safe to say that Bloom admires water for its 'universality', he could hardly be expected to expand that universality as the text indicates:

> its democratic equality and constancy to its nature in seeking its own level: its vastness in the ocean of Mercator's projection: its unplumbed profundity in the Sundam trench of the Pacific exceeding 8000 fathoms [etc.]. (It 185–8)

All such information is retrievable, and in printed form, and has consequently a 'renewed' existence in *Ulysses*, not as the same substance as thought and speech but of *similar* substance. The abstraction of a Bloomian reply to such a question as 'What in water did Bloom, waterlover, drawer of water, watercarrier, returning to the range, admire?' (It 183–4) becomes concretised in the kind of information that Bloom admires, which exists in textbooks, encyclopaedias, brochures, and in the language of such texts. The previous question about the water from the faucet (a simple 'Did it flow?') is immediately answered with a succinct 'Yes' (It 163–4), a reply attributable to any observer in the kitchen, Bloom or Stephen, but all that follows the 'Yes' flows as documentary information in excess of an answer:

Yes. From Roundwood reservoir in county Wicklow of a cubic capacity of 2400 million gallons, percolating through a subterranean aqueduct of filter mains of single and double pipeage [etc.]. (It 164–6)

These two expansive and exhaustive answers are only the 24th and 25th in the series of 309, but they manage at this early juncture to derail the concept of Bloom-at-thought, at some simple variant of stream-of-consciousness. Individual consciousness has reached its outer limits in the Ithacan exposition, as individuality itself, the very fundament of character presentation and development, has already been expanded upon in 'Circe'.

These extreme correctives to the idea of Bloom's mind as exclusive source of Ithacan information have the comic disproportions of Cyclopian giganticism, and function in a similar capacity. Yet an implication of an easily definable distinction between objectivity and subjectivity proves to be tenuous at best. A veneer of objectivity exists in the tracking of the 'parallel courses' of Bloom and Stephen in the first question-and-answer, presuming that two walkers in constant conversation even through familiar surroundings might not be able to reconstruct an exact itinerary. But any mechanical tracking device might falter at defining 'normal walking pace' and 'relaxed walking pace' (It 2, 7–8), judgemental concepts that belong more naturally to the subjective impressions of the walkers. And as the itinerary winds down into final destination, the subject of topography is eventually displaced by a geometrical observation, possible as remembered learning from both walkers but in no way attributable to either: 'the chord in any circle being less than the arc which it subtends' (It 9–10). Extraneous information may have the objectivity of accuracy, but lacks the objectivity of obvious necessity, and to ascertain the limits of needed information is in itself a subjective judgement. When Joe Hynes early in 'Cyclops' introduces the subject of Leopold Bloom, he refers to him as 'the prudent member', apparently grateful that Bloom indicated to him that it was past the middle of the month so that Hynes could draw his pay. The collector of bad debts, as recipient of Hynes's generosity, could be grateful at second remove, but sounds somewhat acerbic in describing the Bloom he has just seen, while a succeeding passage of exalted parody moves to the beat of its own drummer, containing the 'subjective' judgement of prudency introduced by Hynes:

– Sweat of my brow, says Joe. 'Twas the prudent member gave
me the wheeze.
– I saw him before I met you, says I, sloping around by Pill lane
and Greek street with his cod's eye counting up all the guts of
the fish.

Who comes through Michan's land, bedight in sable armour?
O'Bloom, the son of Rory: it is he. Impervious to fear is Rory's
son: he of the prudent soul.   (Cy 211–17)

The technique of 'Ithaca' constantly circumscribes the arc of an
extended circle while as consistently suggesting the subtending
chord.

In contrast to the early water questions a very late query (the
281st) returns the emphasis to Bloom's particular *querencia*, where
the only logical source of information would presumably be
Bloom's mind – and the perspective highly personal. This list of
Molly's supposed lovers, once considered sacrosanct and enlisted
as evidence of Molly's galloping promiscuity, has been called into
question by Ellmann, Adams and Sultan, and thoroughly dispar-
aged by David Hayman, and as a consequence Hayman questions
the nature of the source of such compilations:

the wording . . . indicates that this is a subjective list or at least a
projection arranged by an objective voice in chronological order.
If Bloom is the true author, we must ask what the sources of his
information are and why they are not more reliable. Perhaps the
list is best seen as a product of the narrator's playfulness: a
whimsical pandering to Bloom's apprehensions, Molly's aspirations and the reader's expectations.[22]

The list is only unreliable if those expectations are of legal facts,
although even in a court of law what stands as proven is often seen
as subjective and unreliable. What is ultimately unreliable in this
case is the *source* of the names, but none the less human and
understandable, and admirable in its attempt to be exhaustive and
comprehensive. Bloom has apparently derived some solace from
contending that whereas Boylan considered himself 'to be the first
to enter', he probably was merely 'the last term of a preceding
series even if the first term of a succeeding one' (It 2127–9). To be
able to enumerate twenty-four predecessors is for Bloom a power
to 'reduce' Boylan's accomplishment, a way of slaying the suitors,

although it in no way validates the list nor distinguishes among them along any particular scale.

The question itself is deceptively clinical, the chord subtending the arc of the circle ('What preceding series?'), while the answer is the elliptical arc, direct only in its opening and closing ('Assuming Mulvey to be the first term of his series . . . Hugh E. (Blazes) Boylan and so each and so on to no last term' – It 2132–42). The intervening names are 'known' to Bloom; the four for whom no name is available are known to Bloom by sight; the progression appears to be fairly chronological; the degree of real 'proximity' to Molly at any time varies considerably. Many of these characters classify well as Bloom's detractors, including former employers, and most of them will be categorically dismissed and even derided when Molly thinks of them in her Penelopean reverie. The operative subjectivity resides in Bloom's jealousy of anyone who has at any time in the past admired Molly, but that assumption of a mind fraught with jealous agonisings has almost no basis in previous exposures of Bloom's conscious thinking: most often he delights in Molly's physical attractiveness, as when he is enticing Stephen with her photo, and he has already 'slain' these particular suitors with his display of indifference toward them. The subjective arc is held in place by the objective chord: the list functions as evidence against Boylan's self-estimated importance, and derives from what the generating text can allow as possible within the reservoir of Bloom's mental processes, the scratch material of what he has observed and whom he knows. As an exercise in serial recollection the list has little basis in psychological reality, a feat of 'thinking' as impossible as tracking the Dublin water supply, but as a literary catalogue within the confines of the text it has its claim to a certain kind of reliability: almost half of these putative lovers are also present as part of 'THE HUE AND CRY' that pursue Bloom in 'Circe' (Ci 4326ff.), as much in apposition to Bloom in the one instance as in the other.

Whereas Sultan had been relieved to find that 'Ithaca' 'achieves almost complete objectivity',[23] Hayman is understandably concerned that we are the victims of inexplicable whimsicality, a tenuous state of affairs that so thoroughly disturbs Wolfgang Iser: 'what exactly is the purpose of this inquiry, and why should the narrator be asking all the questions, since he appears to know all the answers anyway?' As Iser continues thinking his way into the problem, the problem itself becomes compounded:

As the narrator asks more and more questions, the answers demonstrate not his knowledge so much as the unobtainability of the right answers – and this is emphasized by the very preciseness of what *is* known. Thus the tendency underlying this question-and-answer process is one that aims at showing the degree of interminability inherent in all phenomena. It is scarcely surprising then that new questions are constantly thrown up which are meant to limit the amount of indeterminancy, but instead – thanks to their very precision – in fact increase it. [24]

Iser's emphasis on indeterminancy in the Ithacan pattern is a vital corrective to outmoded acceptance of computerised or scientific objectivity, but it is weakened by the positing of a Janus-like narrator leaping back and forth between the pitch of the questioner and the wicket of the answerer.

Iser's dilemma might be resolved by applying Kenner's caveat ('The questions and answers are designed for separate contemplation'): only by segregating them and assigning them to their determining sources can we come to assimilate the diverse mass of materials in 'Ithaca', and even then we can expect to be discomfited by the occasional pea underneath the mattresses. Hayman's dilemma arises from the contention that the rogues' gallery of 'lovers' is unreliable because all or almost all of them are easily disqualified as Molly's actual partners in sexual infidelity, but it is in the locating of a viable source for the collective group that a certain kind of reliability can be re-established. S. L. Goldberg offers an important overview applicable in this context, although he first muddies the waters by invoking.

an intelligence utterly superior to the whole action, an ironic *persona* directing us from beyond or above it. But because the technique remains within the terms of an impersonal dramatic art, it is more than merely a device. *It is part of the action, a development from, and of, the material.* [25]

The vocabulary and syntax in which the style of 'Ithaca' is formed, the structures that give it is unique shape, the multifaceted range of its symbolic content are difficulties that require the locating of the elusive and elliptical sources, the materials that determine the techniques. Although Bloom's repository of knowledge accounts for a significant portion, and though the expressive forms develop outside his vocabulary or speech patterns, there is a dynamics within the technique of 'Ithaca', as in each of the eighteen chapters, responsible for the manner of expression, independent of the internalised speech of any of the characters or the narrative style of any 'voice'. What Bloom admires about water only Bloom knows, and the way in which he would voice the admiration remains unknown: its 'universality' and subsequent characteristics literally approximate that admiration, a parallel track reflecting Bloom's silent internalisation. The functional source, however, of the entire entity of that knowledge remains in this case with Leopold Bloom.

FOLLOWING IN GERTY'S FOOTSTEPS

An extreme instance of an indeterminant source can be taken from 'Nausicaa', where no critic has ever challenged the validity of an obvious assumption, but have always taken at face value the truth of the statement that Gerty MacDowell is lame. All preparatory information corroborates the verdict given by Leopold Bloom about her condition, and a capsule portrait has consequently emerged. Gerty is the stereotypical wallflower, the woman-on-the-shelf, condemned to spinsterhood by her deformity. The language of moralistic–romantic Victorian magazine and novelistic prose conceals and reveals simultaneously, and the assertion that 'Gerty would never see seventeen again' (Na 172–3) is later augmented within the ellipses of the narrative style: 'Then they could talk about her till they went blue in the face, Bertha Supple too, and Edy, little spitfire, because she would be twentytwo in November' (Na 220–2). Well beyond the first blush of girlish youth Gerty is systematicaly undercut by the textual presentation, an inexperienced and immature woman mooning over a distinctly younger male still in 'the high school' and only recently out of 'short trousers' (Na 134, 201), so lacking in sophistication that Gerty can only refer euphemistically to the fact that 'Strength of character had never been Reggy Wylie's strong point' (Na 206).

Decoding the Nausicaan style for the clue to Gerty's retarded state of maturity has its obstacles, however, since the style itself is a paragon of retarded immaturity, and the advance notice of Gerty

MacDowell, in a momentary appearance in 'Wandering Rocks', remains silent on the subject of her possible limp:

> Passing by Roger Green's office and Dollard's big red printing-house Gerty MacDowell, carrying the Catesby's cork lino letters for her father who was laid up, knew by the style it was the lord and lady lieutenant but she couldn't see what Her Excellency had on because the tram and Spring's big yellow furniture van had to stop in front of her on account of its being the lord lieutenant.   (WR 1205–11)

Gerty here is on foot and walking, but the narration is silent on the manner of her walk, yet when she reappears in 'Circe' an almost obsessive emphasis is placed on just that aspect of her ('*Gerty MacDowell limps forward*'; '*She glides away crookedly*' – Ci 372, 386). In the interim, of course, Bloom has seen her limp away and declared her lame, determining the gait (as well as the sexual inferences) of her performance in 'Nausicaa', so that Gerty MacDowell is 'fixed' permanently by Bloom's conclusive decision. The narrational style of 'Nausicaa' never allows itself to confront such a conclusion, although events almost force a certain degree of confrontation with the sensitive issue. As long as Gerty remains seated, the narrative can remain silent, although her feet are specifically a subject of consideration – or almost so:

> Her shoes were the newest thing in footwear (Edy Boardman prided herself that she was very *petite* but she never had a foot like Gerty MacDowell, a five, and never would ash, oak or elm) with patent toecaps and just one smart buckle at her higharched instep.   (Na 164–8)

Her 'higharched instep' had already been established (Na 98), and if her feet are a taboo subject, the euphemistic disguise is patent in the cloying comment that status and education were what Gerty needed to have 'patrician suitors at her feet' (Na 103), allying her in fantasy with the Maria of 'Clay' who sings 'I Dreamt that I Dwelt' (*D*, p. 106) but suppresses the stanza that mentions the suitors.

The moment of truth presumably becomes inevitable once Gerty is on her feet and moving away in the dusk, with enough residual light extant to highlight her departure. Despite the self-inflicted limitations of the style, realisation seems inevitable:

Slowly, without looking back she went down the uneven strand
to Cissy, to Edy, to Jacky and Tommy Caffrey, to little baby
Boardman. It was darker now and there were stones and bits of
wood on the strand and slippy seaweed. She walked with a
certain quiet dignity characteristic of her but with care and very
slowly because – because Gerty MacDowell was . . .
    Tight boots? No. She's lame! O!   (Na 766–71)

All the paraphernalia are present for obscuring the truth (stones,
wood, seaweed, the uneven strand itself), but the final sentence
seems destined for revelation, yet remains a blank, trampled upon
by the rush of Bloomian observation – a blank not unlike the one
provided soon after by Bloom's writing in the sand. In characteristic fashion Bloom makes more than one guess (a process seen in
'Circe' when he beholds a glow in the night sky), and his
'corrected' version – 'She's lame! O!' – neatly fits his sexual
inclinations and preferences, and has been valorised into per-
petuity. The verdict, however, does not invalidate the idea of a
Gerty wilfully immobilised by cramming her feet into shoes that
are too small for them, of a crippling vanity to corroborate the
proud contention of a size five foot. Tight boots and lameness are
not mutually exclusive, and Molly Bloom – mature and wordly-
wise on the subject of feminine vanity, and herself the possessor of
highly admired feet – knows all about 'shoes that are too tight to
walk in' (Pe 260). The source that has conditioned the universal
verdict of a lame Gerty is exclusively the twilight observation by
Bloom, and all aspects of the Gerty MacDowell portrait conspire to
substantiate it. Yet the determining source cannot be considered
authoritative; indeed, the process by which authority is rendered
in this scene places that authority on the slippery, ill-lit and uneven
strand.

ENCYCLOPAEDIC READINGS AND RENDERINGS

The 'Cyclops' chapter has permanently placed in disrepute all
facets of the monocular perspective, but when no corroborating
vision is available, the single focus remains preferable to 'blind'
reasoning. Most of the 309 pairings in 'Ithaca' contain the possibilities of multiple readings, although in many cases a primary source

imposes a limiting context. As Bloom and Stephen move through the physical area, a degree of narrational perception records their progress and surroundings, a potentially 'objective' system of observation; and as they interact in conversation in the early segments (and Bloom converses with Molly in the later stages), an indirect mode of presentation replaces the customary dialogue. Internalised commentary, conspicuous in the early chapters of *Ulysses*, gives way in 'Ithaca' to an indirect stylisation of thought process in Bloom and Stephen individually, each indulging at various times in perceiving, remembering, deliberating and (less consciously) drifting into reveries. As well, a repository of information exists outside the perspectives of any of the characters, an encyclopaedic knowledge of reference and resource materials unretainable in the average – even highly knowledgeable – mind, but readily recuperable from other sources: reference books, guides, maps, directories, programmes, brochures, newspapers, journals, circulars and advertisements.

Despite the plethora of such 'gratuitous' information in 'Ithaca', only one of the question–answer units seems attributable exclusively to the encyclopaedic (entry 100), which establishes the points of contact between the Hebrew and Irish languages ('The presence of guttural sounds, diacritic aspirations, epenthetic and servile letters in both languages: their antiquity, both having been taught on the plain of Shinar 242 years after the deluge in the seminary instituted by Fenius Farsaigh [etc.]' – It 747–50ff). The subject arises from the Bloom–Stephen colloquy, but this attending pot-pourri of scholarly and legendary speculation exceeds the expected reservoir of information probable for either of the two conversants. The principle of extended knowledge, of the egregious 'flow' of self-embellishing 'facts', takes possession of the narrational discourse, a 'development from, and of, the material'. Considering the disclaimer in the previous question-and-answer –

Was the knowledge possessed by both of each of these languages, the extinct and the revived, theoretical or practical?

Theoretical, being confined to certain grammatical rules of accidence and syntax and practically excluding vocabulary (It 741–4)

– and the quick shift suggested in the next subject ('What anthem did Bloom chant . . . ?' – It 761), there is little justification in assuming that their conversation included any signifcant portion of the interceding esoterica.

Even the 'purity' of this encyclopaedic Hebrew/Irish item can be challenged, since it is the conversational gambit that instigated the topic, but taken broadly as compartmentisable, approximately three-quarters of the entries can be classified along one of five basic lines of approach. Most of the really interesting ones, however, are the hybrids (again, the closing sentence of 'Cyclops' paves the way for appreciating the sharp shifts of focus in the combined items), as, for example, Bloom's recollection of the 1893 pantomime programme. It can be assumed that the exactness of his memory would not be sufficient for total recall even in the most nostalgic of trivial pursuits, and that the information presented exists basically at its *source*, the printed programme contemporary with the performance. The one serious lapse, the creation of the name 'Nelly Bouverist' (It 437), can be attributed to Bloomian blunder, a conflation of the real Nellie Bouverie with the equally real Kate Neverist, as Adams contends.[26] At the point at which something as concretely authentic and authoritative as a printed pantomime programme presents itself as solid ground in the Ithacan maelstrom, a 'misprint' finds its way into the text, a product of human error and itself diagnostic of the fuller potentials of the weaving–unweaving–reweaving process.

Somewhat different from that particular kind of compilation is the catalogue of participants in the Dignam funeral: this list comes from Bloom's experience refreshed by his recent reading of the *Evening Telegraph* account in the cabman's shelter. But Bloom cannot know for certain that the participants are all actually in bed (no one can), and even if he is justified in a safe assumption at so late an hour, for him the 'fact' is unverified, as for us it is unverifiable. In the instance of the pantomime the actual information is retrievable from a printed source, but in the listing of the dormant mourners there is no available 'encyclopaedia' to provide such information, and in the absence of an omniscient narrator who watches over us all in the night, the reader can only surmise that it is the product of Bloom's deliberative supposition. The subjectivity of the listing becomes apparent when the nature of the censoring is uncovered:

Martin Cunningham (in bed), Jack Power (in bed), Simon Dedalus (in bed), Ned Lambert (in bed), Tom Kernan (in bed),

Joe Hynes (in bed), John Henry Menton (in bed), Bernard Corrigan (in bed), Patsy Dignam (in bed), Paddy Dignam (in the grave).   (It 1238–41)

Understandably absent is Corny Kelleher, whom Bloom had seen only an hour or two earlier arriving in Nighttown, and presumably not yet home in bed. Father Coffey, included by Bloom as one of the unlucky thirteen at the grave (Ha 835), was not included in the newspaper list and therefore fails to appear in the 'Ithaca' list either, perhaps indicative that although the funeral listing here in 'Ithaca' devolves from Bloom's mental processes, it is newly dependent upon a printed source as well for immediacy and accuracy. Assuming that Bloom is purposely cataloguing these names for his own edification, two possible motives are attributable to him: droll humour works toward the conclusion that Dignam is in his grave, so the comedic progress mechanically and repeatedly places the mourners in their beds – and Bloom can now put into practical usage the names he has learned from the newspaper, those of the brother-in-law and the son anonymous to him in 'Hades'.

Various entries in 'Ithaca' mediate between conversation, thoughts and external knowledge, and two of them in particular seem representative of specific types: the first is one of those that basically operates sequentially, while the second seems to function relatively simultaneously. When Bloom listens to Stephen's '*A Pisgah Sight of Palestine* or *The Parable of the Plums*' (It 640–2ff.), he proves no more attentive than the original auditors in 'Aeolus', primarily because he lapses into his own thoughts, the Moses allusion evoking his 'Favourite Hero' as well as the prospect of earning money by publishing such items and entertaining guests by narrating them, until an anticipation of the summer solstice produces in his mind statistics on its actual advent. But when Bloom and Stephen are in the rear garden discussing the stars ('With what meditations did Bloom accompany his demonstration to his companion of various constellations?' – It 1040–1ff.) Bloom's thoughts run parallel to his talk and are pointedly corroborated by statistical facts hardly at his immediate disposal. It is not only a matter of the limitations of the human (non-genius) brain containing these 'Meditations of evolution increasingly vaster' (It 1042), but that the diction bears no resemblance to the familiar thought language hitherto attributed to Leopold Bloom, while it bears a consistent resemblance to the vocabulary and syntax of the astronomy textbook. The final clause, however, 'in comparison with which the years, threescore and ten, of allotted human life formed a parenthesis of infinitesimal brevity' (It 1054–6), contains the biblical phrase that is easily attributable, but not necessarily dependent on, Bloom's mind, an intrusion into the textbook that again replicates the closing clauses of 'Cyclops' – here foreshadowed by 'the parallax or parallactic drift' (It 1052).

Less complex blends are easily understood progressions from observation to internalisation: although a camera could record the furniture in Bloom's parlour, only Bloom's mind harbours an image now of 'the alterations effected in the disposition of the articles of furniture' (It 1279–80); a camera could depict Bloom in the act of lighting incense with the aid of the Agendath Netaim prospectus as a taper (It 1321–9), but Bloom has obviously made a mental decision, once he has recognised the piece of paper for what it is, that it is expendable and can be burned. The urination scene in the garden, on the other hand, includes in a single entry both perceivable action and the simultaneous thoughts of both Bloom and Stephen, the former in his High School achievement ('attaining the point of greatest altitude against the whole concurrent strength of the institution') and the latter on the effect of his drinking on his bladder ('augmented by diuretic consumption an insistent vesical pressure' – It 1195–8). Several entries purposefully collapse their mutual thinking, and one in particular stands out as unique since it offers a basic statement of their *non*-thoughts:

Did either openly allude to their racial difference?

Neither.　(It 525–6)

A nineteenth-century novelist would easily have presented this observation as auctorial comment; many a twentieth-century novelist would as easily have offered it as 'objective' narration. But in 'Ithaca' such items are fixed by the boundaries of the catechism, which produces sets of serial relationships. This question-and-answer development of a specific series begins with the process of Bloom's contemplative mood:

Did he find four separating forces between his temporary guest and him?

Name, age, race, creed.　(It 402–3)

'Creed' may seem inappropriate here since both Stephen and Bloom are *now* nominally Roman Catholics, and if indicative of what Bloom sees as a 'separating force' the distinction points to a residual Jewishness situated on top of Jewish roots, the concern in Bloom's mind with 'race'; and the series continues until the mutual reticence is stated in a 'non-thought', only to be immediately succeeded by the deployment of a convoluted 'trans-thought':

> What, reduced to their simplest reciprocal form, were Bloom's thoughts about Stephen's thoughts about Bloom and about Stephen's thoughts about Bloom's thoughts about Stephen?
>
> He thought that he thought that he was a jew whereas he knew that he knew that he knew that he was not.   (It 527–31)

The shift from proper nouns to personal pronouns, anticipating Molly's multiple shifts in unreferenced masculine pronouns in 'Penelope', undermines the stability of the narrative 'context' here, opening a space between the pronoun and its supposed referent. Since the negation in the preceding entry to any open allusion closes the possibility of dialogue, and the questioning between the two none the less maintains its existence, the thought waves interweave in the space that both separates and joins them.

THROWAWAY RETRIEVED

Yet 'Ithaca' comments obliquely on the limitations of previous methods of narrative presentation in *Ulysses* (each new chapter 'improves' on the style of the previous one, and as often incorporates aspects of the preceding method, acknowledging the limitations of all means of narration). Internalised narrative had intensified the subjective focus, but unlike dramatic soliloquy, where the audience is the intended recipient, the internalised commentaries of the Joycean text are frequently encoded with the personal idiosyncrasies of the 'speaker', frustrating the demands of an unacknowledged 'listener'. As we follow Bloom through the day, his inadvertent 'tip' to Bantam Lyons on Throwaway begins to loom large, although not necessarily for Bloom himself, since the timing of the Gold Cup race at 4 p.m. coincides with the more important assignation of Blazes and Molly – distanced from each other by the difference between Greenwich and Dunsink time. Bloom of course places no bet ('that whiteeyed kaffir? says the citizen, that never backed a horse in anger in his life?' – Cy 1552–3), and the Gold Cup does not figure significantly in his thoughts, so it can also be assumed that it has no actual existence in his consciousness. Is he aware, however, of the accidental 'knowledge' that he had 'named' the winner, and does he not regret having acted on that knowledge and really been, as Lenehan credits him (Cy 1556–7), 'the only man in Dublin has it'? Only in 'Ithaca', where direct questions are the format and extended answers flow untapped, does Bloom's consciousness undergo the necessary interrogation: 'Where had previous intimations of the result, effected or projected, been received by him?' The result is a full recapitulation of the events of the day, and a dry enumeration of the facts in Bloom's mind, indicating rather complete awareness at every juncture of the existence of the Gold Cup event and the existence of Throwaway as the obliquely touted winner. The subjective events, however, are mysteriously elaborated upon, as an intrusive inner subjectivity claims the presented information and carries it into stranger realms:

> when Frederick M. (Bantam) Lyons had rapidly and successively requested, perused and restituted the copy of the current issue of the *Freeman's Journal* and *National Press* which he had been about to throw away (subsequently thrown away), he had proceeded towards the oriental edifice of the Turkish and Warm Baths, 11 Leinster Street, with the light of inspiration shining in his countenance and bearing in his arms the secret of the race, graven in the language of prediction.   (It 334–41)

The unexplained and unprecedented leap from one subject to another (presumably unrelated) subject has its justification in the answer to the next question, where Bloom acknowledges that 'the significance of any event followed its occurrence as variably as the acoustic report followed the electrical discharge' (It 343–5). Accepting the descriptive analysis of his 'mood' regarding the racing and betting event of the day ('He had not risked, he did not expect, he had not been disappointed, he was satisfied' – It 349–50), we find it applied to his moment of inspiration. Having tipped Lyons on

Throwaway had brought 'Light to the gentiles' (It 353) – not that this particular Gentile acted upon his lights – so that the 'acoustic report' of Hugh MacHugh's transmission in the newspaper office of John F. Taylor's rendition of Moses follows the 'electrical discharge' (the lightning):

> *He would never have spoken with the Eternal amid lightnings on Sinai's mountaintop nor ever have come down with the light of inspiration shining in his countenance and bearing in his arms the tables of the law, graven in the language of the outlaw.* (Ae 866–9)

Bloom had not been present in the newspaper office when MacHugh delivered his reverberated speech, any more than he was present in the National Library when Stephen was inspired to hypothesise an imagined walk down Fetter lane with William Shakespeare, but the reverberations persist none the less in strange and mysterious ways, undergoing sea changes. Bloom as Moses/Elijah/Throwaway is credited with his shining inspiration, but there is an immediate comic deflation (he is reduced once again to Bloom) in the realisation that the 'secret of the race' pertains less to the Hebrew race than to the Gold Cup run at Ascot.

A MEETING OF MINDS

The catechismal format of 'Ithaca' is established on the parallelism implied in the first question/answer ('What parallel courses did Bloom and Stephen follow returning?' – It 1) and the colloquy implied in the second ('Of what did the duumvirate deliberate during their itinerary?' – It 11), even when one member of the duumvirate is eventually abstracted and the parallel possibilities are only suggested rather than realised. The Greek meaning of the catechetical, predicated on the presence of an oral teacher, under-lies the printed text of the catechismal of ecclesiastic education, and the first half of 'Ithaca' is dominated by that presence, both Stephen and Bloom sharing the teacher's role. The oral, however, invariably anticipates and gives way to the written, as in the Irish/Hebrew 'lessons' inscribed on 'the penultimate blank page of a book of inferior literary style, entitled *Sweets of Sin*' (It 733–4), the creation of a palimpsest to which Stephen also adds 'by appending his signature in Irish and Roman characters' (It 775). The Stephen who confirmed his role as 'reader' ('Signatures of all things I am here to read', he reminded himself in 'Proteus' – Pr 2) moves tentatively toward the 'writer' who signs his work, now a signatory to *Sweets of Sin*, and soon after when he signs himself in urine under the stars.

Conversation is the impetus in 'Ithaca', separated and 'silenced' into individual thought, and developed into a written text. At several instances a series of entries contains their sources in talk extended into thought, a rise and fall of voiced and unvoiced materials in immediate relationship to each other, as in the triad of queries concerning Mrs Riordan. The spur is contained in the initiating question ('Did their conversation on the subject of these reminiscences reveal a third connecting link between them?'), offering as mutual subject 'Mrs Riordan (Dante), a widow of independent means' (It 477–9) – that is, Bloom's 'Mrs Riordan' in contradistinction to Stephen's 'Dante'. Initially she is Stephen's possession (having 'resided in the house of Stephen's parents'), but she soon becomes Bloom's (at 'the City Arms Hotel' – It 479–82), in each case her residence approximating three years. Yet the conversational emphasis seems to be primarily Bloom's, not only because the first conversational extension is exclusively his (although the second even predates his experiences of her), but because a repeated characterising of her as 'an infirm widow of independent, if limited, means' (It 488–9) focuses directly on the Bloomian perspective, Stephen hardly aware of her from his childhood under that depiction. When the third extension separates the memories of Stephen and Bloom, the latter includes her 'supposititious wealth' (It 504–5), of which the former remains innocent, never having aspired to become her heir. Stephen's 'Dante' has little relevance here and he apparently has no intention of dredging up, much less mentioning, the reason for her quitting the house of Stephen's parents on '29 December 1891' (It 480), although the presence of the date testifies to its relevance to Stephen. (If the Christmas dinner fiasco depicted in *A Portrait* actually took place on Christmas day, Dante took her own good time before slamming the Dedalus door behind her.) Instead Stephen maintains a rather detached, even antiseptic view of 'Mrs Riordan': 'her lamp of colza oil before the statue of the Immaculate Conception, her green and maroon brushes for Charles Stewart Parnell and for Michael Davitt, her tissue papers' (It 506–8) –

Stephen is calculatedly writing the scene, and a careful reading of these 'furnishings' reveals the religious Catholic who will turn violently against the Parnell denounced by the Catholic clergy. Molly would have no trouble reading and corroborating this text, as she remembers 'that old faggot Mrs Riordan that he thought he had a great leg of and she never left us a farthing all for masses for herself and her soul greatest miser ever was' (Pe 4–6).

The tenuous relationships between what is spoken and what is thought in 'Ithaca', as well as what is repressed both in conversation and in the privacy of the mind, also colour the sequence that begins with Bloom's apparent disquisition to Stephen on the art of advertising. Bloom's postulation of 'an illuminated showcart ... in which two smartly dressed girls were to be seated engaged in writing' results in a 'suggested scene ... then constructed by Stephen':

Solitary hotel in mountain pass. Autumn. Twilight. Fire lit. In dark corner young man seated. Young woman enters. Restless. Solitary. She sits. She goes to window. She stands. She sits. Twilight. She thinks. On solitary hotel paper she writes. She thinks. She writes. She sighs. Wheels and hoofs. She hurries out. He comes from his dark corner. He seizes solitary paper. He holds it towards fire. Twilight. He reads. Solitary.

What?

In sloping, upright and backhands: Queen's Hotel, Queen's Hotel, Queen's Hotel, Queen's Ho ... (It 612–20)

The designation of 'suggested scene' does nothing to indicate whether Stephen is imagining or narrating, whether the scene is thought or spoken. The language of 'gesture ... rendering visible ... the first entelechy, the structural rhythm' (Ci 105–7) drunkenly espoused by Stephen in Nighttown takes possession of this vignette, virtually soundless except for the 'Wheels and hoofs' that announce the means of departure for the young woman.

Only when the Ithacan narrative arrives at the specifics of a name does it reveal that Stephen's scene was verbally transmitted, like the telling of the parable to the pressmen, not created silently, like the visit to the Gouldings in 'Proteus'. Bloom reacts to the mention of the Queen's Hotel, a name that Stephen may have chosen at random for its mere commonality, or perhaps because of the appropriateness to the woman writing, but which for Bloom has real and tragic overtones:

> What suggested scene was then reconstructed by Bloom?
>
> The Queen's Hotel, Ennis, county Clare, where Rudolph Bloom (Rudolf Virag) died on the evening of the 27 June 1886, at some hour unstated, in consequence of an overdose of monkshood (aconite) selfadministered.   (It 621–4)

A 'suggested scene' has different tonalities for the two conversants, fictive and real, dramatic and tragic, public and private. Bloom modifies the traumatic impact by 'extending' reality to include not only his father's purchase of poison but also his purchase later that same afternoon of 'a new boater straw hat' (It 629). In the privacy of his own mind Bloom decides that the reference to the Queen's Hotel was merely 'Coincidence', and also decides not to discuss the matter with Stephen:

> Did he depict the scene verbally for his guest to see?
>
> He preferred himself to see another's face and listen to another's words by which potential narration was realised and kinetic temperament relieved.   (It 635–8)

Whatever else remains of Stephen's depiction of the autumnal scene at the hotel disappears, like a train entering a tunnel, lost in the transfer to Bloom's reactive thoughts and calculated decision, and when the train emerges from the tunnel a new narration has displaced the old one, a 'second scene narrated to him, described by the narrator as *A Pisgah Sight of Palestine* or *The Parable of the Plums*' (It 639–41). Stephen has already 'rehearsed' his plum parable earlier in the day, and is now falling back on a familiar narrative instead of attempting the as-yet untried newer one. For Bloom this is a 'second coincidence' (It 639), since he has just burned the image of Palestine in the advertisement for the fruits of Agendath Netaim, and so Stephen's second narration enters an even longer tunnel, lost in Bloom's rambling speculations on Moses and publishing-for-profit, until his thoughts are also swallowed up by the setting off of 'encyclopaedic' facts: 'the increasingly longer nights gradually following the summer solstice on the day but three following, videlicet, Tuesday, 21 June (S. Aloysius Gonzaga), sunrise 3.33 a.m., sunset 8.29 p.m.' (It 654–6). (The informative source has made the necessary transition from Thursday the 16th to Friday the 17th in the computation, and interprets 'but three following' to mean the days *between* the 17th and the 21st – meticulous to a fault.)

'. . . AND SO TO BED'

The 'Ithaca' chapter ends with a fusion similar to the chapter closures that have become a hallmark at least since the end of 'Cyclops' ('Nausicaa' concludes with a reprised Gerty acknowledging the tolling of 9 p.m. by the sound of the cuckoo clock in the Star of the Sea church rectory as Bloom dozes; 'Oxen of the Sun' ends with Lynch noticing the announcement of Dowie's revival meeting at Merrion Hall and taking on the Dowie persona to hawk salvation; 'Circe' dissolves into Bloom's image of the dead Rudy superimposed on the comatose Stephen; and 'Eumaeus' fades as Stephen and Bloom link arms, 'continuing their *tête-à-tête*' – Eu 1889). The constant refinement of subjective techniques in *Ulysses*, the narrowing of focus to the perceptions of the individual characters, is undercut in these later chapters by an expansion beyond functional subjectivity, a phantasmal objectivity comically introduced in the fusion of techniques. Bloom dozing in the last four 'Ithaca' entries recapitulates the sleepy reveries he enjoyed in 'Nausicaa' –

> because it was a little canarybird bird that came out of its little house to tell the time that Gerty MacDowell noticed the time she was there because she was as quick as anything about a thing like that, was Gerty MacDowell, and she noticed at once that that foreign gentleman that was sitting on the rocks looking was
> > *Cuckoo*
> > *Cuckoo*
> > *Cuckoo*.   (Na 1299–1306)

– and Molly's falling asleep at the end of 'Penelope', confusing Gibraltar and Howth, Mulvey and Bloom. The 'Nausicaa' closure moves from Bloomian musings to the 'objectified' dinner scene at the church rectory to an 'interpretive' observation credited to Gerty in the language of the mental wanderings of Leopold Bloom. The irrational fusion in this last paragraph violates rational sources, since not only does Bloom remain innocent that Gerty ever saw him as foreign, but also because he has no inkling of Gerty's surname. A key entry in 'Ithaca' highlights that piece of missing information: Bloom enjoys the 'reflection' that 'his magnetic face, form and address had been favourably received during the course of the preceding day by a wife (Mrs Josephine Breen, born Josie Powell), a nurse, Miss Callan (Christian name unknown), a maid, Gertrude (Gerty, family name unknown)' (It 1844–8).

The ostensibly objective, therefore, has the same questionable validity as the unabashedly subjective, psychological reality constantly being complemented and upstaged by transformational conjecture (if Bloom were Lord Mayor, if Lynch were to announce the advent of Elijah, if Stephen were redeemed by the love of Miss Ferguson, *et cetera*). Lapsing into the irrationality and open-ended possibility of sleep, Bloom is 'the childman weary, the manchild in the womb' who has 'travelled' with 'Sinbad the Sailor' and all his transformed manifestations (It 2317–22). (Molly lying beside him, incidentally, is described as 'in the attitude of Gea-Tellus, fulfilled, recumbent, big with seed' – (It 2313–14), a conflation of encyclopaedic attribution, perceived reality, Bloomian conjecture, and her own intimate awareness – the last an intrusion in the usual sources of 'Ithaca'.) The ultimate aspect of objectified fantasy goes beyond language, the round black dot that 'locates' Bloom in dream-space, while the penultimate entry, the answer to the question 'When?' allows for a last attempt to capture dream-time in a linguistic form:

> Going to dark bed there was a square round Sinbad
> the Sailor roc's auk's egg in the night of the bed
> of all the auks of the rocs of Darkinbad the Bright-
> dayler.   (It 2327–30)

The recently challenged reading of Molly's opening statement that Bloom has actually requested 'his breakfast in bed with a couple of eggs' (Pe 1–2), changes the nature of the missing portions of 'dialogue' between husband and wife lost somewhere before the conclusion of 'Ithaca'. Drowsy dwelling on 'roc's auk's egg in the night of the bed', rather than totally internalised, may have been mumblingly articulated and consequently misinterpreted by the 'listener'. The relationship between the roc and the auk mirrors the relationship between the literal and the imaginative in the narrative setting, distinct from each other yet captured in the web of 'dream reality': the roc is fictional, deriving from such wanderers as Marco Polo and Sinbad the Sailor, and ferocious in its flight, scavaging such enormous land animals as elephants (the name derives from the Arabic); the auk is real, though now extinct, and unable to fly, basically passive (the name derives from the Scandinavian). As birds they are redundant, the one from the *Arabian Nights* perhaps more immediate to Bloom's drowsy thoughts, while the other may well have intruded from one of the books on Bloom's shelf, *In the Track of the Sun*, for example, or more specifically from *Voyages in China* or *Three Trips to Madagascar* (It 1395, 1379, 1374) – or Bloom may actually be mumbling through a request for a breakfast of eggs in bed now that the rain has broken the drought ('Ham and eggs, no. No good eggs with this drouth' – Ca 43–44).

The diffusive techniques of 'Ithaca', allowing for a myriad of sources and a variety of perceptions, have their contrasting simplicity in the technique employed in 'Penelope' (the lamp, the bed, Bloom's sleeping form, the commode, passing trains), and the only viable source for the discourse presented is presumed to be Molly's consciousness. Yet the same singular mind within the span of only a few minutes reminds itself of Boylan's sexual performance of only a few hours before in quite variant numbers: 'he must have come 3 or 4 times'; '4 or 5 times locked in each others arms'; '5 or 6 times handrunning' (Pe 143, 895, 1511–12). Like many of Molly's computations, this expansiveness of design has been easily attributable to temperament, in these cases ranging from sanguine self-satisfaction in the first instance, to contempt for her colleagues – the sexless sopranos – in the second, to furious annoyance with Bloom in the third. Rather than monologue, 'Penelope' is a cantata of Molly's various voices, and no single voice or point of view predominates. The excessive subjectivity that colours Boylan's 'performance' has little to do with Boylan himself, but with the aspect of Molly operative at the moment – and each is as dependent on an external cause as any of the others. The major discrepancy, therefore, is not between three and six (the ultimate numbers) but between three and four, four and five, five and six (the intermediate inconsistency). Reality lies in none of these 'recollections', although a muted reference during an instance of relative tranquillity and recaptured passion may suggest a more specific moment, 'when he made me spend the 2nd time tickling me behind with his finger I was coming for about 5 minutes with my legs round him' (Pe 586–7).

The indeterminate Molly Bloom displays an interest in truth and in the written transmission of truth, as well as a constant realisation of the prevalance of dissembling and discrepancies ('I suppose he thinks I don't know deceitful men all their 20 pockets arent enough for their lies then why should we tell them even if its the truth they dont believe you' – Pe 1235–7). In effect, Molly's is the feminine exposition determined by an awareness of masculine receptivity, an implied male 'listener' conditioned by the dominance of literature and letters written by men ('cant be true a thing like that like some of those books he brings me the works of Master Francois Somebody supposed to be a priest' – Pe 487–9). The elision between truth and deception exists as a reality for Molly, since to her it is more important to fill the void with something. Aware of 'their lies' at all times, she none the less accepts them as necessary, hoping for a love letter from the less-than-highly-literary Blazes Boylan:

> I told him he could write what he liked yours ever Hugh Boylan in Old Madrid stuff silly women believe love is sighing I am dying still if he wrote it I suppose thered be some truth in it true or no it fills up your whole day and life always something to think about every moment and see it all around you like a new world I could write the answer in bed to let him imagine me short just a few words not those long crossed letters Atty Dillon used to write to the fellow that was something in the four courts that jilted her after out of the ladies letterwriter when I told her to say a few simple words he could twist how he liked not acting with precipat precip itancy with equal candour the greatest earthly happiness answer to a gentlemans proposal affirmatively. (Pe 735–46)

Molly's recollections function as an answer to Martha Clifford's letter, as if she herself and not her husband were its intended recipient. 'Do tell me what kind of perfume does your wife use. I want to know', Martha had requested (Lo 259), and the 'Penelope' chapter is redolent with various wafting scents, a constant flow of Molly's variety and complexity, from the Gibraltar girlhood on into her Dublin womanhood. The subliminal acknowledgement that the *word* contains a *world* in Martha's typographical mistake ('I do not like that other world' – Lo 245) is corroborated by Molly, for whom a letter received opens the possibility of 'a new world', while she contends 'that of course some men can be dreadfully aggravating drive you mad and always the worst word in the world' (Pe 237–8). Bloom's most recent letter to Martha Clifford has its own corollary in a letter he sent to Molly when he had first met her, for Molly 'replies' when she notes, 'what a Deceiver then he wrote me that letter with all those words in it how could he have the face to any woman after' (Pe 318–19). 'Tell me the word, mother, if you know now', a desperate Stephen Dedalus demanded of his mother's ghost; 'The word known to all men' (Ci 4191–2). The 'word' in Poldy's letter is by convention unknown to women, to the nubile Molly Tweedy as well as to Martha Clifford, although Martha must known it if she knows enough to know that she does not like it, nor the world it contains. Molly, however, defies the convention and makes her implicit acknowledgement:

> making it so awkward after when we met asking me have I offended you with my eyelids down of course he saw I wasnt . . . and if I knew what it meant of course I had to say no for form sake dont understand you I said and wasnt it natural so it is of course it used to be written up with a picture of a womans on that wall in Gibraltar with that word I couldnt find anywhere . . . then writing every morning a letter sometimes twice a day. (Pe 320–8)

The 'word' always seems to remain known and unknown simultaneously; Molly knows it but cannot acknowledge knowing it, and she even remembers her first encounter with it (written, rather than spoken), and it none the less fails to exist when searched for in an authorative source, apparently a standard dictionary.

Molly Bloom says no 'for form sake', and of course says yes. The conflict between her attitudes is never resolved, each revealing a relevant facet of herself as she faces a contradictory world, and remains resolute in each of her confrontations with that world. The words she knows include the taboo words that are denied to women by the patriarchy, but she is also aware that she is on occasion hampered by not knowing or understanding or remembering words: 'some word I couldnt make out'; 'I couldnt think of the word'; 'where do those old fellows get all the words they have omissions' (Pe 618–19, 750, 1170). (Her substitution in this case of 'omissions' for 'emissions' again points to the missing word(s) at the narrative core.) 'I hope theyll have something better for us in the other world' (Pe 1210–11), she comments soon after, accommodating to the relevance of Martha's letter as a determining source of 'Penelope' – Martha herself only a recent avatar of Molly Bloom, the newest respondant to the predictable 'great Suggester Don Poldo de la Flora' (Pe 1428). The Molly who has been sexually satisfied can retroactively admire Boylan's penis, 'that tremendous big red brute of a thing he has . . . like iron or some kind of a thick crowbar standing all the time' (although she is not unaware of brutishness and the metallic), while the Molly who is scornful of men and their genitalia can comment caustically, 'what a man looks like with his two bags full and his other thing hanging down out of him or sticking up at you like a hatrack' (Pe 144–8, 542–4). Even her own facial characteristics change: when she feels insulted at not being given her due as an Irish soprano, she insists, 'I had the map of it all' (presumably of Ireland all over her face), but when she conjectures on Poldy's initial attraction to her, she attributes it 'on account of my being jewess looking after my mother' (Pe 378, 1184–5). Molly contains multitudes, balanced between the formal No and the informal Yes, and between the Yes as fixity and the Yes as ambiguity.

NOTES

1. A. Walton Litz, 'Ithaca', *James Joyce's Ulysses: Critical Essays*, ed. Clive Hart and David Hayman (Berkeley, Cal.: University of California Press, 1974) p. 398.
2. Anthony Burgess, *Here Comes Everybody* (London: Faber and Faber, 1965) pp. 171, 172; Kenneth Grose, *James Joyce* (London: Evans, 1975) pp. 121, 123; Matthew Hodgart, *James Joyce* (London: Routledge and Kegan Paul, 1978) p. 125; Karen Lawrence, *The Odyssey of Style in Ulysses* (Princeton, N.J.: Princeton University Press, 1981) p. 181.
3. Grose, *James Joyce*, p. 121.
4. Robert M. Adams, *James Joyce: Common Sense and Beyond* (New York: Random House, 1965) p. 163; David Hayman, *Ulysses: The Mechanics of Meaning* (Englewood Cliffs, N.J.: Prentice-Hall, 1970) p. 87.
5. Burgess, *Here Comes Everybody*, p. 172; Adams, *James Joyce*, p. 163.

6. C. H. Peake, *James Joyce: The Citizen and the Artist* (Stanford, Cal.: Stanford University Press, 1977) p. 285.

7. Adams, *James Joyce*, p. 163; Burgess, *Here Comes Everybody*, p. 170; Richard Ellmann, *Ulysses on the Liffey* (New York: Oxford University Press, 1972) p. 156.

8. Clive Hart, *James Joyce's Ulysses* (Sydney: Sydney University Press, 1968) p. 74.

9. Ellmann, *Ulysses on the Liffey*, p. 156.

10. Hodgart, *James Joyce*, p. 125; Peake, *James Joyce*, p. 286.

11. Stuart Gilbert, *James Joyce's Ulysses* (New York: Alfred A. Knopf, 1931) p. 345; Litz, 'Ithaca', pp. 393–4.

12. Hodgart, *James Joyce*, p. 125.

13. *Letters of James Joyce*, vol. 1, ed. Stuart Gilbert (New York: Viking Press, 1957) p. 164.

14. Litz, 'Ithaca', p. 396; Adams, *James Joyce*, p. 165; Hayman, *Ulysses* p. 87.

15. Hugh Kenner, *Dublin's Joyce* (London: Chatto and Windus, 1955) p. 261.

16. Marilyn French, *The Book as World: James Joyce's Ulysses* (Cambridge, Mass.: Harvard University Press, 1976) pp. 221, 227, 239.

17. Michael Groden, *Ulysses in Progress* (Princeton, N.J.: Princeton University Press, 1977) p. 140; Wolfgang Iser, *The Implied Reader* (Baltimore, Md: Johns Hopkins University Press, 1974) p. 219; David Hayman, 'The Empirical Molly', *Approaches to Ulysses*, ed. Thomas F. Staley and Bernard Benstock (Pittsburgh, Pa.: Pittsburgh University Press, 1970) p. 114; Michael Mason, *James Joyce: Ulysses* (London: Edward Arnold, 1972) p. 58; Stanley Sultan, *The Argument of Ulysses* (Columbus: Ohio State University Press, 1964) p. 383.

18. Adams, *James Joyce*, pp. 164–5, 163; Peake, *James Joyce*, p. 296; Hayman, *Ulysses*, p. 87.

19. Kenner, *Joyce's Voices* (Berkeley, Cal.: University of California Press, 1978) pp. 96, 98.

20. Mason, *James Joyce*, p. 58; French, *The Book as World*, p. 223; Groden, *Ulysses in Progress*, p. 140; Peake, *James Joyce*, p. 285.

21. Peake, *James Joyce*, p. 286; Mason, *James Joyce*, p. 58.

22. Hayman, 'The Empirical Molly', pp. 113–14.

23. Sultan, *The Argument of Ulysses*, p. 383.

24. Iser, *The Implied Reader*, pp. 219, 221.

25. S. L. Goldberg, *The Classical Temper* (London: Chatto and Windus, 1963) p. 189.

26. Adams, *James Joyce*, pp. 78–9.

Part Two
Tones and Textures

5
Narrational Evidence

Ulysses exists for us as a highly impregnated text. It confronts a great deal more than it contains; it gives birth to far more characters than it can possibly give life to; it suggests events that never take place within the text, nor could possibly take place even if the text were expanded many times over. None the less, many pieces of 'information' find their way into the elaborate structure more than once, reprised, reconstituted, reactivated, resulting in a format that often turns back upon itself and reopens new possibilities with old specifics. On a rare occasion we are offered an item only once, for a fleeting instance, as in a murder mystery where it would be the single clue leading to the solution (if it is remembered by the reader). Such is not quite the case of Esther Osvalt's shoe, which although mentioned just once, solves nothing that the reader is ever aware of. In Paris Stephen Dedalus had stepped into Esther Osvalt's shoe and was delighted to find that it fit his foot, and someone present at that fitting exclaimed – in French – on the smallness of Stephen's foot. Along Sandymount strand Stephen then remembers trying on Esther Osvalt's shoe. Or, to put it in a way that satisfies the reverse narration of chronological events, in the 'Proteus' chapter of *Ulysses* Stephen remembers trying on Esther Osvalt's shoe during a time in his life when he had been in Paris. The text presents us with a frontal attack on the event, and on Stephen's apprehension of the event, with reverberating connotations of transvestite actions and a love that dares not speak its name. Thereafter the singular Esther Osvalt and her one shoe disappear from the text and from any transcription of Stephen's consciousness in the text.

IN BRIDIE'S SHOES

Bridie Kelly fares a good deal better than Esther Osvalt – or at least twice as well, satisfying our expectation of at least dual reference.

She is no more incarnate in *Ulysses* than Esther, but she *occurs* twice in the textual web. Once in 'Oxen of the Sun' she exists as a recollection in Bloom's thoughts, and later in 'Circe' she acquires the status of an emanation like many others who trouble the reader throughout that enigmatic chapter. It was a convenience for a time to refer to such apparitions in 'Circe' as hallucinatory products of Bloom's mind (or of Stephen's mind when the hallucinatory characters were appropriate to Stephen), and when, even as experienced readers, we could not assign direct attribution, we found ways of circumventing or ignoring those uncomfortable elisions. But the days of drawing a firm line between passages of 'reality' and passages of 'hallucination' are surely long past.

Before confronting the narratological problem in a chapter like 'Circe' – and its amplification in the numerous problems in *Ulysses* – there is first the need to set the narrational situation that introduces Bridie Kelly in 'Oxen of the Sun'. If we assume that all factual materials derive from Bloom's consciousness (and that the style of 'Oxen' therefore is an extension of the possibilities and limitations of interior monologue), we are confronted with the following excerpt of no insignificant proportion:

> He thinks of a drizzling night in Hatch street, hard by the bonded stores there, the first. Together (she is a poor waif, a child of shame, yours and mine and of all for a bare shilling and her luckpenny), together they hear the heavy tread of the watch as two raincaped shadows pass the new royal university. Bridie! Bridie Kelly! He will never forget the name, ever remember the night, first night, the bridenight. They were entwined in nether-most darkness, the willer with the willed, and in an instant (*fiat!*) light shall flood the world. Did heart leap to heart? Nay, fair reader. In a breath 'twas done but – hold! Back! It must not be! In terror the poor girl flees away through the murk. She is the bride of darkness, a daughter of night. She dare not bear the sunny-golden babe of day. No, Leopold.   (OS 1063–74)

The subject of the passage is seduction-leading-to-possible-procreation, and the narrative language is that of Charles Lamb, a Charles Lamb pressed into service by Joyce in lieu of a functioning narrator to narrate events that do not necessarily reflect back on the original Charles Lamb, but advance the narrative format that remains exclusively that of James Joyce. Whatever the degree of parodic tone practised by Joyce on Lamb, and therefore by a Joycean Lamb on the text, the narrative material fluctuates between the attitudes of Leopold Bloom and the language reservoir of Charles Lamb filtered through Joycean channels. What Bloom remembers and conjectures, how he analyses and editoralises, receive corroborative handling in what Joyce surmises would be Lamb's appropriate method of discourse under the circumstances. Any hope that Bloom harbours that the hurried contact engendered a longed-for son is quickly dashed by both the unlikeliness of the coincidental conception and the proscriptives fostered by his own moral code. But what are the implications about Bridie Kelly? Whereas it is acknowledged that this had been Bloom's initiation into sex, is it also hers? Is it her 'bridenight', or does Bloom prefer to think so – and how could he know? Which one is the 'willer' and which the 'willed'? We may also speculate as to why the consummation takes place on Hatch street, although we notice that Gilbey's bonded stores are just around the corner from the High School that Bloom attended. If Bridie is a prostitute, she unfortunately lacks the basic rudiments of the profession, a place of business. Plying her trade *al fresco* in the crannies of a well-policed street hardly signifies professional status, yet there exists the tradition of 'tuppeny uprights' along Dublin's bridges.

On the basis of this passage and the one in 'Circe', Bridie has been referred to categorically as a prostitute by various readers. Those who contend that Bloom pays for her services point to that 'bare shilling', but even if the shilling is literally in play at the time, it could represent a gratuitous donation rather than a contracted payment (Bloom sends Martha Clifford a money order on a far flimsier excuse). And where then does the 'luckpenny' pertain? It seems to be Bridie's already, and there is no reason to think that it changes hands at all. Nor are there any indications that the coins are coincidental with the night of the seduction. Even allowing for something more than merely metaphoric language, the moralistic designation of Bridie as a 'child of shame' may account for the reference to payment in exchange for sexual favours. When asked to share the universal responsibility for Bridie Kelly ('yours and mine and of all'), the reader (even the reader trained in participatory response to Victorian novels) may be understandably reluctant – but is it her *sin* or her *sinful conception* that is the issue advanced in the passage? Whatever prostitution is invoked here may refer to an incident that engendered the 'poor waif' herself, not the one in which she may have created Bloom's hypothetical offspring. Such is the nature of moral imprecation, that it transcends the limitations of the 'real' aspects of a fictional text, or the potential for such 'reality'.

Leopold Bloom would undoubtedly find Lamb's language base a difficult responsibility to bear, even if he found the moral basis one that he assumes that he could readily accept. And since the linguistic stream always overspills its boundaries, meandering into convenient eddies, Lamb might find Bloom's discourse a distraction. 'Never forget the name, ever remember the night': where have we heard this pattern before? The existing intertext does not seem to derive from Charles Lamb, but echoes the rhythmic phraseology of the Masonic pledge of secrecy that locates itself again in the final moments of 'Circe', directly from Bloom: 'swear that I will always hail, ever conceal, never reveal, any part or parts, art or arts' (Ci 4951–2). The language of admonition that the parodist can extract from Lamb has its linguistic counterpart in the admonitory proscription of the Freemason: language generates parallels in language at the coincidental interstices throughout *Ulysses*.

Bridie's 'reappearance' in 'Circe' is usually cited as conclusive proof that she follows the world's oldest profession. Her spectre accosts Bloom in Nighttown, reminds him of their previous encounter (over two decades earlier), and re-solicits, although pursued and presumably captured by a 'burly rough' before Bloom can respond (Ci 361–7). The setting is appropriate; the name is the same; she has presumably been hard at it all these years and still outdoors at night, but at least the rain has stopped, although she is still '*rainbedraggled*'. Our sceptical minds easily disallow the Bawd's claim that Bridie is a virgin. Our ironic minds note that the price has gone up to 'ten shillings', with no assurance that the burly rough intends paying anything. The price is contingent on Bridie's being a virgin, yet the Bawd continues to offer her at that price to Bloom even after the rough has had 'his pleasure' (Ci 369). And Gerty MacDowell, a latter-day Bridie with better claims to virginity, is next in line to solicit Bloom.

The Bridie enigma lies in the method of reading 'Circe', as different from all other chapters of *Ulysses*. The conventional approach accepts as functioning reality those events that could conceivably happen, and relegates to some form of psychological reality (or *surreality*) those which violate verisimilitude. In Bloom's guilty mind Bridie was desecrated to the status of a whore in the Lamb passage, his own violation of her the incident that branded her and sent her permanently into the streets. Under those conditions, the Bridie of Mabbot street is as likely a figment of Bloom's guilt, and no more real than the Gerty who succeeds her. Her attainment of professional standing becomes problematic, and only the evidence of the recollection transmuted through Charles Lamb remains applicable.

Bloom's apprehensiveness that she became a prostitute certainly does not make her one, and there is little enough indication that that is his actual apprehension. His concern in 'Oxen' centres on the chance that he made her pregnant rather than that he made a whore of her (the setting in Nighttown does that). When disabused of the expectation that she might have borne his child, Bloom's motive may have undergone a change. 'It must not be!' sounds suspiciously like religious imprecation, and the disembodied 'voice' that labels Bridie a 'bride of darkness, a daughter of night' may have as its concern her status as a non-Jew – an abomination. The recovery of Bridie follows immediately upon an image of the paternal Rudolph Bloom (né Virag), 'the head of the firm, seated with Jacob's pipe after like labours in the paternal ingle' (OS 1057–8), while the conjuring up of Bridie Kelly in Nighttown is also preceded by his father's appearance and his stern questioning: 'Are you not my dear son Leopold who left the house of his father and left the god of his fathers Abraham and Jacob?' (Ci 261–2). The consubstantial father Virag and the transubstantial father Jacob in both instances provide the pre-text for the presence of Bridie Kelly, 'bride of darkness', the Gentile who sinned against the light in a mirror context of Mr Deasy's condemnation of dark Jews who sinned against *his* Christian version of the light.

The two 'instances' of a defined Bridie Kelly in *Ulysses* may not actually provide a total account of that mysterious character, who may have an antecedent existence as definite as that of Charles Lamb (or Stephen Dedalus). As readers of Joyce's texts we recall another night scene, a 'gloomy secret night' when 'the yellow lamps would light up, here and there, the squalid quarter of the brothels' (*AP*, p. 102). In this case the focus is on Stephen Dedalus in a comparable 'nighttown' and the text is *A Portrait of the Artist as a Young Man*. Stephen has recently been initiated into sexual experience and hears a whore's voice saying: 'Hello, Bertie, any good in your mind?' (*AP*, p. 102), just as Bloom will presumably hear Bridie in Nighttown echoing, 'Hatch street. Any good in your mind?' (Ci 364). Whereas the solicitation in *A Portrait* was 'Number ten. Fresh Nelly is waiting on you' (*AP*, p. 102), in *Ulysses* the Bawd hawks 'Ten shillings a maidenhead. Fresh thing was never touched' (Ci 359–60), with Fresh Nelly having made the transition into *Ulysses* as a character in Buck Mulligan's travesty, '*Everyman His Own Wife*' (SC 1187).

Of more potent significance, however, may be the manner of Bridie Kelly's attempted flight from the burly rough, '*With a squeak she flaps her bat shawl and runs*' (Ci 365), awakening as it does other recollections from the preceding text, where Stephen brooded over the peasant woman as 'a type of her race and his own, a batlike soul waking to the consciousness of itself in darkness and secrecy and loneliness' (*AP*, p. 183). He later endows Emma with the same characteristics, 'a figure of the womanhood of her country, a batlike soul waking to the consciousness of itself in darkness and secrecy and loneliness' (*AP*, p. 221), until he arrives at his own determination in relation to the woman with the batlike soul, the daughter of the Irish peasant:

> How could he hit their conscience or how cast his shadow over the imagination of their daughters, before their squires begat upon them, that they might breed a race less ignoble than their own? And under the deepened dusk he felt the thoughts and desires of the race to which he belonged flitting like bats, across the dark country lanes.   (*AP*, p. 238)

Bridie Kelly, potential progenitor of Bloom's sons, joins Emma and the Irish peasant woman, the daughter of the squire, as a belated woman of her race, Bloom having already invoked her tremulous image in Nausicaa as an avatar of Gerty MacDowell: 'Ba. What is that flying about? Swallow? Bat probably' (Na 1117), Gerty immediately replacing Bridie in accosting Bloom in Nighttown.

PEELING REALITY APART

'Circe' is a deep, dark well into which many things are dropped that never reach bottom and never make a sound. Attempts to achieve a finite separation of that which is 'reality' from that which

is presumably someone's 'hallucination' have been relatively un-
successful, and readers should become suspicious of anything
taking place in 'Circe' that cannot be proven retrospectively – and
then to continue to question that 'proof'. The chapters that follow
'Circe' should be read for indicators that in the relative normality of
the 'Nostos', Circean events actually cast their shadows and can
therefore be validated, allowing for the styles of each chapter to
achieve their own margins of unreliability.

Bracketing the enormity of 'Circe' are the closing moments of
'Oxen of the Sun', when Stephen and Lynch are heading for
Nighttown, with Bloom trailing behind, and the beginning of
'Eumaeus', when Bloom is helping Stephen to his feet and
brushing him off. Soon after, Bloom's thoughts inadvertently
supply the necessary pieces of exposition on what occurred prior to
the events in 'Circe'. In his conversation with Stephen he merely
refers to 'what occurred at Westland Row station' (Eu 250–1),
engendering no specific response, but soon after he silently recapitulates (allowing for no rejoinder or correction):

> the very unpleasant scene at Westland Row terminus when it
> was perfectly evident that the other two, Mulligan, that is, and
> that English tourist friend of his, who eventually euchred their
> third companion, were patently trying as if the whole bally
> station belonged to them to give Stephen the slip in the
> confusion, which they did.   (Eu 263–7)

Stephen is ill-disposed to think about, much less talk about, his
Circean experiences, and consequently only bits and pieces bob up
in 'Eumaeus'. Nor is Bloom particularly well-disposed toward
discussing *his* Circean adventures when he is reunited with Molly
in the early hours of 17 June 1904. Consequently the last chapter of
the 'Nostos' with its locus in Molly's thoughts is totally devoid of
any aftermath of Nighttown.

In the central chapter of the 'Homecoming', however, certain
factors re-emerge, surviving vestiges of Circean wreckages,
although some specifically quantifiable evidence has been lost in
the transition. Bloom's double-entry book-keeping ticks off the day
in retrospect, meticulously ignoring the unsavoury visit to Bella
Cohen's ten-shilling house. The presence in the text of the compilation of the day's expenditure is in itself legerdemain, and can
hardly be 'objectively' credited (although in its austere format it

masks itself as accurate and complete). Given the imperative
statement, 'Compile the budget for 16 June 1904' (It 1455), two lists
devolve, with eighteen items under *Debit* and three under *Credit*.
The seven nocturnal entries in the debit column read as follows:

Tramfare	[one penny]
1 Pig's Foot	[four pence]
1 Sheep's Trotter	[thruppence]
1 Cake Fry's Plain Chocolate	[one shilling]
1 Square Soda Bread	[four pence]
1 Coffee and Bun	[four pence]
Loan (Stephen Dedalus)	[one pound, seven shillings]
refunded	(It 1469–75)

The coffee and bun can be discounted as expenditures at the
cabman's shelter (after 'Circe'), as can the fare for the tram that
brought Bloom back from Sandymount (before 'Circe'), but how
did Bloom get from Holles street to Nighttown? He was admittedly
present at the Westland Row terminus, but no train fare is
recorded. If we trust Bloom's account in 'Circe', apparently mum-
bled to himself, he had a third class ticket that he would be
expected to have bought: 'Nice mixup. Scene at Westland row.
Then jump in first class with third ticket. Then too far' (Ci 636–7).
But, along with the ten shillings paid for the privilege of visiting
the brothel (Ci 3583–4) and another shilling for the smashed lamp
(Ci 4312), the train fare has mysteriously been censored, an
indiscretion that cannot appear in the ledger.

What survives from the sojourn in Nighttown is exclusively an
account of Bloom's payments for food, almost none of which
Bloom was actually observed to have eaten there. The pig's foot
and the sheep's trotter were presumably purchased at Olhousen's
just as the pork butcher was about to close up his shop (Ci 155–9),
and the chocolate and bread a short while before ('*Bloom appears,
flushed, panting, cramming bread and chocolate into a sidepocket*' – Ci
142–3), but only the chocolate reappears later on: he gives it to Zoe,
who then in turn offers pieces to Kitty and Lynch, and eventually
to Bloom, which he accepts (Ci 2699–739). The unkosher meats,
which he carefully concealed from his father (Ci 256), are later
disposed of surreptitiously, fed to the stray dog (Ci 672): 'O, let it
slide', he comments, adding, 'Two and six' (Ci 671–2). His calcula-
tion remains mysterious, since the meats cost him all of seven

pence, and even with the chocolate and soda bread, the tab comes to only one and eleven. And the disposition of the soda bread also remains a lingering mystery.

Bloom's temporary role as Stephen's banker offers another mysterious element. Both the debit and credit columns record the loan as one pound, seven shillings – so that receiving and returning the money create an even cancellation. Yet events in 'Circe' belie the evenness of the amount, since Bloom actually took one pound, six shillings and eleven pence into safekeeping ('That is one pound six and eleven. One pound seven, say', says Bloom – Ci 3613), and in 'Ithaca' he repays Stephen the latter amount ('The former returned to the latter, without interest, a sum of money (£1-7-0), one pound seven shillings sterling' – It 957–8). Stephen in actuality does receive one penny in interest, but that penny would have had to come out of Bloom's own money and should have shown up as a discrepancy in the balance between debit and credit. If the added penny had been Bloom's, and the 'Circe' event really occurred, then another instance of juggled book-keeping has been practised to excise the brothel scene entirely from Bloom's account of his night. Determining which is the 'true account' can be risky, since the events in 'Circe' could have taken place and still not show up on the bowdlerised ledgers. Two overlapping texts exist, therefore, both quite plausible and each in its own way contributing to a facet of the narrative of *Ulysses*, although it is also apparent that each undercuts the other, challenging the assumed notion that a literary text inevitably posits a singular 'reality'.

In stripping away all hallucinatory matter from the bare bones of the literal narrative of 'Circe', readers have usually agreed on a skeletal plot that can be summarised as follows: Bloom tracks Stephen and Lynch into Nighttown, locating them at Bella Cohen's, where drunken Stephen smashes a lampshade, runs out into the street, is accosted by Private Carr and knocked down, having been deserted by Lynch. Bloom then rescues him and brings him out of Nighttown. Yet even these time-honoured 'facts' will not quite withstand precise scrutiny if we demand corroboration from their residue in the ensuing chapters. Omitted from Bloom's account of the day's events to Molly, and therefore solid negative evidence, is any mention of 'the visit to the disorderly house of Mrs Bella Cohen, 82 Tyrone street, lower, and subsequent brawl and chance medley in Beaver street' (It 2054–6). What he does relate to Molly, replete with the 'modifications' he makes in order to gloss over the unsavoury truths, concerns 'a temporary concussion caused by a falsely calculated movement in the course of a postcenal gymnastic display, the victim (since completely recovered) being Stephen Dedalus' (It 2260–3). From the doctored version advanced and the true account withheld we can verify that Stephen was hurt in connection with a brawl in Nighttown, although Private Carr's name is never mentioned after his appearance in 'Circe', neither Stephen nor Bloom ever having heard it. We might disentangle the 'brawl' from the 'chance medley' (locating the first in Bella Cohen's establishment and the second as taking place with the two British soldiers in Beaver street), in which case Stephen's torn coat can be assumed to derive from the former event. In his kitchen Bloom considers the 'reparation of a fissure of the length of 1½ inches in the right side of his guest's jacket' (It 374–5), which was presumably torn when he ran from Bella Cohen's, as a whore in the doorway so nakedly reported: 'He tore his coat' (Ci 4273). On the other hand, the limited focus of language arrangement here allows for either simultaneity or sequence, dependent on context or determining meaning, so that a 'brawl and chance medley' may be a compound referring to one and the same event, in which case the one verifiable element (the torn coat) hangs loose without a source in a contextual 'reality'.

The 'chance medley', usually so vital to a reading of the narrative of the chapter, is none the less shrouded in mystification when the evidence from 'Ithaca' is sifted. As they approach Eccles street Stephen and Bloom are discussing, *inter alia*, the subject of 'prostitution' (It 12) – but this may merely be an extension of their talk in the cabman's shelter about the haggard streetwalker (Eu 728–38) – as well as the subject of 'Stephen's collapse' (It 17). Being knocked senseless by an irate Private Carr is hardly the same as suffering a collapse, a term that suggests an internal, self-sustained process, while a chance medley implies a mêlée (in its archaic meaning) and certainly a mingling of more than one (in any of its meanings). The fault once again is with the limitations of language, which denotes more about the character of the person using it than the intention of that person's discourse. Stephen and Bloom have reached a point of euphemistic reference to whatever transpired in Beaver street, and prefer to debate the causes of what they term Stephen's 'collapse' (it is worth noting that 'prostitution' as a subject of discussion is listed between 'woman' and 'diet' – It 12–13). But their disputed causes are unrelated to Private Carr's fists:

The collapse which Bloom ascribed to gastric inanition and certain chemical compounds of varying degrees of adulteration and alcoholic strength, accelerated by mental exertion and the velocity of rapid circular motion in a relaxing atmosphere, Stephen attributed to the reapparition of a matutinal cloud (perceived by both from two different points of observation, Sandycove and Dublin) at first no bigger than a woman's hand.   (It 36–42)

Stephen's resilience and coordination may well have been marred by either his physical condition or the influence of a little cloud, while the First Cause of his collapse may none the less be attributable to the bellicose Private Carr. The parallax of observation is paralleled by the parallax of language: *chance medley* and *collapse* stem from one language source in *Ulysses*, the heightened narrational thrust of the developing narrative, while 'give him a kick in the knackers. Stick one into Jerry' (words spoken to Private Carr by Private Compton – Ci 4484) to another and equally valid language source, the colloquial discourse appropriate to the setting in the brothel district.

While on the subject of the 'root' language of 'Circe', it is pertinent to glance at and savour that particularly salient word used in this same instance in the chapter: 'trenchancy'. The word is spoken so trippingly on the tongue of none other than Cunty Kate, in response to the comment by Biddy the Clap regarding 'Professor' Dedalus's handling of language:

BIDDY THE CLAP

He expresses himself with such marked refinement of phraseology.

CUNTY KATE

Indeed, yes. And at the same time with such apposite trenchancy. (Ci 4442–5)

Nighttown is certainly the natural habitat of Biddy the Clap and Cunty Kate, but such trenchant refinements of phraseology are not quite naturalistically theirs. Transformational magic has been at work, altering their discourse to conform not with literal verisimilitude but with the context of what is being said. A comment on refined phraseology itself becomes refined into existence as phraseological refinement, and one suspects a parodist once again in the wings. 'Trenchancy' in particular is the property of Tom Kernan and already parodied in 'Hades' when Martin Cunningham presumably quotes Kernan as saying, '*His singing of that simple ballad, Martin, is the most trenchant rendering I ever heard in the whole course of my experience*', and Jack Power adds, '*Trenchant*. . . . He's dead nuts on that' (Ha 146–9). Kernan himself, on hearing the same ballad, will comment ingenuously in 'Sirens': 'Most trenchant rendition of that ballad, upon my soul and honour it is' (Si 1148–9). In this 'retrospective arrangement', the parody precedes the formative statement, so that the more benign 'rendition' follows after the somewhat unusual 'rendering'. None the less, we may well wonder what is Cunty Kate to Tom Kernan or Tom Kernan to Cunty Kate that 'trenchancy' should be their common password? 'Circe' retains, reprises and restructures not only plot elements of the Ulyssean day, but the language elements as well, as the constantly fluctuating context of worlds-within-worlds would seem to dictate.

LASCIATE OGNE SPERANZA VOI CH' INTRATE

The retensions, reprises, and restructurings operative in 'Circe' are immediately apparent as the curtain rises on '*The Mabbot street entrance of nighttown*' (Ci 1), and a prologue of sorts reintroduces the principal characters. The initial lighting determines that alternating (and highly coloured) perspectives will dominate, and the opening stage directions account for the methods by which narrative elements will be retained while changed, revealed but concealed: '*skeleton tracks, red and green will-o'-the-wisps and danger signals*' (Ci 2–3) – the keys to the Circean treasures. What may appear at first to be stunted adults are exposed as children, a '*pigmy woman*' actually a child on a swing, although immediately after the '*gnome*' may very well be a stunted rag-and-bone man (Ci 25–9). The danger signals are in constant operation, so that when the first 'reprised' character appears, the incongruence between past 'reality' and the present re-presentation becomes apparent. Cissy Caffrey, that 'Madcap Ciss with her golliwog curls' from 'Nausicaa' (Na 270), first intrudes on the 'Circe' narrative as a voice heard singing: '*Cissy Caffrey's voice, still young, sings shrill from a*

lane' (Ci 41–2). Just as we wonder what that proper young girl from
sedate Sandymount is doing in the red-light district at midnight
singing an obscene song, we might also wonder by what process
she has *aged* (if indeed she has) in the intervening hours, that her
unaging voice needs to be characterised as 'still young'. The tracks
lead from 'Nausicaa', the colouring focuses change, and the danger
signals are up: we listen to her voice, which has been signalled as
possibly reliable (still young – therefore retained from the previous
text), and find little correspondence with the voice of Cissy Caffrey
heard in 'Nausicaa'.

The minimal amount of dialogue allowed by the gushing narration in 'Nausicaa' gives the reader few opportunities to hear
Cissy's speaking tones, and those few are often involved in dealing
with children. Her first speech (and the initiating bit of dialogue in
the chapter) sets up a 'colloquy' with an infant, in which her direct
statement has its distored corollary:

– Now, baby, Cissy Caffrey said. Say out big, big. I want a drink
of water.
   And baby prattled after her:
– A jink a jink a jawbo.   (Na 26–8)

The distortion of speech is paralleled in 'Circe', where the children
attempt to taunt a semblance of talk from the babbling Idiot, whose
responses are merely 'Ghahute!' and 'Ghaghahest' (Ci 20, 24) – not
quite as good as the infant. Language sets up a mirror by which
two facets of conflicting speech pose as communicative dialogue,
statement and corrupt restatement: every analogue in 'Circe'
succeeds in confounding its source. The actual gambit of dialogue
in the chapter proves to be something not human at all, but
'Whistles' that *'call and answer'* (Ci 9):

THE CALL

Wait, my love, and I'll be with you.

THE ANSWER

Round behind the stable.   (Ci 10–13)

[Just as the 'Circe' chapter has its link with the earlier 'Nausicaa',
so does it have its originating source in 'Sirens', the luring

transmission of sounds and visual apparitions ('M'appari') coalesc-
ing. Leopold Bloom's response to Richie Goulding's whistling,
itself an echo of Stephen Dedalus's recall in 'Proteus' of his uncle's
whistle, sets the stage for 'Circe': 'Taking my motives he twined
and turned them. All most too new call is lost in all. Echo. How
sweet the answer. How is that done? All lost now. Mournful he
whistled. Fall, surrender, lost' (Si 633–6). 'Call' and 'answer' are
contained in the 'whistled'.]

It is not just that speech has been allowed to non-articulate
sounds, but that a discrepancy immediately presents itself between
the staid and romantic call (worthy of the tone of 'Nausicaa') and
the direct and suggestive answer (*chez* 'Circe'). Despite her nasty
'leg of the duck' ditty (Ci 44–7ff.), Cissy is merely a disembodied
voice at this early stage, hardly the vicious hoyden of the closing
portion of the chapter, where she blatantly announces herself as
'only a shilling whore' (Ci 4383). However one accounts for this
Circean Cissy transformed from the basically proper maiden of
'Nausicaa', it is in her few lines of speech that we seek whatever
parallels exist or distortions are made. The earlier Cissy was quite
capable, despite her bourgeois respectability, of suggestive word
play ('I'll run ask my uncle Peter over there what's the time by
his conundrum' – Na 535–6) and coy euphemisms ('–On the
beeoteetom, laughed Cissy merrily' – Na 263), although her
speeches are linguistically framed by the mode of the Nausicaan
narration: '– O my! Puddeny pie! protested Ciss. He has his bib
destroyed' (Na 613). Even within 'Nausicaa' the bourgeois Miss
Caffrey has two voices, 'Uncle Peter' apparently remembering her
quite discreet question as 'Would you mind, please, telling me the
right time' (Na 900–1), so that we read the elision between her
announced intentions and her polite action.

Cissy's companion in 'Nausicaa', the thoroughly bland and
inoffensive Edy Boardman, also makes an immediate appearance
in 'Circe' (along with the young twin brothers of Cissy Caffrey),
and her single speech belies the innocence of her previously
established character:

> (*bickering*) And says the one: I seen you up Faithful place with
> your squarepusher, the greaser off the railway, in his cometobed
> hat. Did you, says I. That's not for you to say, says I. You never
> seen me in the mantrap with a married highlander, says I. The
> likes of her! Stag that one is! Stubborn as a mule! And her

walking with two fellows the one time, Kilbride, the engine-
driver, and lancecorporal Oliphant. (Ci 91–6)

This spiteful gossip may seem rather gratuitous as intruded into
the Nighttown scene, but it too has its antecedent in an innocent
state in 'Nausicaa', where Edy begins the coy interrogation of
Tommy Caffrey on the same subject: '–Tell us who is your
sweetheart, spoke Edy Boardman. Is Cissy your sweetheart?' (Na
66–7). The subject matter (who loves whom? with Edy hoping that
she is at the centre) is Edy Boardman's, controverted into a higher
intensity of maliciousness in 'Circe'. And the auditor of the two-
voiced monologue is none other than Bertha Supple, mentioned as
another friend but never present in 'Nausicaa'. Consequently,
when 'present' in 'Circe', Bertha, who has never had a voice of her
own, merely listens. To establish 'Nausicaa' as an authentic text
that is 'violated' in 'Circe' is to deny it its own element of distorted
narration: the cosmetic handling of reality in the first is as
unreliable as the gross transformations of the second.

The appearance of Stephen Dedalus engenders a backlog of
echoes from the preceding chapters of *Ulysses*, analogues of
exposition that recreate the new 'essentials' of character for the
'Circe' environment: 'Way for the parson', announces Private
Compton; 'What ho, parson!' echoes Private Carr (Ci 75, 77). No
stage direction is necessary to describe the black clothes and Latin
Quarter hat fixed as his attire in 'Telemachus': the soldiers corroborate the misattribution made by the Denzille lane boy on the
basis of that attire: 'Jay, look at the drunken minister coming out of
the maternity hospal!' (OS 1444–5), which then and there established the self-styled Reverend Stephen Dedalus S. J. as 'Parson
Steve' (OS 1451). At this initial confrontation with Stephen the
Tommies are jovial and even deferential; at the concluding encounter they will prove uncontrollably hostile. The distorting mirror of
Circean transformation operates from the benign to the malignant,
turning even British soldiers into swine.

When Stephen enters Nighttown chanting '*with joy the* introit *for
paschal time*' (Ci 73–4), he certainly behaves out of character for
anyone's idea of a Protestant parson. Instead, he performs as an
ironic counterpart to Buck Mulligan's initial appearance in 'Telemachus', when he 'intoned': '*Introibo ad altare Dei*' (Te 5). In the face
of the teasing redcoats, the singing Cissy and gossiping Edy, as
well as the soliciting Bawd, Stephen persists in his ecclesiastical

chant. To complement Buck holding the shaving bowl aloft, Stephen *'flourishes his ashplant, shivering the lamp image, shattering light over the world'* (Ci 99–100), a salutory and triumphant gesture that impresses no one except the growling dog that *'slinks after him'* (Ci 100–1). This benign gesture will have its malignant aftermath in Bella Cohen's, distorted into damage and menace and exorcism: *'He lifts his ashplant high with both hands and smashes the chandelier. Time's livid final flame leaps and, in the following darkness, ruin of all space, shattered glass and toppling masonry'* (Ci 4243–5). (The paralleling situations at beginning and end will have their later responses in *Finnegans Wake*, where Justius 'points the deathbone and the quick are still. *Insomnia, somnia somniorum. Awmawm'*, while Mercius 'lifts the lifewand and the dumb speak' – *FW*, p. 193, ll. 29–30; p. 195, l. 5.)

Stephen at this juncture is a compendium of past selves, as throughout 'Circe' he and Bloom create an auditory sense of *déjà vu*, recapitulating aspects of themselves and extending vast possibilities of their selves. The 'translation' from the previous existences into the present is effected in physical animation, as Stephen suggests once he has stopped chanting: 'So that gesture, not music not odour, would be a universal language, the gift of tongues rendering visible not the lay sense but the first entelechy, the structural rhythm' (Ci 105–7). [The implied transition is between such narrational techniques as those in 'Lotus Eaters' (*odours*) and 'Sirens' (*music*) and the new universe of 'Circe'.] Stephen is reliving his performance in 'Scylla and Charybdis' for Lynch's benefit, conjuring up the essence of himself in changing forms ('But I, entelechy, form of forms, am I by memory because under everchanging forms' – SC 208–9), and the 'selves' who constitute his intellectual past: 'We have shrewridden Shakespeare and henpecked Socrates. Even the allwisest Stagyrite was bitted, bridled and mounted by a light of love' (Ci 111–12). In the National Library Stephen had given form to a Shakespeare who 'like Socrates . . . had a shrew to wife' (SC 665) and an Aristotle who was a 'Stagyrite schoolurchin and bald heathen sage' (SC 720) – in his earlier manifestation in 'Proteus', 'Bald he was and a millionaire, *maestro di color che sanno'* (Pr 6–7). Each segment of *Ulysses* rewrites itself, and 'Circe' in particular proves to be a palimpsest through which previous writings and rewritings are constituted and reconstituted. In the spirit of such 'resurrections' Lynch returns to an earlier stage of his existence when he exclaims, 'Damn your yellow stick' (Ci

120), an echo of his 'Damn your yellow insolence' that had caused Stephen to remark: 'It was a great day for European culture ... when you made up your mind to swear in yellow' (*AP*, p. 204). The echo from *A Portrait* returns the character to his 'birth' in that narrative, to his first conversation with Stephen Dedalus on aesthetics, which Stephen in 'Circe' is now revitalising and am-plifying. (The concluding paragraph of 'Oxen of the Sun' had set the stage for 'Circe' when Lynch demanded, 'who's this excrement yellow gospeller on the Merrion hall?' – OS 1579.)

The Bloom who subsequently appears after Stephen and Lynch have left the stage (and after the Caffrey children have been frightened away by the drunken navvy, whose natural milieu they have inexplicably invaded) is in a state of agitation unlike any previous appearance in *Ulysses*: '*Bloom appears, flushed, panting*' (Ci 142–3). He encounters distortion almost immediately:

> *From Gillen's hairdresser's window a composite portrait shows him gallant Nelson's image. A concave mirror at the side presents to him lovelorn longlost lugubru Booloohoom. Grave Gladstone sees him level, Bloom for Bloom. He passes, struck by the stare of truculent Wellington, but in the convex mirror grin unstruck the bonham eyes and fatchuck cheekchops of jollypoldy the rixdix doldy.*   (Ci 143–9)

Composite portraits and concave/convex mirrors are the contorting effects of Circean 'magic', inexplicable changes wrought by un-usual parallactic stances, so that Bloom sees an aspect of himself set against eminent upholders of the British Empire, whose coiffeurs may have been eminently imitable – in a section of Dublin devoted to catering to British soldiers. The Bloom that concavely composes itself to him is the Bloom of 'Sirens', where songs of love and war, of sexual consummation, and of British political treachery, affected him deeply at a time when Boylan was on his jaunty way to Molly – and singing and sexual consumma-tion.

The transformations of Bloom in 'Sirens' are mirrored again in Gillen's distorting glass [from 'Bloowhose', 'Bloohimwhom', 'Lugugugubrious', 'I feel so lonely Bloom' of 'Sirens' (Si 149, 309, 1005, 1136–7)) to '*lovelorn longlost lugubru Booloohoom*' and '*blowing Bloohoom*' of 'Circe' (Ci 146, 157)]. That it is all done with mirrors had been anticipated in 'Sirens', where Bloom sits in the dining-room of the Ormond listening to the singing from the Ormond saloon and regarding the barmaids through the open door reflected in the bar mirror: 'Doesn't half know I'm.... Bronze gazed far sideways. Mirror there. Is that best side of her face?' (Si 1044–6). Visual reflection is soon translated into auditory 'reflection' as Bloom thinks, 'Ventriloquise. My lips closed. Think in my stom' (Si 1095). Now in Nighttown he indeed thinks in his stomach: the image of his own reflected '*Fatchuck cheekchops*' sends him in quest of more substantial fare than the bread and chocolate already purchased, and he rejects fish-and-chips in favour of '*a lukewarm pig's crubeen*' and '*a cold sheep's trotter*' (Ci 158–9). How he sees himself in relation to such august personages as Nelson–Wellington–Gladstone will be recapitulated later in 'Circe' when he and Stephen look into Bella Cohen's glass to capture William Shakespeare in their combined selves.

The '*puffing Poldy, blowing Bloohoom*' (Ci 157) is temporarily dispossessed of the 'equanimity' with which he has conducted himself throughout the day and with which he will be specifically credited in 'Ithaca' (It 2177), a victim of 'Circean' imbalance, a lack of equanimity (of equal mind) and equilibrium. In 'Lotus Eaters' Bloom stood firm and balanced outside the post office, ostensibly listening to M'Coy but carefully watching the woman outside the Grosvenor Hotel, waiting for a glimpse of her ankle as she steps up into her carriage. But a 'heavy tramcar honking its gong slewed between' (Lo 131) and Bloom's effort was frustrated: 'Lost it. Curse your noisy pugnose' (Lo 132). In Nighttown, decidedly off-balance, with a pain in his side ('Stitch in my side. Why did I run?' – Ci 163), he '*darts to cross the road*' (Ci 175) in order to avoid the drunken navvy who had previously succeeded in scaring the Caffrey twins from his terrain: 'I'll miss him. Run. Quick. Better cross here' (Ci 174). He had lulled himself into a false sense of security, aware that the blaze he sees in the southern sky could not be from his own house but might be from Boylan's, and in running again he is 'grazed' by a bicycle and again suffers from a stitch in his side: '*halts erect, stung by a spasm*' (Ci 183). Yet he runs across the street once more, this time endangered by a sandstrewer:

He looks round, darts forward suddenly. Through rising fog a dragon sandstrewer, travelling at caution, slews heavily down upon him, its huge red headlight winking, its trolley hissing on the wire. The motorman bangs his footgong....
The brake cracks violently. Bloom, raising a policeman's whitegloved

hand, blunders stifflegged out of the track. The motorman, thrown forward, pugnosed, on the guidewheel, yells as he slides past over chains and keys. (Ci 184–93)

Always on the alert for coincidences Bloom investigates the possibility of the motorman as the same person who drove the tramcar past him that morning (the unlikelihood of a tram driver by day moonlighting as a sandstrewer driver by night exists in the same realm as 'madcap Ciss' doing double duty as a shilling whore). But Bloom is caught within the web of Circean duality, red and green signals alternating, and considers the possibility: 'Insolent driver. I ought to report him. . . . Might be the fellow balked me this morning with that horsey woman. Same style of beauty' (Ci 204–6). Bloom has equated the pugnoses with each other, but the text provides other echoes as well – from 'Lotus Eaters': 'A heavy tramcar honking its gong slewed between'; from 'Circe': 'slews heavily down. . . . bangs his footgong'. The reprise has been thoroughly restructured, yet a coincidence of language retains aspects of the original in the reproduction. Whatever Bloom's traffic policeman's gesture might be interpreted as having been, the white glove on his hand is thoroughly gratuitous, written into the text by the transformational circumstances – will-o'-the-wisps – of the particular event. The morning incident was governed by the accident of inadvertence: M'Coy and the horsey woman and the pugnosed driver are unaware of Bloom's particular focus, and the driver passes Bloom without observation or comment. The nocturnal incident is goverend by the laws of 'skeleton tracks, red and green will-o'-the-wisps and danger signals': even at a caution the sandstrewer endangers Bloom, just as his responding gesture endangers the motorman.

The mild coincidence of lookalike drivers (although the vehicles are drastically different) produces the situational instance in Nighttown, yet the unexpected economy of language (slew, heavy, gong) determines the tighter restructuring, the recycling of a coincidental event in similarly coincidental linguistic terms. This linkage remains trivial, especially when one becomes aware of a hyperbolic restructuring built into the ancillary aspect of the encounter with menacing vehicles – the stitch in the side (cured, incidentally, by the 'close shave' with the strewer – Ci 199). Subliminally present is a piece of past history, the encounter with a bee that Bloom had experienced several weeks earlier. Despite its triviality, it is casually remembered by Bloom in 'Hades' ('Nice young student that was dressed that bite the bee gave me' – Ha 380–1) and as casually reremembered in 'Lestrygonians' ('Still I got to know that young Dixon who dressed that sting for me in the Mater' – Le 429–30). In both cases the focus is primarily on the nice young medical student Dixon, leading toward the re-encounter that evening at the lying-in hospital, where Mandevillean language transposes him into a 'young learningknight yclept Dixon' (OS 125). The allegorical methods of 'Oxen of the Sun', and the linguistic contortions that give them their shapes, work their magic on the insignificant bee and its sting: 'the traveller Leopold came there to be healed for he was sore wounded in his breast by a spear wherewith a horrible and dreadful dragon was smitten him' (OS 128–30). Once such an augmentation has taken place within the allegorising process of 'Oxen of the Sun', a concomitant process becomes possible within the frame of Circean transformations, where Bloom is *stung* by a spasm and encounters a *dragon* sandstrewer (which at best was 'draggin''). The bee sting is reprised tangentially, restructured into a near-obscurity, but held together by the reiteration of key words, a ventriloquism that has its verbal sources in the preceding episodes of the text.

'DUBBING OF GHOSTERS'

The imminence of danger and violence at the beginning of the chapter is corroborated at the end of the chapter, and far more significant for most readers of 'Circe' than Stephen's defeat at the hands of Carr has been the symbolic victory won by Stephen Dedalus in his spirited attack on Bella Cohen's chandelier. The stage direction insists that '*He lifts his ashplant high with both hands and smashes the chandelier*', yet 'THE GASJET' utters a rather pathetic 'Pwfungg!' on contact (Ci 4247). Bella of course maintains that 'The lamp's broken' (Ci 4269) and claims ten shillings damages, but Bloom relights the lamp, examines the '*crushed mauve purple shade*' and announces that 'Only the chimney's broken' (Ci 4284–6), leaving only a shilling in payment. The grandiose gesture and its concomitant symbolic meaning, Stephen's exorcism of the shade of his dead mother, are deflated even within the context of the 'Circe' chapter, yet the Stephen Dedalus who emerges from the experience seems soberer and calmer. Negative evidence carries weight in *Ulysses*, as we observe Stephen in 'Eumaeus' and 'Ithaca', essentially relieved of the 'ghoul-and-corpse-chewer' rhetoric that had characterised him throughout the day.

Perhaps the clue to Stephen's sense of peace with his conscience can be found in one other carryover from the closing moments of 'Circe' to the closing moments of 'Eumaeus': sentimental Bloom, looking solicitously at the face of the comatose Stephen, muses, 'Face reminds me of his poor mother' (Ci 4949), and then as they head toward Eccles street, 'He looked sideways in a friendly fashion at the sideface of Stephen, image of his mother' (Eu 1803–4). In the latter instance Stephen and Bloom are discussing music, and in the former Stephen is mumbling the words of 'Who Goes with Fergus', a song he remembers having sung to his dying mother (Te 249–50). May Dedalus is undoubtedly a topic of discussion and thought as the two commune over cocoa in the Eccles street kitchen. Stephen presents himself as 'eldest surviving male consubstantial heir of Simon Dedalus of Cork and Dublin and of Mary, daughter of Richard and Christina Goulding' (It 537–9), and Bloom mentions his first having met Stephen 'in 1887, in the company of Stephen's mother, Stephen then being of the age of 5' (It 468–9). These reminiscences seem to evoke no strong reaction in Stephen, although the 'objectified' technique of the chapter may be responsible for masking emotional responses. None the less, two significant items break through the restraints of the narrative method and reveal more than can be concealed: Bloom 'suppresses' any mention of the death of May Dedalus by considerately avoiding mentioning her funeral (It 949–53), and Stephen has a nostalgic memory of 'his mother Mary, wife of Simon Dedalus, in the kitchen of number twelve North Richmond street on the morning of the feast of Saint Francis Xavier in 1898' (It 142–4), a milestone in Stephen's early life, when he could still feel the positive force of his religion in saving him from guilt and despair (as witness Chapter 3 of *A Portrait of the Artist as a Young Man*).

A third significant incident caps the laying of the ghost of May Dedalus, but not without an equivocal aspect. Our last glimpse of Stephen in Bloom's back garden has him listening to the chimes tolling the hour from St. George's Church. Although to Bloom they once again echo the death knell for Paddy Dignam in a tone of gentle mockery, '*Heigho, heigho*' (Ca 546–8; It 1233–4), for Stephen they return the litany for the dead that caused him such anguish in the morning:

Liliata rutilantium. Turma circumdet.
Iubilantium te virginum. Chorus excipiat.
(It 1230–1; see also Te 276–7)

But as Stephen fades from view, no invective follows that litany as
it did on the tower gunrest that morning ('Ghoul! Chewer of
corpses! / No mother! Let me be and let me live' – Te 278–9). If we
read the intaglio for the cameo, the post-Circean Stephen may have
reached a point of stasis in the death-struggle with his mother's
ghost, evidence of an event in 'Circe' that has lasting reverberations throughout the closure of *Ulysses*. In Sir Arthur Conan
Doyle's 'Silver Blaze' Sherlock Holmes is asked, 'Is there any point
to which you would wish to draw my attention?' and replies, 'To
the curious incident of the dog in the night-time.' When he is
reminded that 'The dog did nothing in the night-time', Holmes
responds, 'That was the curious incident'. Whatever may or may
not have occurred in Nighttown, whatever magical transformations may have been accomplished in Circe's cave, the negative
evidence that resounds through the post-Circean chapters suggests a sense of permanence as a residue in the Ulyssean text.

'Circe' is a long, dark, labyrinthine tunnel in which many dogs
do not bark in the night-time, with a enormous aperture at the
beginning and a tiny aperture at the end, through which barely
more than a trouser-button emerges – and a missing trouser-button
at that. An integral part of the text of *Ulysses*, 'Circe' is also a text
unto itself. An almost infinite number of possibilities are played
out upon its magical stage, loosely based on the suggestive
materials of the first fourteen chapters of *Ulysses*, and as befits an
open-ended text, certain improbabilities and even some impossibi-
lities are the logical extensions of those suggestions. As such
'Circe' is the ultimate development of the Dedalian aesthetic
pronounced (for better or worse) in *A Portrait of the Artist*:

> The dramatic form is reached when the vitality which has flowed
> and eddied round each person fills every person with such vital
> force that he or she assumes a proper and intangible esthetic
> life. . . . The esthetic image in the dramatic form is life purified in
> and reprojected from the human imagination. (*AP*, p. 215).

Once the magic of dramatic purity is dissipated – and nothing can
dispel it as baldly as a sentence like the one that begins 'Eumaeus'

('Preparatory to anything else Mr Bloom brushed off the greater bulk of the shavings and handed Stephen the hat and ashplant and bucked him up generally in orthodox Samaritan fashion which he very badly needed' – Eu 1–3) – the reader of the 'Nostos' once again requires the quasi-certainty of certain probables: Bloom probably followed Stephen and Lynch into Nighttown, located them in Bella Cohen's, and eventually brought Stephen out of Nighttown, somewhat the worse for wear and tear. And although we will never be able to get a conviction in a court of law, Stephen had probably been knocked down by a British soldier. Even Bottom the Weaver could not have achieved that much probability when he recovered from his *Midsummer Night's Dream*, itself a variant of 'Circe'.

6

Literary and Narrational In/Validities

The allusive methods favoured by the modernist poets – and utilised by Joyce as well – prove upon examination to be unusually diverse, handled quite individually by each practitioner. Yet the basic assumption remains that if the original source can be located, its 'meaning' isolated and determined, and its applicability to the new text illustrated, a neatly constructed unit becomes apparent that establishes a specific meaning within the new text, enlarging the operative 'context'. Characterising Joyce's allusive method, however, has often eluded the allusionists, although the principle of direct confrontational usage continues to define the methodology. What must we know about Dante Alighieri to be able to appreciate 'the spiritual-heroic refrigerating apparatus' that Stephen so caustically credits him with having 'invented and patented in all countries' (*AP*, p. 252)? Will Dante's heroic effort to sublimate Eros in favour of Agape in his appreciation of pre-nubile Beatrice Portinari suffice to substantiate a similar transition in Stephen's attitude toward Emma, even if we acknowledge that Stephen's is rather disingenuous and forced? Direct application would endow Stephen Dedalus with Dante's perfected spiritualism, but his ironic tone favours an inexact application, no matter how sincere his love for Dante might otherwise appear. Dante's heroic spirituality loses something in the translation, even if Dante emerges unscathed, and can go on to provide Stephen with triple feminine rhymes in *Ulysses* (Ae 717–19).

Joyce's titling of *A Portrait of the Artist as a Young Man* has called itself to our critical attention often enough, and the sub-text locates in a convention (that of a painter's self-portrait) rather than in a specific allusion. The device allows for a certain degree of anonymity, yet the artist's signature is almost always there on the portrait. If we can authenticate the facial features as having belonged to the same person who signed the painting, we reinforce identity, although it may never have occurred to us to challenge it. Name of author corresponds to name of subject (a museum may retitle the painting to read 'Self-Portrait of Rembrandt', but Rembrandt himself had no need for such redundancy). Yet Joyce's portrait subject is endowed with a name quite different from that of the author, so that an important element of distancing superimposes itself on the obviousness of the convention. And whereas a painter at work on a self-portrait may take a day or a week or even months to produce the completed likeness, too lengthy a creative process would result in distortions due to physical changes; and the convention assumes that the version specifically framed as a single portrait determines a heterogeneity of time, even if titling allows for the ambiguous designation of 'as a young man'. Joyce's portrait of Stephen Dedalus begins with an infant, soon progresses to a child, and then to an adolescent – but at what juncture is Stephen a 'young man?' This title (like Faulkner's *As I Lay Dying*) may actually have a time-orientation that allows for a certain area of the text, but is only suggestive for, if not inapplicable to, the remainder of the text. Joyce's title has aspects of inexactness that belie the artistic convention: distancing between the age of the author (which in itself changed considerably between 1907 and 1914) and that of the character (a gap of some twenty years); distancing between identities of artist-signatory and artist-designate; distancing between the painting artist (hypothetical) and the writing artist (assumed). What process of portraiture then can prepare us for the Circean experiment with self-reflexiveness when '*Stephen and Bloom gaze in the mirror. The face of William Shakespeare, beardless, appears there, rigid in facial paralysis, crowned by the reflection of the reindeer antlered hatrack in the hall*' (Ci 3821–4), especially when later the experiment is compounded: '*The face of Martin Cunningham, bearded, refeatures Shakespeare's beardless face*' (Ci 3854–5)?

'A SONG IN THE AIR'

Finding a specific painting as text is as difficult as finding a musical text that would approximate, much less anticipate, the opening cacophony of 'suggestions' in 'Sirens' (Si 1–63). Only literary texts present themselves as adequate pre-representations for Joycean allusions, duplications *in kind*, and these of course have the expansive range from Homer's *Odyssey* to the lyrics of Alfred

Bunn. The latter is significantly represented in *Dubliners*, where the singing of 'I Dreamt that I Dwelt' is afforded a privileged position. No other lyricist or librettist receives as much display as Bunn with his six lines of song in the slight, eight-page story (Polly Mooney's song in 'The Boarding House' runs for only three lines, and the third line of 'The Lass of Aughrim' – a song strongly keyed to Gretta Conroy – fades out incomplete). Not that Bunn enjoys any acknowledgement in 'Clay' as the author of the lyrics sung; instead the Dublin-born composer Michael Balfe is fully applauded, and it may be more than a moot point whether Joe Donnelly really means to credit the music rather than the words when he declares that there is 'no music for him like poor old Balfe' (*D*, p. 106). Joe fully intends to shift the emphasis from pathetic Maria to the song, and even then might actually be adroit in specifying the music rather than the incriminating lyrics. And given its exalted position in the story, the first stanza of the Bunn–Balfe song has received a great deal of attention from allusion-hunters, although not nearly as much attention as the second *stanza*, absent as it is from the text. The prevailing assumption is that Joyce as a gnomonic allusionist 'features' the missing portion of the song, validating the literary allusion by allowing it to cast a long shadow over the baldly presented first stanza: 'when she came to the second verse she sang again [the first verse]. . . . But no one tried to show her her mistake' (*D*, p. 106).

That missing verse has surfaced easily enough since the extant two-verse song exists, and pre-exists 'Clay', and has been the subject of scrupulous examination. Which came first – an analysis of verse two that disclosed its potent contents, or the assumption that since Maria must have repressed that second verse, it contains potent contents? Inductively or deductively, the critical method employed assumes that the absence of the second verse eclipses the double presence of the first. The second deals exclusively with 'suitors', and consequently on impending marriage, although the particular inamorato persists as still attentive and loving – and obviously preferred. But that lover exists under the same terms in the first stanza, since those closing lines are repeated at the end of each. In various ways the first stanza contains much more material impossible to associate with Maria (incredible wealth and noble status), yet the mere mention of 'suitors' (in the plural) gives the second a prominent position as too amorously vivid for Maria not to repress it. If she already has the desired lover in the first stanza, why balk at numerous suitors in addition in the second? Sexual repression should logically be absolute, not merely monogamous. The Freudian assumption is that Maria identifies with the persona of the song, and consequently prevents herself from allowing that identification to become too uncomfortable – which only happens if differentiation succeeds identification. Should she be able to distance herself from the persona, she can sing about 'riches' and 'a high ancestral name' and that 'you loved me still the same' (*D*, p. 106) with impunity, and probably then of 'suitors' with equal impunity.

The *literary* validity of the pre-existing text, presumably signalled by Joyce's insistence on Maria's mistake, may yet hold up if we continue to read verse two as somehow more erotic than verse one, but the *narrational* validity of Maria's forgetfulness remains intact. While safely within the confines of the Dublin by Lamplight laundry she does not forget to cut the barmbrack nor to set her clock back an hour for early rising for Mass on All Saints Day, but once on the tram she manages to forget the plumcake and now she forgets to sing the second verse. (Worse still, having just sung the first verse, she forgets that she has and sings it again.) Maria's failing powers, the intimations of incipient premature senility, are suggested by the narrative – rather than by the literary allusion. One can hardly expect that the generally insensitive Joe Donnelly is 'very much moved' by a realisation that Maria still yearns for a marriage that is hardly even a remote possibility. More likely he has had an indication that she is nearing dotage, and may become unemployable soon and a burden, or – allowing him a somewhat greater measure of sensitivity – that someone he once loved as his 'proper mother' is becoming pathetically forgetful.

Even greater selectivity is operative in the presence of 'The Lass of Aughrim' in 'The Dead'. By the time Gabriel becomes aware of his wife listening on the top of the stairs, and enough silence is obtained through the closing of the hall door that the singing can be heard, it is the third stanza of the song that makes itself audible – thereby allowing itself to be fixed in the print of the text. The elimination of the song after two-and-a-half bars is occasioned by the voices of Mary Jane and Aunt Kate, commenting that Bartell D'Arcy had refused to sing, so that now that they have the opportunity to hear him sing, they cancel out his singing. The song has no referentiality to them, and D'Arcy himself afterwards has to offer the title. Only for Gretta does the song have essential validity because of 'a person long ago who used to sing that song' (*D*, p. 218), although obviously she does not have any reason to identify with the lass seduced and abandoned by a noble lover. Instead, it is the poor Michael Furey who sang the totally inappropriate song, although his own eventual death allies him with the suggested death of the maiden in the song. The words that had filtered through to Gabriel's hearing ('*O, the rain falls on my heavy locks / And the dew wets my skin, / My babe lies cold . . .*' – *D*, p. 210) oddly corresponds to Michael Furey's situation in the rain under Gretta's window: 'The window was so wet I couldn't see so I ran downstairs as I was and slipped out the back into the garden and there was the poor fellow at the end of the garden shivering. . . . I implored of him to go home at once and told him he would get his death in the rain' (*D*, p. 221). The association of Michael Furey with the lass – and of Gretta with Lord Gregory – probably offends the literary validity of the allusion, yet the selection of those particular lines seems deliberate enough in the face of the rainy-night tale that Gretta then relates, so that the narrational validity of the allusion remains operative.

A selective method verging on bowdlerisation informs the opening song used in *A Portrait of the Artist*, a snatch of which is offered as being sung by a very young Stephen Dedalus, probably when he is essentially still baby tuckoo, and with no title given:

> O, the wild rose blossoms
> On the little green place.   (*AP*, p. 7)

Edited out of the text is the source of Stephen's knowledge of the song (we only learn that 'He sang that song. That was his song' – *AP*, p. 7), and except for the two lines quoted, we have no idea how much more of the song he knows. Locating H. S. Thompson's song, 'Lilly Dale', probably changes drastically the literary validity of the lines in Joyce's text, since it is so obviously a song of death and burial. The verses take us through the deathbed request for a specific and idyllic burial site, although the chorus (with one exception) seems innocuous enough; the 'poor lost Lilly Dale' of the verses becomes simply 'sweet Lilly, dear Lilly Dale'. The child could have at his disposal only the chorus, and with the word 'grave' changed to 'place', as it is in Stephen's version, all aspects of death are nicely removed. Someone has made a significant impact on the mourning song, teaching it to Stephen in an excised and censored version – or he himself may have heard the song and 'approximated' a word within his own vocabulary (place) for a word as yet outside it (grave). Someone else, however, has not been as coddling with the young Stephen, if genteel censorship was being practised generally in the Dedalus household. When Stephen is spending his first term at Clongowes Wood, he is well enough aware of death, even anticipating his own in the school infirmary:

He said over to himself the song that Brigid had taught him:

> *Dingdong! The castle bell!*
> *Farewell, my mother!*
> *Bury me in the old churchyard*
> *Beside my eldest brother.*
> *My coffin shall be black,*
> *Six angels at my back,*
> *Two to sing and two to pray*
> *And two to carry my soul away.*   (*AP*, pp. 24–5)

Brigid, the servant in the Dedalus household, obviously had no genteel compunctions, but the Stephen at Clongowes seems quite able to handle the death motif, and even to wallow in it luxuriantly and self-pityingly.

Locating this lugubrious 'song' outside the Joyce text has not been easy, although it has been identified as an anonymous Scottish nursery rhyme. Its provenance remains suspect, and it exists primarily as the property of servant Brigid, secondarily as the assumed property of young Stephen, and only tertiarily as an autonomous piece of doggerel in the 'literary' marketplace. With 'I Dreamt that I Dwelt' the exact words are fixed by identified authorship and publication; with 'The Lass of Aughrim' (also known as 'Lord Gregory') the wording is variable, and only those words actually presented in 'Clay' have full credibility; with the titleless 'Dingdong' ditty the only credibility exists inside the frame of the literary text. If an extant version were actually recovered which conformed precisely to the one printed in *Dubliners* (with or without a second verse), the narrational validity of Joyce's use would necessarily diminish, a preceding literary text acknowledged as exactly fitting the author's needs and therefore incorporated *in toto* by him. Given the nebulous origins of such nursery rhymes and children's songs, the chances are that variations would pre-exist Joyce's usage, and whatever differences are apparent must necessarily be attributed to Joyce, and their narrational validities would take precedence. The relationship between *Ding-dong! The castle bell!* and Stephen Dedalus may seem tenuous, since he has no eldest brother either dead or alive, but a surrogate of sorts had just been introduced in the person of the dead Little ('Then he would have a dead mass in the chapel like the way the fellows had told him it was when Little had died' – *AP*, p. 24). The close affinity of 'Lilly Dale' and 'Dingdong' as burial-request songs exists on the literary level, however, with no bridge existing in the text between 'the little green place' and 'the old churchyard'.

'HOLDING UP A MIRROR'

Allusions that lend literary support generally inform the new text that subsumes them, those of narrational validation are absorbed so completely as to expand their original shapes into transformed guise and significance. The lifeline back to a source can only be traced once we suspect that such a source exists, although it is apparent that a marked quotation, a piece of verse or lyric, or a gratuitous name triggers the pursuit for the allusion. Some of these may be deceptive, and names in particular we learn in *Ulysses* are externally imposed. When the style of Thomas Babington Macaulay offers a view of Bloom as 'that vigilant wanderer, soiled by the dust of travel and combat and stained by the mire of an indelible dishonour', one tends to be suspicious, even when we are informed that 'but from whose steadfast and constant heart no lure or peril or threat or degradation could ever efface the image of that voluptuous loveliness which the inspired pencil of Lafayette has limned for ages yet to come' (OS 1217–22). The Marquis de Lafayette may be known to every schoolboy, but it was hardly his pencil that caught the beauty of Molly Bloom, rather that of James Lafayette, the Dublin photographer. Patience is rewarded when in the cabman's shelter Bloom shows the photograph of Molly to Stephen, 'Lafayette of Westmoreland street, Dublin's premier photographic artist, being responsible for the esthetic execution' (Eu 1435–6). Direct verisimilitude, rather than extended allusion, also provides the Dublin landmark of 'Henry and James's wax smartsuited freshcheeked models, the gentleman Henry, *dernier cri* James' (WR 1215–16). The fashionable clothiers had their shop there in Dublin, yet so much of the mode of presentation in 'Wandering Rocks' nudges the literary reader toward that stylishly outfitted and fashionably modern author Henry James, whose literary style may do its bit to inform the style of presentation of the clothiers' mannikins. The added presence in a previous segment of 'Wandering Rocks' of Jimmy [James] Henry, Dublin assistant town clerk, plays its oblique part as well in elliptically enriching the narrative condition.

The reader of *Ulysses* suspects that Joyce was not only profligate in his vast choices of allusive areas for exploitation, but contrived his own, self-contained allusive trails that never left the Joycean compound. In 'Circe', where narrative sources are often suspect because of narrational transformations, the appearance of the entire grieving Dignam family proves to be an embarrassment of exactness in detail. Prior to 'Circe' the reader has only been privileged with a glimpse of the oldest son Patsy, at his father's funeral (where Bloom saw him) and during his aimless meanderings in 'Wandering Rocks'. We have learned from 'Hades' that the deceased left a widow and 'Five young children' (Ha 540), and suddenly they make their mysterious appearance in 'Circe' as Bloom is babbling about the dead Napoleon:

> *Mrs Dignam, widow woman, her snubnose and cheeks flushed with deathtalk, tears and Tunney's tawny sherry, hurries by in her weeds, her bonnet awry, rouging and powdering her cheeks, lips and nose, a pen chivvying her brood of cygnets. Beneath her skirt appear her late husband's everyday trousers and turnedup boots, large eights. She holds a Scottish Widows' insurance policy and large marquee umbrella under which her brood run with her, Patsy hopping on one shod foot, his collar loose, a hank of portsteaks dangling, Freddy whimpering, Susy with a crying cod's mouth, Alice struggling with the baby. She cuffs them on, her streamers flaunting aloft.* (Ci 3837–47)

The narrative source for this family group portrait derives from the non-text, that gap between 'Cyclops' and 'Nausicaa' during which Bloom visited the Dignam home and assisted in resolving the problems concerning insurance. Consequently, the presence of all six survivors is accepted in this context, as is the placement of the insurance policy (the 'marquee umbrella' covering a swan and her offspring has its source in the logo of the Scottish Widows' Assurance Society). At least one anomoly exists in Mrs Dignam wearing a bonnet, since it is assumed that the visit, with sherry offered, took place indoors. The 'deathtalk' could well have brought back images of the Glasnevin interment to Bloom, and his observations may then be responsible for the superimposition of an incident from 'Hades':

> Mourners came out through the gates: woman and a girl. Leanjawed harpy, hard woman at a bargain, her bonnet awry. Girl's face stained with dirt and tears, holding the woman's arm, looking up at her for a sign to cry. Fish's face, bloodless and livid.   (Ha 517–20)

The exact transfer of 'her bonnet awry' from the woman at the cemetery to the widow indicates that the 'Hades' passage has its locus not in objective narrative but in Bloomian observation, unless the overly zealous reader supposes that Mrs Dignam and her daughter Susy actually visited the cemetery prior to the funeral, arriving early on their own and leaving just as the coffin was being brought in for burial. Dismissing such illogical behaviour, the reader instead reads the 'Circe' text as dependent on the 'Hades' text, with Bloom as the subjective medium of transfer. Even the anonymous girl's 'Fish's face' has its analogue in Susy's 'cod's mouth', which in turn ironically echoes Bloom's own 'cod's eye' (Cy 214), attributed to him consistently by the anonymous narrator in 'Cyclops'.

The 'Hades' vignette in turn can be traced to a literary pre-text, Joyce's *Stephen Hero*, where a funeral service preceding that of Stephen's sister Isabel's produces a similar pair of mourners:

> A girl, one hand catching the woman's skirt, ran a pace in advance. The girl's face was the face of a fish, discoloured and oblique-eyed; the woman's face was square and pinched, the face of a bargainer. The girl, her mouth distorted, looked up at the woman to see if it was time to cry: the woman, settling a flat bonnet, hurried on towards the mortuary chapel.   (*SH*, p. 167)

Mrs Dignam's bonnet has now travelled back in time to a source that actually has no literary validation, a discarded text that assumes the validity only of an early draft, but none the less serves to reassure the overzealous reader that Mrs Dignam was not present at her husband's funeral. Even for *Stephen Hero* this vignette was not a new text, having its previous existence in a Joycean epiphany, in only a slightly different format:

> The girl, one hand catching the woman's skirt, runs in advance. The girl's face is the face of a fish, discoloured and oblique-eyed; the woman's face is small and pinched, the face of a bargainer. The girl, her mouth distorted, looks up at the woman to see if it is time to cry; the woman, settling a flat bonnet, hurries on towards the mortuary chapel.[1]

In his own lifetime William Shakespeare's face made a transition from beardless to bearded, as extant efforts at portraiture attest; in *Ulysses* Shakespeare's face ages within the portrait frame of a mirror, beardless for reflected images of Stephen and Bloom, bearded for Martin Cunningham (Stephen had set the stage for the ageing process when he asserted that in *Hamlet* 'The boy of act one is the mature man of act five' – SC 1020). Mrs Dignam's face, on the other hand, is snubnosed with her cheeks flushed (the shape of the nose fixed, the complexion transitory), eclipsing for Bloom the leanjawed visage of the harpy at Glasnevin, now that he has had an actual view of Paddy Dignam's widow. The harpy's predecessor in *Stephen Hero* had a face that was 'square and pinched', while *her* predecessor's in the epiphany was 'small and pinched'. No fixed person (no Shakespeare) is a prescribed source, even if Joyce is transcribing someone seen while attending his mother's funeral – or that of his brother George – and no literary validation is available, but only a nebulous source like that of the 'Dingdong' rhyme, anonymously Scottish. Changes from epiphany to *Stephen Hero* to 'Hades' are determined by Joyce's creative inventiveness; the change from harpy to Mrs Dignam is authenticated by narrational necessity. When Stephen declares to Bloom that Shakespeare's name is a commonplace (Eu 362–4), he also cites that of Napoleon, and it is a reference to the dead Napoleon in 'Circe' that prefigures the configuration of the widow and orphans. Just as Shakespearean quotations and tags abound in the post-Shakespearean world (although he himself is as dead as a doornail), so do phrases from the Shakespearean ambience of 'Scylla and Charybdis' pervade the atmosphere in the chapters that follow the library scene.

The single most mysterious reverberation concerns the William Shakespeare that Stephen has set in motion down Fetter Lane (SC 651–3) who duplicates himself (Si 905) with a near-exactness that borders on 'quotation'. That Mrs Dignam as mother of five offspring should appear as 'a pen chivvying her brood of cygnets' resounds as overly literary, and echoes far too exactly Stephen's narrative in 'Scylla and Charybdis':

> Shakespeare has left the huguenot's house in Silver street and walks by the swanmews along the riverbank. But he does not stay to feed the pen chivying her game of cygnets towards the rushes. The swan of Avon has other thoughts. (SC 159–62)

What Shakespeare will not feed, the Scottish Widows' Assurance will, now that Bloom has helped adjust the policy, Bloom himself (a generous doner of five shillings for the orphans – WR 975–6) having fed the Liffey gulls in lieu of Thames swans.

One can easily brood over the 'pen chivying her game [or brood] of cygnets', which folds so neatly into the two contexts, savouring delicately of Shakespearean diction but not recuperable from any known Shakespeare text. Nor does the sentence seem to have its provenance in any of the biographical conjectures that Joyce used for Stephen's information in 'Scylla and Charybdis' (in Georg Brandes or Sidney Lee or Frank Harris), yet the repetition of its antique verbiage suggests the possibility of an allusion where none has been uncovered. If a close-enough version were to appear, then once again that allusion, its source and its original context, would become germane to its positioning in *Ulysses*. Without external source corroboration the phrase, redolent of archaicism, joins several such phrases (as in the 'nuncle Richie' vignette – Pr 61–103) of Joycean manufacture intended to replicate the language of a pre-existing but merely suggestive context. That the words 'pen' (Old French *penne* for feather/plume) and 'cygnet' are both used in heraldry may be of significance in terms of the Scottish Widows' logo – the advertising sign as modern variant on the heraldic escutcheon. The Circean image, therefore, of Mrs Dignam and her children is emblematic of the fatherless Dignam family as viewed simultaneously through the 'literary' device of a coat of arms and the 'narrational' device of an advertisement, the strength of the latter validation not necessarily invalidating the intimation of the former. When the playwright/novelist holds 'The mirror up to nature' (Ci 3820), it can understandably produce Lynch's reaction of mocking laughter, especially since it may actually be Gillen's convex/concave distortion glass.

GERTY REVISITED

Literary and narrational validities vie with each other in particular in such 'extra-literary' chapters as 'Nausicaa', where the Gerty-centred half owes its stylistic rationale to both a general type and a specific attribution, Maria Cummins's *The Lamplighter*, a book with a Gerty in it. Gerty MacDowell herself is responsible for signalling the allusion, and although she claims to have read the book, she fails to comment on the coincidental name (Molly Bloom has no such reticence: 'I dont like books with a Molly in them like that one he brought me about the one from Flanders' (Pe 657–8) which she obviously did not read very carefully). 'Nausicaa' presumably separates at the point at which the romantic, sentimental perspective loses its light with Gerty's departure, and the 'realistic' perceptions of Leopold Bloom in the dark take possession of the narrative as he himself remains on the scene. Oddly enough, Gerty's rather offhanded use of literary attributions has its source in quite mundane reality, the 'gathering twilight' that she observes (Na 624), and whereas romantic fiction imposes 'the last glimpse of Erin' (Na 624–5) as the crepuscular setting, reality intrudes in the form of a bat 'with a tiny lost cry' (Na 626–7) – Count Dracula would have appreciated the sight of Gerty MacDowell at dusk. Gerty is caught between the world of dream-potential and real inadequacies, highlighted by her very precise awareness of her actual surroundings:

And she could see far away the lights of the lighthouses so picturesque she would have loved to do with a box of paints because it was easier than to make a man and soon the lamplighter would be going his rounds past the presbyterian church grounds and along by shady Tritonville avenue where the couples walked and lighting the lamp near her window where Reggy Wylie used to turn his freewheel like she read in that book *The Lamplighter* by Miss Cummins, author of *Mabel Vaughan* and other tales.   (Na 627–34)

Molly Bloom knows enough about Moll Flanders to know that she was a 'whore always shoplifting anything she could cloth and stuff and yards of it' (Pe 659) – the cloth and stuff immediately making her aware that her blanket is too heavy – but how does Gerty know *The Lamplighter* and to what personal advantage to her? Lamplighters as such co-exist in the real world as necessary functionaries and in the fictional world of the Miss Cumminses as romantic, even shadowy figures. Gerty attempts to distance herself from herself (and from the hovering bat) and reaches out for the lighthouses, which she would distance further by painting them. Her inadequacy in being unable to paint a man instead ('easier than to make a man') impinges upon her thoughts, so that the hypothetical lamplighter, with whom she has no direct relationship, becomes a necessary surrogate. Yet she cannot remain oblivious to what the lamplighter inadvertently sheds his light on ('where the couples walked'), nor can she avoid coupling herself with the elusive Reggy Wylie, a subject too real and discomfiting for her. Fiction is therefore conveniently introduced to eclipse the world in which no Reggy Wylie freewheels by her window any longer, for even the literal lamplighter of Tritonville avenue illuminates Gerty's empty life – something that Maria Cummins's lamplighter never would do. 'The Lamplighter by Miss Cummins, author of *Mabel Vaughan* and other tales' reads suspiciously like a title-page, rather than a reader's recollection of a narrative, and Gerty reveals nothing beyond that 'cover' page, either from the book or from her disappointment regarding the freewheeling Reggy:

> For Gerty has her dreams that no-one knew of. She loved to read poetry and when she got a keepsake from Bertha Supple of that lovely confession album with the coralpink cover to write her thoughts in she laid it in the drawer of her toilettable.
> (Na 634–7)

The Gerty segment of 'Nausicaa' is a blank, unwritten confession concealed by its coralpink cover, locked away in a toilettable drawer, 'which, though it did not err on the side of luxury, was scrupulously neat and clean' (Na 637–8).

When not completely concerned with reading the book of himself, and writing it as a vague message in the sand, Leopold Bloom attempts his own reading of the concealed Gerty, revealed to him primarily by her exposed limbs. What Gerty is apparently concealing – and all the stylistic techniques of a Miss Cummins and her colleagues abet in the concealment – is the deformed foot that persists as her valid text, so that the point of demarcation in the chapter between Gerty–romance–deception–fiction and Bloom–reality–investigation–life exists in the ellipsis of an incomplete sentence:

> She walked with a certain quiet dignity characteristic of her but with care and very slowly because – because Gerty MacDowell was...
> Tight boots? No. She's lame! O!   (Na 769–71)

The 'author' whose style determines the narrational thrust of the opening part of Nausicaa is being phased out, since that particular authorial validity remains only as long as Gerty (and available light) remain on the scene. The fading sentence itself has a 'certain quiet dignity', a certain 'care', and moves 'very slowly', quite uncharacteristic of the gush and lushness that had hitherto been its stock-in-trade. Bloom, when he has the narrational responsibilities thrust upon him, displays his usual preference for an easy solution, the painless explanation (as noted in 'Circe' when he prefers any theory to the realisation that Dublin is ablaze: 'A flasher? Searchlight', he at first conjectures, then '*Aurora borealis* or a steel foundry?' – Ci 166–70). Gerty may intentionally have delayed her departure until the cover of darkness was sufficient, but time ran out and even the protective darkness can reveal what it is concealing. The dark and treacherous terrain conspire against her: 'Slowly, without looking back she went down the uneven strand to Cissy, to Edy, to Jacky and Tommy Caffrey, to little baby Boardman. It was darker now and there were stones and bits of wood on the strand and slippy seaweed' (Na 766–9).

To put into question the verifiability of Gerty's vitally important lameness equally challenges any assertion that Gerty *does not* limp, and creates a dialogue within the reader of the text, paralleling the dialogue that Arthur Power records having had with Joyce after a first reading of the manuscript of *Ulysses*:

> I found myself confused by its novelty and lost in the fantasia of its complicated prose, not knowing if a thing had really happened or was just a Celtic whorl. In fact I later irritated Joyce by

enquiring into the details of what actually occurred during
Bloom's encounter with Gerty MacDowell on the beach.
– Nothing happened between them, he replied. It all took place
in Bloom's imagination.[2]

Yet, as tempting as it might be to consider Gerty's disability as a
feature of Bloom's romantic imagination, Gerty's interpretation of
what she must conceal hovers somewhere within the vicinity of
that confession album, 'for she felt that the years were slipping by
for her, one by one, and but for that one shortcoming she knew she
need fear no competition and that was an accident coming down
Dalkey hill and she always tried to conceal it' (Na 649–51). Bloom,
however, has no access to Gerty's thoughts or confession album,
and his reading of the situation, no matter how close it may come
to Gerty's concealed secret, has its own subjective reasons for
being.

The constant tension between cover and content, between the
polite explanation and the glaring revelation, has its corollary in
the dual nature of language in 'Nausicaa', the diffused lighting of
the Gertyan euphemism and the harsh spotlight of Bloomian
reportage. Only at that one interstice, on the perilous cusp of an
ellipsis, is Gerty's lameness validated: thereafter she has 'limped
away' (Na 772), as Bloom interprets her faulty footsteps, once he
has irrevocably decided that she is lame, and darkness swallows
her up so that no one can ever re-investigate or re-evaluate the
manner of her walk. At the crucial instance Gerty's lameness is in
the eye of the Bloomian beholder, and at no point in the earlier
phase of 'Nausicaa' is there visual evidence of a deformity. If her
lameness is manifest only when she is walking, her determined
sedantariness on the rock prevents any demonstration of her
manner of walk. In 'Wandering Rocks', where she made her only
pre-'Nausicaa' appearance, one wanderer among many, she was
certainly as ambulatory as any of the others, but nothing in the
manner of narrational presentation seems to have allowed for a
diagnosis:

Passing by Roger Greene's office and Dollard's big red printing-
house Gerty MacDowell, carrying the Catesby's cork lino letters
for her father who was laid up, knew by the style it was the lord
and lady lieutenant but she couldn't see what Her Excellency
had on because the tram and Spring's big yellow furniture van

had to stop in front of her on account of its being the lord
lieutenant.   (WR 1205–11)

(Gerty may read fictional romances and women's magazines, but
she does know how to tell Lady Dudley 'by her style', and the
reader will learn in 'Nausicaa' how to tell Gerty by *her* style.) With
no Bloom present to observe how she walks, with all eyes
ostensibly on the processional, and with no *observational* narrative
style operative that would monitor such events, the manner of
walk passes unrecorded. Actually, the negative evidence in 'Wandering Rocks' (for what it is worth) is that Gerty does not limp – or
does not necessarily limp, and that negative evidence carries over
into the first half of 'Nausicaa' as well. Present in 'Nausicaa',
however, is an operative detective, intent on solving a mystery that
for him has a particular fascination: Bloom may not be aware that
he is reading a troublesome text in which Gerty's unusual behaviour, her languorous inertness and her secret self-exposure,
remains for him inexplicable. By waiting out the operative situation
he forces Gerty's hand, and she reveals the 'secret'. For the reader,
however, dubious perhaps of the subjective detective, the literary
text provides the single clue about Dalkey hill, easily overlooked
and never repeated.

The boy of act one may well be the man of act five – maturation is
a natural concomitant of character development – but a Gerty
MacDowell firm of limb in the afternoon cannot, without an
interceding accident, be a limping Gerty in the evening. Only the
focus of observation can determine the validity or invalidity of her
lameness, and that focus in 'Wandering Rocks' differs stylistically
from that of 'Nausicaa'. The capsule appearance of Gerty in the
earlier chapters remains ungoverned by either the effusiveness of
Maria Cummins or the preoccupations of a Leopold Bloom, as each
'observer' of the Lord Lieutenant's cavalcade decides the nature
and focus of his or her observation. When 'On Ormond quay Mr
Simon Dedalus, steering his way from the greenhouse for the
subsheriff's office, stoodstill in midstreet and brought his hat low'
(WR 1199–1201), only Simon Dedalus knows that he has just
visited the public urinal and that his lowered hat may be concealing the buttoning of his flies, so that when 'His Excellency
graciously returned Mr Dedalus' greeting' (WR 1201–2), he may
have misinterpreted that outspoken Nationalist's unspoken
gesture.

The sentence that depicts Gerty's presence in Dublin City is the only one in *Ulysses* that reveals Gerty's thoughts in language approximating her own, transparent narration that contains her particular perspectives (both the printing house and the furniture van are 'big', despite the presumed difference in size between a building and a vehicle – and of course their colours are vivid), her euphemism regarding her father's hangover ('he was laid up'), her interests (women's clothes), her politely covered annoyance ('had to stop in front of her'), her confusion about titles (the 'lady lieutenant'), and her less than literate turns of phrase ('on account of its being the lord lieutenant') – no Miss Cummins is present to help her over that stile. Unlike Bloom, Gerty does not bother to notice whether the tram driver is pugnosed, but the coincidence of obstructed views reminds us that it was a well-turned ankle that Bloom had hoped to see. When we are informed in 'Cyclops' that 'Gerty MacDowell loves the boy that has the bicycle' (Cy 1494), the style is that of neutral statement, a literary indulgence that has no definite validity since it has no course other than literary style.

Common ground stands between such literary exemplars as *The Lamplighter* and 'I Dreamt that I Dwelt', and 'Nausicaa' specifically locates that ground in the introduction to Gerty:

There was an innate refinement, a languid queenly *hauteur* about Gerty which was unmistakably evidenced in her delicate hands and higharched instep. Had kind fate but willed her to be born a gentlewoman of high degree in her own right and had she only received the benefit of a good education Gerty MacDowell might easily have held her own beside any lady in the land and have seen herself exquisitely gowned with jewels on her brow and patrician suitors at her feet vying with one another to pay their devoirs to her.   (Na 96–104)

Fixed in deliberate Victorianisms the language of the Gerty portion easily absorbs such expressions as 'of high degree' and 'suitors at her feet' from Alfred Bunn without dropping a stitch, and Gerty's figure as a Maria seems as predictable as that of Eveline's. Her hypothetical position 'beside any lady in the land' was close to being realised in 'Wandering Rocks', when the viceregal procession passed close to Gerty, who was not alone in sharing the assumption that a cat may look at a king: 'the reverend Hugh C. Love, M.A., made obeisance unperceived, mindful of lords deputies whose hands benignant had held of yore rich advowsons' (WR 1202–4). And the Anglican Love shares his veneration of the aristocracy with the Roman Catholic reverend John Conmee S.J., who early in 'Wandering Rocks', even without the excuse of the viceregal cavalcade, 'walked and moved in times of yore' and 'smiled at noble smiling faces in a beeswaxed drawingroom, ceiled with full fruit clusters' (WR 174–7). At such instances the language of 'Wandering Rocks' anticipates that of 'Nausicaa'.

Joyce's own depiction of the technique of 'Nausicaa' as 'written in a namby-pamby jammy marmalady drawsery (alto là!) style with effects of incense, mariolatry, masturbation, stewed cockles, painter's palette, chit chat, circumluction, etc., etc.'[3], fixes in its own rights the language of derision, directness, hauteur, innuendo, double entendre, and excess that confronts the stylistics of the chapter, that sets it apart and calls attention to what it highlights and conceals under layers of paint. To establish Gerty's age, for example, requires two separate pieces of oblique information: the first refers to 'the fluttering hopes and fears of sweet seventeen (though Gerty would never see seventeen again)' (Na 172–3), where the familiar sixteen is altered to allow for the age of Homer's Nausikaa. The second is Gerty's petulant assertion that 'they could talk about her till they went blue in the face, Bertha Supple too, and Edy, little spitfire, because she would be twentytwo in November' (Na 220–2), where the vague referent might conceivably attribute the age to Edy instead of where it belongs, with Gerty. The writing style refuses to be direct and precise, but the matter of age cannot logically be ignored, and the implied 'authoress' opts for grammatical obtuseness rather than fail to fulfill an authorial obligation.

With Gerty so precisely the focal point of concern, the evasiveness dictated by Victorian propriety none the less concentrates on accounting for her unfortunate position – 21 years old and still unmarried. The text attempts to shy away from whatever infirmity of foot she may have, but cannot help but glance frequently at just that part of her anatomy, especially once it has asserted that under different circumstances Gerty MacDowell could have had 'patrician suitors *at her feet*'. Since a description of female attire is essential as part of the literary convention, it is only a matter of time before shoes are included: 'Her shoes were the newest thing in footware (Edy Boardman prided herself that she was very *petite* but she never had a foot like Gerty MacDowell, a five, and never would, ash, oak or elm) with patent toecaps and just one smart

buckle over her higharched instep' (Na 164–8). If feet are a taboo
subject in this genteel arena, then the text skirts dangerously close,
although clothing is fashioned for concealment of naked reality,
and fashion practises even subtler concealments. Yet the next
sentence unabashedly takes up the forbidden subject, insisting
that 'Her wellturned ankle displayed its perfect proportions beneath her skirt and just the proper amount and no more of her
shapely limbs encased in finespun hose and highspliced heels and
wide garter tops' (WR 168–71).

Assuming that Gerty has the lame foot that Bloom attributes to
her, we read the deceptiveness of this description in the interplay
between shoes in the plural and foot in the singular, the use of the
generic foot presumably to represent the two feet generally. The
category of shoes, toecaps and heels vies with the singular foot,
ankle and instep as if no discrepancy existed (proposition: let
Gerty's one good foot stand for her two feet). Nor is there any
omniscience apparent in the narrative source, which may contend
that the genteel Gerty does not now and never has revealed more
of her limbs than is properly permitted, but cannot at this stage be
responsible for Gerty's future indiscretions only a few minutes
away, at which time 'she revealed all her graceful beautifully
shaped legs' (Na 698), so that eventually Bloom

> could see her other things too, nainsook knickers, the fabric that
> caresses the skin, better than those other pettiwidth, the green,
> four and eleven, on account of being white and she let him and she
> saw that he saw . . . and she was trembling in every limb from being
> bent so far back that he had a full view high up above her knee
> where no-one ever not even on a swing or wading.   (Na 724–9)

The literary tone has necessarily shifted with the narrational
content to that of mildly pornographic literature (never very far
beneath the surface in prissy romances), apologetic and preten-
tious, although the various censoring devices remain apparent,
even to an inclusion of the price of a pair of knickers.

WHERE IS MOLLY THEN, MOLLY AND HER MEN?

Throughout *Ulysses* one text masks another, as one character masks another. Bloom momentarily tries to squeeze Gerty's feet into tight boots, an aspect of feminine vanity that he is familiar with from home: Molly is quite aware of male foot fetishes, as she remembers Boylan's interest in her feet: 'I saw his eyes on my feet going out through the turning door he was looking when I looked back and I went there for tea 2 days after in the hope but he wasnt now how did that excite him because I was crossing them when we were in the other room first he meant the shoes that are too tight to walk in' (Pe 256–60). While on the subject Molly quickly moves toward self-criticism ('I dont like my foot so much' – Pe 262–3), remembering a sexual experience that places Poldy even more directly within the area of foot fetishism: 'still I made him spend once with my foot the night after Goodwins botchup of a concert' (Pe 263–4) – an interesting parallel to Bloom's masturbation over Gerty's self-exposure. That Bloom and Boylan tend to mask each other in Molly's thoughts soon becomes apparent as she continues to pursue the matter of feet, beginning with the night of the Goodwin concert:

he asked to take off my stockings lying on the hearthrug in Lombard street west and another time it was my muddy boots hed like me to walk in all the horses dung I could find but of course hes not natural like the rest of the world that I what did he say I could give 9 points in 10 to Katty Lanner and beat her what does that mean I asked him I forgot what he said because the stoppress edition just passed. (Pe 265–71)

The 'confusion' of Bloom and Boylan is based on their mutual preoccupation with women's feet (the archetypal male is characterised and charactonymed in *Finnegans Wake* as 'Mr Anklegazer' – *FW*, p. 193, ll. 11–12), a tendency they share with others remembered by Molly, 'the man with the curly hair in the Lucan dairy' and 'Bartell dArcy too' (Pe 271–3).

Just how pervasive the Bloom–Boylan co-identity can be is corroborated within the passage in which the attempt is made to determine which of the two compared Molly's feet with those of the London dancer. We can easily suppose that both men are aware of Kitty Lanner and her talents, most obviously Boylan because of his position as an impresario. Bloom's credentials are validated by less tangible evidence: the ballet mistress is 'present' with him in Bella Cohen's brothel when Maginni the dancing master invokes her name: 'Deportment. The Katty Lanner step. So. Watch me!' (Ci 4043–4). But like the grammatical inadvertence that conflates Gerty and Edy regarding age in 'Nausicaa', the Molly sentence makes no definite commitment to either fetishist. Bloom is the immediate antecedent, but Boylan the preceding one, so that if the sequence leads in with Bloom it may just as quickly revert to Blazes, especially since it was he who that evening had interrupted his dalliance with Molly to buy a stop-press edition in order to find out about the Gold Cup results. Stop-press editions, however, are a daily occurrence, and at some time in the past Bloom too could have broken off his commentary to his wife to buy a newspaper. Like two actors auditioning for the same role, antagonists Bloom and Boylan easily fit the part.

We can logically assume that Molly herself is fully aware of which fetishist she is featuring in this vignette. Literary convention, and particularly Joycean manipulation of the conventions, allows for the language of thought but no visual image, yet the thinker none the less retains a firm hold on the visual. The possibility that Molly is confused or inexact in her conceptualisation of the incident seems remote. Although she exhibits a basically nebulous reproduction of some people's names, especially from her distant past, her girlhood in Gibraltar, her Dublin recollections have an uncanny preciseness, as witnessed by her classification of 'Gardner lieut Stanley G 8th Bn 2nd East Lancs Rgt' (Pe 389), which for a lover seems exceedingly bland and even antiseptic, suggesting a mailing address or a heading of transfer orders or even an obituary notice, a parallel to Gerty's reproduction of *The Lamplighter* title page or dust cover. Since Lieutenant Gardner's romantic predecessor was Lieutenant Mulvey, we could assume that Molly has as full a remembrance of him as well – yet that hardly seems the case.

Bloom, who apparently has been kept ignorant of the existence of Lieut. Gardner, does know about Lieut. Mulvey, since Molly has apparently seen fit some time in the past to provide Poldy with an awareness of her past 'lover' by lending him a book 'with Mulveys photo in it so as he see I wasnt without' (Pe 655–6). At four instances on 16 June 1904 Bloom conjures Mulvey up in his mind, twice in 'Nausicaa': 'Molly, lieutenant Mulvey that kissed her under the Moorish wall beside the gardens' (Na 889–90) and '*señorita* young eyes Mulvey plump bubs me breadvan Winkle red slippers she rusty sleep wander years of dreams return' (Na 1282–3).

Bloom could hardly have gleaned information about the kiss from a photo found in a book, so Mulvey obviously was a subject of conversation and Bloom therefore privy to Molly's reminiscences. The other instances both occur in 'Ithaca' where 'lieutenant Mulvey, British navy' (It 870) is vaguely 'hallucinated' as a blond progenitor of the blond Milly Bloom, and where 'Assuming Mulvey to be the first term of his series' (It 2133), that remote and tentative lover leads the procession of Molly's putative admirers. Molly herself remembers that Mulvey 'was rather fair' (Pe 819) and even acknowledges that 'Mulveys was the first' (Pe 748), referring to the first love letter she ever received.

Nowhere in Bloom's arena of knowledge does Mulvey's first name ever surface, and it does seem rather strange that if Molly has been telling her husband about him that she should have referred to the lieutenant so formally. The supposition persists that Molly may not know Mulvey's given name – that Molly has retained no clear recollection of it. The given name has dropped out of her mind over the years, and perhaps the new liaison with Blazes has reawakened romantic memories, including those about Mulvey. Molly makes a concerted effort to give Mulvey a name, after recapitulating in detail the events of their time together in Gibraltar. The belated attempt at dredging up the name arrives at 'Molly darling he called me what was his name Jack Joe Harry Mulvey was it yes I think a lieutenant he was' (Pe 817–19), and we are led to assume that the last term of that series is the definite find, rather than only one more speculation. Molly treats it (Harry) as definitive and applies it to him thereafter, although only once more, as if trying it out: 'Harry Molly darling' (Pe 861). Her acceptance of the suggested name gives it very little validation, for her last thoughts of him revert back to merely Mulvey (Pe 1582), kissing her under the Moorish wall. 'Jack' and 'Joe' seem casually tossed off as only experiment, but 'Harry' may actually have some substantial basis: Molly is remembering her girlhood love when she was fifteen years old – Milly Bloom's present age. She thinks of her daughter being 'courted' at age fifteen: 'now shes well on for flirting too with Tom Devans two sons imitating me whistling with those romps of Murray girls calling for her can Milly come out please shes in great demand to pick what they can out of her round in Nelson street riding Harry Devans bicycle at night' (Pe 1023–7). Milly, like Gerty MacDowell, has a boy with a bicycle, and if his name is really Harry, that might be the source for Molly's deciding on Harry Mulvey. Conversely, having first determined that Mulvey was named Harry, she might inadvertently now be applying the same name to one of Tom Devan's two sons. Mulvey and young Devan may be actors auditioning for the part of 'Harry'.

Molly's images of Gibraltar are incredibly vivid, and she is particularly interested in recuperating names as indicators of exact references, 'like those names in Gibraltar Delapaz Delagracia they had the devils queer names there father Vilaplana of Santa Maria that gave me the rosary Rosales y OReilly in the Calle las Siete Revueltas and Pisimbo and Mrs Opisso in Governor street O what a name' (Pe 1463–6). There is an aura of precise nomenclature and total recall in this cataloguing, especially in the juxtaposition of people and places. Molly seems quite definite about an old servant names Mrs Rubio, and consistent both in her characterisation of her and her name, yet the intrusion of a 'Captain Rubio' ('I went up Windmill hill to the flats that Sunday morning with Captain Rubios that was dead spyglass' – Pe 856–7) may seem rather coincidental, unless there is some way to establish a hypothetical relationship between the old servant woman and the dead captain. What sort of 'captain' was he? naval or fishing boat? (Unlikely the British Navy if his name was really Rubio.) Was it just an honorific for a local fisherman with his own boat? In which case is he the dead husband of Mrs Rubio, or does one name merely mask another? 'Rubio' may substitute for another name when memory is inexact, although Molly does not stumble over the captain's name as she did over Mulvey's. Nor is there any way of determining whether her father's crony in Gibraltar was named Captain Grove or Captain Groves, the former version appearing twice ('regards to your father also captain Grove' – Pe 622–3; 'I was with father and captain Grove' – Pe 644), and the latter also twice: 'only captain Groves and father' (Pe 689–90) and 'father and old captain Groves' (Pe 1583). (No amount of textual editing of *Ulysses* manages to eliminate the discrepancy.)

None the less, it is possible to sort out the areas in which errors of memory may have been intruded in Molly's thoughts regarding the binomial captain. Hester Stanhope may actually be the culprit responsible, since the first mention of the captain comes from her postcard ('write soon kind she left out regards to your father also captain Grove' – Pe 622–3). The careless Hester may have reduced Groves to Grove, and only moments later Molly could perpetuate the error in her thoughts. In which case, she soon rights herself and establishes Groves as the name she will repeat a good while later. Alternatively, Grove may be correct (Hester notwithstanding – it is after all the more common version), and Molly's third usage may have jumped the rails because of a series of plurals consecutive in her thoughts: 'keys to lock the gates and bagpipes and only captain Groves and father talking about Rorkes drift' (Pe 689–90). Once having got on track she retains the correct version at the end, never aware that there had been any slippage at all.

Nor is Hester Stanhope all that easily acceptable as the real name of Molly's Gibraltar acquaintance, that is, 'fathers friend Mrs Stanhope' (Pe 612), about whom Molly wonders, 'whats this her other name was' (Pe 614). Mr Stanhope, that vague sort of husband, is reduced merely to his wife's pet name for him, 'wogger she called him' (Pe 616) – the lack of capitalisation a phenomenon of the wife's postcard. Molly soon arrives at 'Hester' as a given name for Mrs Stanhope, based on the signature on the card (which is already established as a suspect document), whether as a belated recall or an easy attribution, considering the possibility that Molly had heard of the famous Hester Stanhope and made a subliminal substitution. The common ground between the historical Hester and Molly's conjuration is that of exotic foreign travel, an area that Gibraltar-born Molly Tweedy could not then lay claim to but the now Dublin-based Molly Bloom could. In any event, toward the close of her night thoughts, Molly reassembles her cast of characters on the reconstituted Gibraltar stage, perhaps in the most accurate or near-accurate form (no 'Harry' for Mulvey, no 'wogger' for Hester's husband, but a definite 'Hester' for the wife): 'Mulvey and Mr Stanhope and Hester and father and old captain Groves' (Pe 1582–3). At this instance of finality, at the establishing of a definitive, if only temporary, text, Hester Stanhope persists as implicit in the narrative, endowed with narrational validity (she belongs to Molly, who has the final word on her naming), although still lurking in the shadows of literary invalidity, since there is no gainsaying the permanent existence of the legendary explorer, the eighteenth-century personage, *the* Hester Stanhope.

BLOOM ON TRIAL

Joyce's *Ulysses* accumulates the baggage of numerous pre-existing texts, a repository of literary left luggage that adds its own accumulations as they take shape along the way. Stephen's entrance into Nighttown, for example, is heralded with his incantations of the Introit for paschal time and his recapitulation of comments he himself made in the National Library earlier in the day, while his companion Lynch reprises his yellow oaths from his previous existence in *A Portrait*. Bloom's entrance soon develops into his arrest and trial, an extended scene in which various texts play their parts: Mosenthal's *Leah, Charms and Invocations of the Most Blessed Abbot Peter Salanka*, Mosaic law, da Ponte's *Don Giovanni*, the 'U.P.: up' postcard, *Sweets of Sin, Ruby: the Pride of the Ring*, 'Matcham's Masterstroke', the Agendath Netaim advertisement, the letters Bloom wrote to Martha Clifford, as well as H. Rumbold's letter, the Old Testament, works of Sacher Masoch and Paul de Kock, the *Freeman's Journal* obituary column for 16 June 1904, and the tentative House of Keyes advertisement. And many of the earlier Bloom chapters of *Ulysses* contribute their bits and pieces, as witness the constituency of the jury, all twelve good men and true having encountered Bloom in person earlier that day: Martin Cunningham, Jack Power, Simon Dedalus, Ned Lambert, John Henry Menton, Tom Kerman ('Hades'); Myles Crawford, Lenehan ('Aeolus'); Paddy Leonard, Nosey Flynn ('Lestrygonians'); M'Coy ('Lotus Eaters'); and The Nameless One ('Cyclops'). The judge in the case is Sir Frederick Falkiner, whom Bloom observed entering the Freemason's Hall toward the end of 'Lestrygonians'.

The expanding circumstances that lead to Bloom's 'Troubles' with the law seem to develop from two sources, one direct (the recollection of the 'horsey woman' obscured by the passing tram) and the other indirect (the recollection of 'That awful cramp in Lad lane. Something poisonous I ate' – Ci 207–8). On the basis of these thoughts and his admitted weariness, the psychodrama begins with the first apparition:

(*A sinister figure leans on plaited legs against O'Beirne's wall, a visage unknown, injected with dark mercury. From under a wide-leaved sombrero the figure regards him with evil eye.*)

BLOOM

Buenas noches, señorita Blanca. Que calle es esta?   (Ci 212–16)

Bloom's licit sexuality is linked to the 'Spanish' Molly, and his illicit sexuality has already been graphically depicted in his photo of the nude torero and señorita and the 'thoughts' in 'Nausicaa': *'Buenas noches, señorita. El hombre ama la muchacha hermosa'* (Na 1208–9). Other aspects of residual guilt soon intercede as well, as in his confrontation with his dead father, where he finds himself accused of having abandoned his heritage: 'Are you not my son dear Leopold who left the house of his father and left the god of his fathers Abraham and Jacob?' (Ci 260–2) – an odd accusation coming from the Rudolf Virag who converted from Judaism. Bloom responds cautiously, allowing the sins of his father to be visited on the son, 'I suppose so, father', adding obliquely, 'Mosenthal. All that's left of him' (Ci 264). Bloom is relying on a text he thinks he knows, one that presumably links him to his father, since he had contemplated attending a performance of *Leah* that evening:

Hello. *Leah* tonight. Mrs Bandmann Palmer. Like to see her again in that. Hamlet she played last night. Male impersonator. Perhaps he was a woman. Why Ophelia committed suicide. Poor papa! How he used to talk of Kate Bateman in that. Outside the Adelphi in London waited all the afternoon to get in. Year before I was born that was: sixtyfive. And Ristori in Vienna. What is this the right name is? By Mosenthal it is. *Rachel*, is it? No. The scene he was always talking about where the old blind Abraham recognises the voice and puts his fingers on his face.
(Lo 194–202)

The confusion of 'texts' here is multiple, since Bloom has already been transposing the alternate titles of the Mosenthal original and the English translation, and is further conflated in the two Abrahams, the biblical patriarch and the blind father in the drama, creating a palimpsest in which his own defection is superimposed on that of the fictional Nathan. Nor is Jacob (of fathers Abraham and Jacob) without strings attached: whereas Bloom in 'Lotus Eaters' conjures up a father Abraham as a surrogate for his own, in 'Oxen of the Sun' he visualises his father 'with Jacob's pipe' in the 'paternal ingle' (OS 1057–8), so that in 'Circe' he has deftly shifted the emphasis away from religious defection (patriarch Abraham) to the lesser sin of leaving his father's house (substituting the fictional Abraham).

Similarly, at Bloom's trial Father Coffey manages to conflate the biblical Jacob with the Dublin company that manufactures Jacob's Biscuits in his version of *'Domine vobiscum'*: 'Namine. Jacobs. Vobiscuits. Amen' (Ci 1241–2), anticipating the instance in *Finegans Wake* where the single word 'Jacobiters' (*FW*, p. 111, l. 4) invokes the biscuits, Scottish rebellions against England, and Shem the Penman. The 'confusion' of Jacob and his brother Esau by their blind father Isaac accounts for a confusion of texts, *Hamlet* and the Old Testament, when the ghost of Paddy Dignam testifies in Shakespearean echoes, only to have Bloom combine the˙ blind Abraham of the Mosenthal text with the blind Isaac:

PADDY DIGNAM

Bloom, I am Paddy Dignam's spirit. List, list, O list!

BLOOM

The voice is the voice of Esau.   (Ci 1217–20)

The pervading biblical aura of the trial scene has been determined by Mosaic law, and failed attorney J. J. O'Molloy takes on the visage of John F. Taylor to invoke the 'Mosaic code' that 'superseded the law of the jungle' (Ci 969–70), himself transmitting the Taylor invocation of Moses that he heard from Professor MacHugh in the newspaper office. Everything Mosaic conspires during the judicial proceedings to reiterate Moses and magnify the persona of Moses (even Mosenthal suggests the valley of Moses): 'A VOICE FROM THE GALLERY' gratuitously chants, 'Moses, Moses, king of the jews, / Wiped his arse in the *Daily News*' (Ci 846–8); Bloom had earlier remembered 'Marcus Tertius Moses, the tea merchant . . . with his daughter, Dancer Moses' (Ci 571–2); O'Molloy has designated Bloom's 'native place' as 'the land of the Pharaoh' (Ci 946–7); 'THE SLUTS AND RAGAMUFFINS' jeer Bloom as 'Ikey Mo!' (Ci 1040–1), echoing Mulligan's sneer ('What's his name? Ikey Moses' – SC 607); and hardly unexpectedly, Falkiner the trial judge assumes the features of Michelangelo's Moses, *'in judicial garb of grey stone . . . stonebearded. . . . From his forehead arise starkly the Mosaic ramshorns'* (Ci 1162–5). Moses *is* the Law, the legal text; he is himself the stone embodiment of the words set in stone, *'the tables of the law, graven in the language of the outlaw'* (Ae 868–9). A multiplicity of Moseses provides the graphic pattern, the stylistic mosaic.

The most oblique Mosaic reference – and perhaps the most significant – relates to the 'Jewish' pork butcher from whom Bloom purchased his kidney in the morning. Dlugacz's only other 'appearance' in *Ulysses* is here at the trial, the only instance in which a first name is given for him – Moses. The context in which he appears reconstitutes the Agendath Netaim advertisement first located on the butcher's counter by Bloom. The Circean replication reads:

> *The image of the lake of Kinnereth with blurred cattle cropping in silver haze is projected on the wall. Moses Dlugacz, ferreteyed albino, in blue dungarees, stands up in the gallery, holding in each hand an orange citron and a pork kidney.* (Ci 986–9)

The 'Circe' chapter, like 'Oxen of the Sun', is a repository of given names that had not previously existed in the developing chapters of *Ulysses* ('Ithaca' will expand on this phenomenon extensively), and the contextual unreliability of the 'renaming' of characters remains an open question. Although some biographical evidence (always an area of suspect relationship to the fictional text) supports the actual existence of a Moses Dlugacz of Joyce's acquaintance in Trieste, the delay in placing the given name into contention calls suspicious attention to it, especially since the linkage with Dlugacz's initial position carries its own weight. The basic version in 'Calypso' reads:

> He took a page up from the pile of cut sheets: the model farm at Kinnereth on the lakeshore of Tiberias. Can become ideal winter sanatorium. Moses Montefiore. I thought he was. Farmhouse, wall round it, blurred cattle cropping. (Ca 154–7)

Sir Moses Montefiore, the English philanthropist and Zionist, provides the fictional Dlugacz with the Mosaic name he hitherto did not have, and even the accusing Mrs Bellingham, who soon follows Dlugacz on the Circean stage, displays an unusual familiarity with the language of the advertisement when she refers to 'the model farm' (Ci 1035). Certain oblique assumptions are made (by Bloom – and by the overly casual reader of *Ulysses*): 'I thought he was' apparently assumes that Dlugacz the pork butcher is Jewish, at least as Jewish as Bloom himself; the Agendath Netaim on his counter presumably identifies him as a Zionist, and yet these 'cut sheets' are for wrapping meat and in no way implicate the butcher in prosetylising for either the faith or the farm. 'Circe' makes explicit that which has never been more than vaguely implicit, dramatising the potential reality that lurks within conjectural presentation. The characters in 'Circe' are actors playing the characters conceptualised earlier in the text: Josie Breen, for example, takes her turn playing Molly Bloom, and responds with *'Voglio e non'* to Bloom's *'Là ci darem la mano'* (Ci 469–73), Bloom standing in for Molly's singing partner, J. C. Doyle.

Authorship – and therefore implied authorship – is always speculative under circumstances in which one character masks another, and the source of the postcard to Denis Breen becomes an arena of speculation at Bloom's trial. Bloom had narrowed the field to only two possible candidates when he first heard of the incident: 'U.p: up. I'll take my oath that's Alf Bergan or Richie Goulding. Wrote it for a lark in the Scotch house I bet anything' (Le 320–1). Bloom is not a betting man and is cautious in taking oaths (language often masks 'other' language, the idiomatic 'representing' the literal meaning), and in eliminating all other Dublin pranksters in favour of a simple choice between Bergan and Goulding he displays the arbitrariness of a literary text that reduces all of Dublin to a manageable number of active characters – of actors impersonating Dubliners – but also allows the innocent person to hide the guilty perpetrator. 'Sirens' and 'Cyclops' provide forums in which first Goulding and then Bergan can act out their putative relationships to the offending postcard: Goulding seems oblivious of it while Bergan enjoys the joke immensely, one of them therefore 'confessing' while the other acts out his innocence.

Attributing guilt to Bergan and innocence to Goulding seems mandatory on the basis of their behaviour, yet in a world in which actors perform, the former may be relishing an event that he did not precipitate and the latter may be effectively hiding his complicity. 'Circe' then offers them both an opportunity to replay their parts, especially since a trial is in progress (Bloom's 'I'll take my oath' lands him in the dock) in which neither one is the defendant in the case. Bergan once again jeers at Breen ('U.p: up' – Ci 485) and Goulding continues to be indifferent to the situation, only his immediate presence and proximity to Bergan reminding us that he was once actually 'accused'. At the initial meeting with Mrs Breen, Bloom calls her attention to the 'performance' of the eccentric Cashel Boyle O'Connor Fitzmaurice Tisdall Farrell, in effect calling

attention away from the eccentric Denis Breen, one looney masking another, making them virtually indistinguishable from each
other. But no sooner has Bloom taken leave of Josie Breen, having
announced to himself the verdict that Breen is 'Meshuggah. Off his
chump' (Le 314) and that Farrell is 'that other mosey lunatic' (Le
318), than he passes the offices of the *Irish Times*, remembering the
advertisement he had placed *under an assumed name* that generated
the correspondence with Martha Clifford, the anonymous postcard
serving as a cover for the pseudonymous letters.

In his attempt to 'change the subject' away from the 'U.p: up'
card (Le 274–5), Bloom shifts to that of Mina Purefoy, but his *lapsus
lingua* creates the fictious personage of a 'Mrs Beaufoy' (Le 276) that
Josie Breen immediately sees through and corrects, Bloom acknowledging to himself the source of the mistake: 'Philip Beaufoy I was
thinking. Playgoer's Club. Matcham often thinks of the masterstroke. Did I pull the chain? Yes. The last act' (Le 278–9). The
signed *Titbits* story joins the unsigned postcard and the falsely
signed lascivious letters in setting up the circumstances that lead to
Bloom's 'arrest' and 'judgement' in 'Circe', and as his mental
association between the literary text and defecation ('Did I pull the
chain?') attests, the cloacal text becomes of major importance in
Ulysses. Myles Crawford was an early participant in the creation of
that associative process when he viewed the 'existence' of a
missing text, that which had been torn by Stephen from Mr
Deasy's letter for the writing of a bit of verse: 'Who tore it? Was he
short taken?' (Ae 521).

Bloom's recall of 'That awful cramp in Lad lane. Something
poisonous I ate' contributes to preparing the trial setting, especially
when he is confronted by his father while in the possession of a
non-kosher pig's crubeen ('*Yellow poison streaks*' are a feature of
Virag's '*drawn face*' – Ci 250–1), which he feeds instead to the
sniffing dog. In his address to the '*sinister figure*' who leans '*against
O'Beirne's wall*' as '*señorita Blanca*' Bloom 'translates' a Nausicaan
euphemism attributed to Madcap Ciss: 'when she wanted to go
you know where she said she wanted to run and pay a visit to the
Miss White' (Na 273–5). Incipient food poisoning and the absence
of a public convenience then sets the stage for the anecdote related
by 'THE GAFFER' for the edification of 'THE LOITERERS': 'And when
Cairns came down from the scaffolding in Beaver street what was
he after doing it into only into the bucket of porter that was there
waiting on the shavings for Derwan's plasterers' (Ci 584–7). The

loiterers prove to be an appreciative audience ('Jays, that's a good
one. Glauber salts. O jays, into the men's porter' – Ci 595), and
Bloom makes his own associations: 'Coincidence too. They think it
funny. Anything but that. Broad daylight. Trying to walk. Lucky
no woman' (Ci 593–4). Whatever once happened to Bloom and
where remain clouded in secrecy, but Cairns's experience has
become public gossip (although the 'he' of the anecdote has on
occasion been identified instead as Bloom by readers of *Ulysses*).
Cairns and Bloom mask each other, the pugnosed tramdriver
having already singled out Bloom when he called out to him 'Hey,
shitbreeches, are you doing the hat trick?' (Ci 195). The public
'trying' of Cairns is enough to add that remote incident from
Bloom's own 'awful cramp' for the configuration of trial material
against him, and the plasterers's 'shavings' will serve as setting for
the trial by combat of Stephen Dedalus in Nighttown, '*At the corner
of Beaver street beneath the scaffolding*' (Ci 4365).

By again compounding a 'Mrs Beaufoy Purefoy' (Ci 640–1) – in
this case one assumes that the latter 'corrects' the former – Bloom
calls up from the vasty deep the irate Philip Beaufoy, who accuses
him of being 'A plagiarist. A soapy sneak masquerading as a
littérateur' (Ci 822–3). Bloom has not only read 'Matcham's Masterstroke' and hoped to emulate it, but has also used it after the
reading as toilet paper ('cut sheets', similar to those used by
Dlugacz for wrapping meat, are also used by the Blooms in the
jakes, as Molly acknowledges: 'Im glad I burned the half of those
old Freemans and Photo Bits leaving things like that lying about
hes getting very careless and threw the rest of them up in the W C
Ill get him to cut them tomorrow for me' – Pe 600–3). Beaufoy then
can complain about 'a specimen of my maturer work disfigured by
the hallmark of the beast' (Ci 844–5), and editor Crawford can
answer the telephone for the '*Freeman's Urinal* and *Weekly Arsewipe*'
(Ci 812), while the 'THE VOICE FROM THE GALLERY' can jeer the
Moses who 'Wiped his arse in the *Daily News*' (Ci 848).

It remains only for Bloom to admit his guilt, to authenticate the
diarrhetic experience as his own, and assume authorship of the
offending text:

The crossexamination proceeds re Bloom and the bucket. *A large bucket.
Bloom himself. Bowel trouble. In Beaver street. Gripe, yes. Quite bad. A
plasterer's bucket. By walking stifflegged. Suffered untold misery.
Deadly agony. About noon. Love or burgundy. Yes, some spinach.*

Crucial moment. He did not look in the bucket. Nobody. Rather a mess.
Not completely. A Titbits back number. Uproar and catcalls. Bloom in a
torn frockcoat stained with whitewash, dinged silk hat sideways on his
head, a strip of stickingplaster across his nose, talks inaudibly.
(Ci 929–37)

What in the daylight world of 'Sirens' had merely been a slight case
of flatulence, blamed on the burgundy at lunch ('Must be the cider
or perhaps the burgund' – Si 1268) is transmogrified in the
nightmarish theatrical circus of 'Circe' as the creation of the cloacal
text. Just as Bloom shoulders the guilt of defecating in the plasterers'
porter, the ghost of Paddy Dignam relieves him of that guilt and
takes the burden upon himself. Dignam interrupts his life (and
death) story by asking for a lamp, explaining, 'I must satisfy an
animal need. That buttermilk didn't agree with me' (Ci 1234–5). As
Bloom seemed willing to serve as scapegoat for Cairns, Dignam
volunteers to serve for Bloom, and the 'inspirational source'
progresses from Glauber salts to burgundy to buttermilk.

A DARKNESS AT NOON

A major displacement in *Ulysses* (perhaps *the* major displacement)
occurs in the transition from day to night, from sight to blindness,
from the easily perceivable to the dependency on senses and
faculties other than just vision for perception. The early morning
sunlight from the top of the Martello tower allowed for the most
minute observations, even for the Stephen Dedalus whose
eyesight has often been the topic of critical speculation: he juxta-
poses sightings from near and far, close up and remote, even
improbably remote. When confronted by Mulligan, he interprets
the sophistry emanating from the goldtoothed mouth, its 'Chrysostomos' significance (Te 26); when confronted by Mulligan's
mirror he views both is own face and the crack in the glass, a trick
of refocusing for glances *at* and *into* the looking-glass. At the
tower edge Stephen 'gazed at the fraying edge of his shiny black
coatsleeve' (close up) and then 'Across the threadbare cuffedge he
saw the sea' (distant), and beyond that, 'looking towards the blunt
cape of Bray Head that lay on the water like the snout of a sleeping
whale' (remote, impossibly remote) (Te 101, 106, 181–2). That it is

assumed to be impossible to see Bray Head from the Sandycove tower without a telescope does not invalidate the directional suggestion ('looking towards') or the situational existence of the promontory: in the early sunlight the text distinguishes not only the location of Bray Head and its blunt shape, but also allows for the sort of metaphorical observation ('like the snout of a sleeping whale') that Stephen would be qualified to make, improving on Shakespeare.

For Leopold Bloom also at the same time of morning images are sharp, both those his eyes observe and those determined by complementary inner vision. Once outdoors heliotropic Bloom immediately gravitates to the 'bright side' of the street (Ca 77) while the 'sun was nearing the steeple of George's church' (Ca 78). He had no difficulty in the glare of 'avoiding the loose cellarflap of number seventyfive' (Ca 77–8), either because he sees it clearly or knows in advance to look out for it, despite the apparent glare: 'His eyelids sank quietly often as he walked in happy warmth' (Ca 81). His imagination allows him mentally to 'Travel round in front of the sun' (Ca 84–5), a hypothetical journey to the East in pursuit of his own racial origins, although the overly romantic picture that plays along the screen of his mind he realistically dismisses afterward in a succinct review: 'Probably not a bit like it really' (Ca 99). At the pork butcher's, however, he is offered a second opportunity to make the sentimental journey to the East, to the model farm at Lake Tiberias, where the 'blurred cattle cropping' in apparently glaring sunlight reactivate the call. Yet once again the critical reviewer intercedes: 'Nothing doing. Still an idea behind it' (Ca 200). His interest in following the servant girl is also cancelled when, instead of making her journey eastward home, she turns westward, while prudent Bloom opts for a straight return home – to the east.

The juxtapositioning of real and imaginary 'sightings' also includes his thoughts on what seems to be an imaginary book with a 'Sunburst on the titlepage' ('Kind of stuff you read: in the track of the sun' – Ca 99–100), but that image probably has its origins in a book that is actually on Bloom's shelf, as witnessed by the inventory in 'Ithaca' that includes '*In the Track of the Sun* (yellow cloth, titlepage missing, recurrent title intestation)' (It 1395–6). That its title-page is missing indicates either that it is remembered by Bloom from before it went missing, or that he is transposing a sunburst from the titlepage of one of his other books – or the origin of the thought is simultaneous with the 'in the track' concept rather than following close upon it. The source of the mental image might clarify itself if a transposition has been made from the succeeding image of the banner of the *Freeman's Journal* to the hypothetical titlepage, as Bloom re-experiences Griffith's quip about a 'homerule sun rising up in the northwest from the laneway behind the bank of Ireland' (Ca 102–3). Retaining that image, Bloom can then translate it not only to the nonexistent titlepage but to immediate perception, the sighting of Larry O'Rourke inside his pub looking out, 'Baldhead over the blind' (Ca 111).

Later in the morning the bright sunshine continues to dominate, and in 'Lotus Eaters' Bloom focuses often on the effects of heat and light, overemphasising the warmth of the day in order to wipe his brow and manoeuvre the Henry Flower card from the headband in his hat. The chapter presents a Bloom who is alert to see and careful not to be seen, but the brilliant glow of the sun makes him obvious and vulnerable, while at times the glare interferes with his perceptions. The various ploys regarding the claiming of Martha's letter include rearranging his copy of the *Freeman's Journal* into a baton that he casually taps against his leg as he enters the post office: 'Careless air: Just drop in to see' (Lo 50–1), making sure that there is no one else there who might see (and recognize) him. As he waits for his mail he both gazes away from the grille ('at the recruiting poster' – Lo 56–7) and masks himself with the news-paper ('held the tip of his baton against his nostrils, smelling freshprinted rag paper' – Lo 57–8), an effect similar to his envision-ing Molly wearing a yashmak. Yet M'Coy spots him immediately after, just as Bantam Lyons will spot him and descend upon him outside the chemist's shop later on. As M'Coy holds forth, Bloom's focus is across the road at the horsey woman, and he manoeuvres himself around M'Coy for a better view: 'Mr Bloom gazed across the road' (Lo 98); 'Drawing back his head and gazing from beneath his vailed eyelids he saw the bright fawn skin shine in the glare, the braided drums. Clearly I can see today. Moisture about gives long sight perhaps' (Lo 110–13). His immediate disadvantage, regardless of his assumption that he can see clearly in the moist air, is that in facing westward with his back to the post office, he is staring into the glare of the hotel windows ('Watch! Watch! Silk flash rich stockings white. Watch!' – Lo 130). The anticipated view flashes before the mind's eye, but the obstruction prevents any such glimpse of stocking, and all he eventually apprehends is the

'Flicker, flicker: the laceflare of her hat in the sun: flicker, flick' (Lo 139–40).

For much of the time Bloom is seeing with his fingers like a blind man, reading the significance of pin and flower from the letter while it remains safely hidden in his pocket – out of sight. Deserted Cumberland street finally affords him a chance to read the contents of the letter, where one of the very few observers is a 'wise tabby, a blinking sphinx' who 'watched from her warm sill' (Lo 234). Refuge in All Hallow's Church soon after allows him time to manipulate the card back into the headband, take stock of his situation, fantasise at leisure, but also 'read' the message on the priest's chasuble, 'Letters on his back: I. N. R. I? No: I. H. S.' (Lo 373). He realises that how one reads what is written at times depends on one's vantage-point, from where one sees, as the initial 'I' remains in place while the anticipated 'N' turns into 'H' – and the rest of the message becomes self-evident although still unseen. The church experience may have sharpened his perceptions ('Hello. Were those two buttons of my waistcoat open all the time?' – Lo 452–3), but as he emerges into brightness, he is immediately blinded by the change from the dim light within: 'He passed . . . into the light. He stood a moment unseeing by the cold black marble bowl' (Lo 458). At the second unforeseen and undesired encounter, being approached by Lyons for a look at his paper ('Show us a minute. . . . I want to see about that French horse' – Lo 520–6), Bloom is disclosed as more often seen than seeing, and he quickly heads for the nearest baths, relying now exclusively on inner vision, imagination: 'He foresaw his pale body reclined in it at full, naked. . . . He saw his trunk and limbs riprippled over and sustained' (Lo 567–9). The 'Lotus Eaters' episode had begun with Bloom's constant perceptions of external reality (although even from the beginning he was an object of attention, spied upon from the first: 'A smaller girl with scars of eczema on her forehead eyed him' – Lo 6–7), as he reads recruiting posters, 'multicoloured hoardings' (Lo 193), the initials on the priest's back, etc., but finding himself *being read*, he retreats into privacy and anticipated masturbation.

Each of the daytime outdoors chapters repeats the continued interaction of the carefully perceptive Bloom as the object of the observations of others, even after the 'secret agent' guise used in 'Lotus Eaters' for the veiling of Martha's letter has run its course. As soon as Bloom settled himself in the funeral carriage in 'Hades' he 'looked seriously from the open carriagewindow at the lowered blinds of the avenue' and immediately noticed 'an old woman peeping' (Ha 11–12). At the end of the chapter Bloom has spotted a dent in Menton's hat and called his attention to it: 'John Henry Menton stared at him for an instance without moving' (Ha 1019), and when Cunningham seems to be rebuking Menton for the snub, Bloom observes carefully: 'Martin laying down the law. Martin could wind a sappyhead like that round his little finger, without his seeing it' (Ha 1028–30). The inobservent Menton is then dismissed by Bloom as 'Oyster eyes' (Ha 1031). In 'Lestrygonians', Bloom is so busy watching a 'sugarsticky girl shovelling scoopfuls of cream for a christian brother' that he is caught unaware by a 'sombre Y.M.C.A. young man, watchful among the warm sweet fumes of Graham Lemon's' who then 'placed a throwaway in a hand of Mr Bloom' (Le 1–6). At chapter's end Bloom has recovered his skills at being the first to observe that seem so important to him, and has the advantage of detecting Blazes Boylan before Boylan can spot him, focusing immediately on the 'Straw hat in sunlight. Tan shoes. Turnedup trousers' (Le 1168), taking him in from head to toes. He is apparently spared Boylan's powers of observation, presumably because of the bright sun, Bloom's ally ('Didn't see me perhaps. Light in his eyes' – Le 1175), so he reverts to 'secret agent' behaviour and pretends to be searching for something in his pockets: 'Look for something I'; 'Where did I?'; 'Busy looking'; 'I am looking for that'; 'Where did I?' (Le 1182–9).

The searching process continues thereafter, and that more idle and carefree Bloom who had been looking outward at the world at large, noticing things about everyone around him, concentrates instead on his own affairs, the quest for the *Kilkenny People* at the National Library, a book for Molly at the bookstalls. The near-collision with Boylan may well have cured the heliotropic Bloom from following the sun, his cavalier attitude of the morning ('set off at dawn. Travel round in front of the sun, steal a day's march on him. . . . Dander along all day. Might meet a robber or two. Well, meet him' – Ca 84–92) no longer applicable now that he has come so close to meeting the robber of his own home. He searches his pockets for the particular item that will ward off the intrusion of Blazes Boylan on his privacy and internal security, as earlier he had scrutinised his fingernails in the carriage rather than encounter Boylan's gaze ('the white disc of a straw hat flashed reply' to

Cunningham's salute – Ha 198–9). At first he fails to find the exact antidote, the 'moly' or talisman for self-protection. He rejects the Agendath Netain advertisement (the lure of the East and his own origins), as he does his copy of the *Freeman's Journal* and his handkerchief, and even the potato preservative that is his mother's means of protecting him: 'His hand looking for the where did I put found in his hip pocket soap lotion have to call tepid paper stuck. Ah soap there I yes. Gate. / Safe!' (Le 1191–3). The soap that had washed his body in the bath ('his pale body ... naked ... sustained' – Lo 567–9) is called upon to provide the security for his physical self ('Enjoy a bath now. . . . This is my body' – Lo 565–6). In 'Circe' the solar soap celebrates and sustains Bloom when he '*points to the south, then to the east. A cake of new clean lemon soap arises, diffusing light and perfume*':

THE SOAP

> We're a capital couple are Bloom and I.
> He brightens the earth. I polish the sky.

(*The freckled face of Sweny, the druggist, appears in the disc of the soapsun.*)   (Ci 335–41)

'CHARACTICULS DURING THEIR BLACKOUT'

Night falls gradually in the closing segment of 'Nausicaa', and indeed Bloom's observations become almost completely internalised. When he does make himself aware of external conditions, counting the flashes of the Bailey light, he notes that it is 'lightingup time' (Na 1070), but that there is 'Some light still' (Na 1075). He differentiates between the qualities of light and dark as if in terms of safety and danger, commenting that 'Light is a kind of reassuring' (Na 1071) and that 'People afraid of the dark' (Na 1070–1). At the water's edge Bloom assumes the role of mariner as he watches the 'lighting up' of the stars, calculating that 'When three it's night' (Na 1077). His thoughts come full circle back to the first venture out into daylight that morning:

> Were those nightclouds there all the time? Looks like a phantom ship. No. Wait. Trees are they? An optical illusion. Mirage. Land

of the setting sun this. Homerule sun setting in the southeast. My native land, goodnight. (Na 1077–80)

Whereas to Gerty the lamplighter is both a literary personage and a remembered experience, it is for Bloom that evening that the lamplighter (mysteriously unacknowledged) accomplishes his lighting up: 'And among the five young trees a hoisted lintstock lit the lamp at Leahy's terrace' (Na 1172–3) – in tones reminiscent of Gerty's favourite reading.

The closing moments of 'Nausicaa' anticipate the 'Oxen of the Sun' chapter (the three stars that verify night are paralleled by the three-part triple invocation that opens the first night-time chapter), where the sacred oxen of the sun god are sacrificed in darkness. Bloom in 'Nausicaa' commiserates with sailors and worries about 'Big brutes of oceangoing steamers floundering along in the dark, lowing out like seacows. *Faugh a ballagh!* Out of that, bloody curse to you!' (Na 1148–50), recapturing a street collision that he himself did not witness, that of the looney Farrell with the blind piano tuner in 'Wandering Rocks': ' – God's curse on you, he said sourly, whoever you are! You're blinder nor I am, you bitch's bastard!' (WR 1119–20). 'Nausicaa' had begun with benign security, with the promise that night would be kind and protective, that 'dear old Howth' would be 'guarding as ever the waters of the bay' (Na 4), but at the close of the chapter, Bloom's night thoughts are of shipwrecks, ironically composed after the storm in just such benign serenity as the opening had promised: 'Then you have a beautiful calm without a cloud, smooth sea, placid, crew and cargo in smithereens, Davy Jones' locker, moon looking down so peaceful' (Na 1163–4).

The National Maternity Hospital on Holles street embodies shelter and sanctuary, where various 'mariners' cast adrift find refuge, and embryonic Mortimer Purefoy, belying his given name, finally emerges from the amniotic fluid to maternal and medical care. The storm that breaks that evening (Bloom had worried that 'Lots must be killed in storms. . . . Dreadful life sailors have' – Na 1147–8) spares the celebrants in the commons room, but catches Mulligan and Bannon unaware so that they too take shelter belatedly in the lying-in hospital. The protective element is reinforced by the continual narrational 'voice-overs', literary validation constantly being supplied in predictable chronological sequence with only occasional, hardly perceptible lapses, until time runs out and the chances of a last round of drinks drives the celebrants to Burke's pub, propelling them into the uncharted streets. Time has run its course, language has begun to disintegrate, secure haven replaced by perilous voyage (down a single street), and between hospital and pub Bloom takes on the responsibility of navigating ('Righto, Isaacs, shove em out of the bleeding limelight' – OS 1447). Bloom's navigational strategy, like that of the general on the battlefield, may actually be effected from *behind* the contingent, since he has held back from the others when they all started out ('Bloom stays with nurse a thought to send a kind word to happy mother and nurseling up there' – OS 1401–2), and his scattering of the Denzille lane boys, dangerous rocks that unexpectedly bob up in the narrow sea, seems to prevent them from marauding from the rear. In the dark street no spotlight illuminates the stage, and no external narration offers guidance as the group moves out of the hospital. Only the 'voices' of the participants themselves actualise the nature of their activities, hollow voices in the darkness.

Bloom in the rear is not the last of the ten who set out. Dixon and Costello are apparently even further back, since one of the others asks where they are and calls back to them: 'Where the Henry Nevil's sawbones and ole clo? Sorra one o' me knows. Hurrah there, Dix! Forward to the ribbon counter. Where's Punch?' (OS 1442–4). The concern for the laggards also includes Bloom, designated here by the anti-Semitic characterisation as a vendor of old clothes and a merchant of ribbons – probably because it is likely that he is viewed as possessing the money necessary to stand the drinks. 'Sawbones' Dixon has had an attack of stomach pains, and Punch Costello has remained with him, as we hear when they finally arrive at Burke's: 'Got a pectoral trauma, eh, Dix?' (OS 1472). These closing pages of 'Oxen' are an exercise in reading blind by listening to the ten voices, distinguishing their varied modes of facetious and drunken colloquy and commentaries, reading past their comic disguises as they babble and rant in unison. No narrational map exists for the reading, only voices in the dark, the 'literary' structures that had supported the bulk of the chapter having been displaced and rendered inoperative.

Several of the authors commandeered by Joyce into service for the bulk of the 'Oxen' chapter had taken pains to identify the celebrants around the refectory table, to delineate each of them in appropriate literary language, and a few also undertook to catalogue the *dramatis personae*. Sir John Mandeville, for example, set the scene:

There was a sort of scholars along either side the board, that is to wit, Dixon yclept junior of saint Mary Merciable's with other his fellows Lynch and Madden, scholars of medicine, and the franklin that hight Lenehan and one from Alba Longa, one Crotthers, and young Stephen that had mien of a frere that was at head of the board and Costello that men clepen Punch Costello all long of a mastery of him erewhile gested (and all of them, reserved young Stephen, he was the most drunken that demanded still of more mead) and beside the meek sir Leopold. (OS 188–95)

Bloom and Stephen and Lynch and Lenehan have their previous existences in *Ulysses*, while Dixon is already known through Bloom's recollection of him, so that Costello, Crotthers and Madden appear as the new characters to be assimilated within the constructs of the 'Oxen' chapter. When it is John Bunyan's turn to re-present these personages, he opts for his own allegorical language and succeeds in classifying seven of the eight along his own lines: 'So were they all in their blind fancy, Mr Cavil and Mr Sometimes Godly, Mr Ape Swillale, Mr False Franklin, Mr Dainty Dixon, Young Boasthard and Mr Cautious Calmer' (OS 467–70). Bunyanesque perspective defines the boasting nature of Stephen Dedalus and the cautious nature of Leopold Bloom, while Dixon is directly named. But the others require that Bunyan has access to previous parts of the text, that the literary validity that he brings to judgemental description none the less depends on the narrational validity of a cumulative process. Mandeville had already characterised Lenehan as a 'franklin' and Costello as a swiller of ale, so Bunyan has determined for his own purposes how to 'read' Mandeville even as we are in the process of realising how to 'read' Bunyan.

When Samuel Pepys takes possession of the narrational responsibilities, he follows through on what Mandeville had promised ('on young Malachi they waited for that he promised to have come' – OS 195–6). But Pepys has access to the more recent turn of events, aware that Mulligan has met Alec Bannon along the way ('Mal. Mulligan . . . chanced against Alec. Bannon' – OS 495–7), and the full complement of the ten male members of the party are now assembled. When Pepys counts up, however, he also misses out one of the group, as had Bunyan before him, although his is a different omission:

> There Leop. Bloom of Crawford's journal sitting snug with a
> covey of wags, likely brangling fellows, Dixon jun., scholar of
> my lady of Mercy's, Vin. Lynch, a Scots fellow, Will. Madden, T.
> Lenehan, very sad about a racer he fancied and Stephen D.
> (OS 504–7)

Whereas Bunyan had somehow lost Crotthers entirely, Pepys fails
to name him, dismissing him lightly as a 'Scots fellow', while
losing the drunken Costello instead (Crotthers and Costello become lost in each other). The loss of the Crotthers name seems
particularly mysterious since Pepys indulges in the use of first
names and initials hitherto unavailable in *Ulysses*, 'Will. Madden,
T. Lenehan' – nowhere else in the text will Lenehan's given name
ever appear. The power of naming has its own particular validity in
Ulysses, and the absence of a name implies a significant weakness,
as when Bloom admits that for nurse Callan 'Christian name
unknown' and for Gerty 'family name unknown' (It 1847–8), and
he is aware of the deficiency.

Even more prodigious than Pepys is Thomas Babington
Macaulay, who takes it upon himself to contain all ten members in
his summary, although only nine are now physically present,
Dixon having gone up to attend to Mrs Purefoy in the delivery
room. A closer attention is now paid to the placement of the
drinkers around the table, as they arrange themselves in a
tableau:

> Crotthers was there at the foot of the table.... There too,
> opposite to him, was Lynch.... Next the Scotchman was the
> place assigned to Costello ... while at his side was seated in
> stolid repose the squat form of Madden. The chair of the resident
> indeed stood vacant before the hearth but on either flank of it the
> figure of Bannon ... [and] Malachi Roland St John Mulligan.
> Lastly at the head of the board was the young poet ... while to
> right and left of him were accommodated the flippant prognosti-
> cator ... and that vigilant wanderer.   (OS 1204–18)

Macaulay had been so diligent in identifying everyone by name
that the four instances in which he resorts to mere designations
seem peculiar. It is perhaps understandable that the Dixon who is
not there might lose his name, but Stephen and Lynch and Bloom

become all the more significant by their loss of nomenclature, trailing after the others and especially after the fullblown enumeration of the Mulliganian trail of names.

That the most important characters of *Ulysses* are presented without their names may attest to how little of the full narrational process each temporary stylist in 'Oxen of the Sun' has absorbed, and is more than compensated for by the luxurious appellation for the Buck, a four-part elaboration of which the two middle terms are nowhere else validated in the text. Mulligan himself had almost immediately made much of his musical name when he announced in 'Telemachus', 'My name is absurd too: Malachi Mulligan, two dactyls. But it has a Hellenic ring, hasn't it? Tripping and sunny like the buck himself' (Te 41–2). The Buck in this instance feels compelled to exploit his real given name, although the text throughout persists in employing his nickname, Mulligan in effect attempting to be the literary author of his own characterisation. When only a few minutes before Stephen has indulged in the allusionist's art and read the name 'Chrysostomos' in Buck's goldtoothed mouth, he had failed to specify in the allusion which of the two orators of that name was intended – that is, if he bothered to distinguish between the two for his own purposes. But Macaulay in his meticulosity has now taken the trouble to make a distinction by inserting the 'St John', presumably opting for the ecclesiastical Chrysostomos of that name.

Biographical evidence has long since presented us with a prototype for Mulligan in Oliver Gogarty of the two dactyls, whose middle name was St John as well, but Roland arrives as a gratuitous addendum. Is Roland actually germane to the text of *Ulysses*? Does it have a permanent status along with St John as part of Mulligan's name at all times, or is it only in the Macaulay context that it has its temporary validity? Further play with the intrusive biographical evidence positions Roland as an analogue for Oliver, so that the *Chanson de Roland* surfaces as a literary pre-text, and a new interplay of Stephen and Buck as 'devoted' friends along the lines of Roland and Oliver has its ironic echo ('Hast thou found me, O mine enemy?' Stephen commented without equivocation – SC 482). For his own purposes perhaps our newly conscripted author cannot be held responsible for the *Chanson*, himself too busy describing the 'primrose elegance and townbred manners' (OS 1212–13) of the Buck.

DECODING BLIND

Once literary authority has run its course and language remains as the naked vehicle of narrational development, there is no projection of light focusing on the ten who make their way from the House of Horne to Burke's pub, that amorphous 'dedale of lusty youth' (OS 1394–5). Although also mysteriously classified as 'noble every student there' (OS 1395), only three have been named as medical students, Lynch, Madden and Mulligan (Crotthers seems to be a possible fourth), and Bloom is certainly no youth. In addition, this contingent is also described by Thomas Carlyle rather cavalierly as 'a tag and bobtail of all them after, cockerel, jackanapes, welsher, pilldoctor', plus 'punctual Bloom' (OS 1391–3), an indication that – as with John Bunyan – an interfering perspective is operative in 'locating' the characters of the impending drama. Since 'dialogue' throughout 'Oxen' has also been governed by the prevailing literary determinants at every stage, the 'narrational' voices of each of the ten have been replaced by literary approximations of a previous age for each of the literary contexts, so that when allowed to be heard in their own voices, the new additions to the cast (Costello, Crotthers, Dixon, Bannon, Madden) have no known resonances for easy identification. Stephen, for example, can easily be held responsible for the ecclesiastical Latin that is intruded, especially when *'Benedicat vos omnipotens Deus, Pater et Filius'* arrives as a response to having been identified as a 'drunken minister' (OS 1444–6) by the ignorant street arabs, but Mulligan has also been known to chant Introits and perform masses.

On the other hand, the bits and pieces in French that filter in could also be attributed to Stephen, recently rearrived from Paris, although Punch Costello should not be overlooked, he who 'had been indentured to a brandyshipper that has a winelodge in Bordeaux and he spoke French like a gentleman too' (OS 552–4). In addition, Lenehan has also been known to use the French language in vain for his own jocular purposes (*'Pardon, monsieur'*, he says to Bloom in 'Aeolus', and to O'Molloy, *'Thanky vous'* – Ae 417, 468). During the session at Burke's Lenehan departs early, once he has sighted Bantam Lyons (with a characteristic 'Horryvar, mong vioo' – OS 1522), leaving several French phrases thereafter to the provenance of others: when Bannon decamps at the sight of Bloom he utters a Lenehanian *'Bonsoir la compagnie'* (OS 1536), both of them are, of course, taking French leave. On the other hand, a subsequent toast, '*À la vôtre!*' (OS 1545), can be almost anyone's property, and the mock-French '*Tiens, tiens*, but it is well sad, that, my faith, yes' (OS 1558) can best be laid at Costello's doorstep, even if it is hardly the French of a gentleman.

The paragraph of transition that takes the group through the lane is the only one in the segment located outside the hospital that contains a narrative device to describe activity, the opening sentence asserting, 'All off for a buster, armstrong, hollering down the street' (OS 1440). Thereafter, like dramatic action without the benefit of stage directions, the speaking and hollering voices take complete charge. Only on the basis of direct address or direct reference in this transitional paragraph can identities make themselves known (Dix, Punch, Isaacs, Mullee, Mulligan, Parson Steve), with Mulligan in particular making his distinctive voice heard (distinctive on the basis of his manner of speaking). His presence on this last-drink jaunt seems assured, despite the possibility of misreading his absence as due to his having left the hospital with Haines (who was not present in the hospital at all): when Buck was recounting the appointment he made with Haines earlier that evening at George Moore's, it was a 'retrospective arrangement' of past action narrated in the present tense, the Gothic rendering of 'Malachias' tale' (OS 1010). In Holles Street the same Mulligan hollers, 'To be printed and bound at the Druiddrum press by two designing females. Calf covers of pissedon green. Last word in art shades. Most beautiful book come out of Ireland my time' (OS 1454–7), repeating his witticisms of the morning and afternoon:

about the folk and the fishgods of Drundrum. Printed by the weird sisters in the year of the big wind ...   (Te 366–7)

A new art colour for our Irish poets: snotgreen ...   (Te 73)

The most beautiful book that has come out of our country in my time.   (SC 1164)

Specific echoes such as these form the primary means of identifying the speaker-in-the-dark, but few such clear returns of actual speech exist in the closing segment. Instead, there is only speculation that it is Lenehan who has trod on someone's feet and apologises for it in a somewhat distinctive manner: 'You hurt?

Most amazingly sorry!' (OS 1464). The speculation, however, is dependent on Lenehan's comment when he 'bumped against' Bloom in 'Aeolus' and heard Bloom apologise: 'Are you hurt? . . . Sorry' (Ae 416–23). (The 'most amazingly' modifier logically transfers the comments from the staid Bloom to the flamboyant Lenehan.) Nor is there much chance that it was Bloom who was trod on in the later instance, since it is unlikely that he would exclaim, 'Wow, my tootsies!' (OS 1463–4).

Not only does this paragraph have its roots in past events, but it will also provide a source for a recapitulation in 'Circe', where on a highly lit stage identities are defined and gestures clarified: the narrational thrusts of the 'stage directions' provide light-in-darkness where no such illumination was available in 'Oxen of the Sun'. The eight who headed so resolutely for Burke's (other than Stephen and Bloom) are present in 'Circe' by name and in costume, conjured up by Stephen's incantation, 'Blessed be the eight beatitudes' (Ci 2236–7). Stephen had previously announced his 'apostates' creed' (OS 1451) *en route* to Burke's as 'British Beatitudes! . . . Beer, beef, business, bibles, bulldogs, battleships, buggery and bishops' (OS 1453–60), which were immediately modified into a succinct 'Beer, beef, trample the bibles' (OS 1460–1). In 'Circe' the 'actors' become the eight beatitudes incarnate summoned forth, all performing as 'medicals' regardless of their actual occupations ('noble every student there'):

(*The beatitudes, Dixon, Madden, Crotthers, Costello, Lenehan, Bannon, Mulligan and Lynch in white surgical students' gowns, four abreast, goosestepping, tramp fast past in noisy marching.*)

THE BEATITUDES

(*incoherently*) Beer beef battledog buybull businum
barnum buggerum bishop.   (Ci 2238–43)

The have their 'identities' from 'Oxen', where they were far less co-ordinated in the dark but none the less approached Burke's with their 'March! Tramp, tramp, tramp, the boys are (atitudes!) [*sic*] parching' (OS 1458–9). The close attention to detail that marks 'Circe', especially in personages and costuming, presents the sharp focus of a spotlighted arena, yet does not provide accuracy in speech or in characterisation. The mode of Circean presentation colours and distorts in one direction (concentrated specificity within transformational fantasy), just as the mode of Oxenian presentation had coloured and distorted in another (residual familiarity affected by darkness and drunkenness), so that any real semblance of actuality necessarily resides in the space between the chapters, in the interaction between the two modes of presentation read against each other.

With only dialogue to carry the narration – and demotic, disguised and almost demented dialogue at that – it may seem precarious to sketch a scenario for the 'events' at Burke's pub, yet certain factors seem to defy the dark. Two rounds of drinks are bought and consumed during the few remaining minutes before closing, and there is every indication that it is Stephen (although perhaps reluctantly) who pays for both rounds. His temporary affluence has not gone unnoticed ('Seed near free poun on un a spell ago a said war hisn. Us come right in on your invite, see?' – OS 1501–2), and he might have been even more forthcoming for the second round: 'You move a motion? Steve boy, you're going it some. More bluggy drunkables?' (OS 1528–9). At least five of the drinkers are quick to plead poverty at the outset when the 'Query' is posed as to 'Who's astanding this here do?' (OS 1465), each in a variant phrase that captures the communal colloquial without in any particular way individualising the speaker:

> Proud possessor of damnall.
> Declare misery.
> Bet to the ropes.
> Me nantee saltee.
> Not a red at me this week gone.   (OS 1465–7)

Since none of these five can be assumed to be either Bloom or Stephen, and such well-dressed swells as Mulligan and Bannon might also be exempt (along with the sick Dr Dixon), the disclaimers can then be attributed at least in general to Crotthers, Costello, Madden, Lynch and Lenehan – the last two rather well-known sponges. Mulligan is the first to place his order (in Nietzschean self-identification), 'Mead of our fathers for the *Übermensch*', seconded by someone with a succinct 'Dittoh' (OS 1467). The call then for 'Five number ones' (OS 1467–8) – of Bass's ale, the prevailing drink at the hospital commons room – assumes that gestures were made that added three more of the same. Bloom opts for 'Ginger cordial' (OS 1468) and Stephen for 'Absinthe' (OS 1470), while somewhat later there are two calls for Guinness ('Two Ardilauns' – OS 1476), the delay probably occasioned by a private discussion of Molly Bloom's sensual body by Dixon (certainly) and Lenehan (probably), as well as one other person (perhaps). When the belated orders are added to the others and the drinks have arrived, they are counted up as 'Five, seven, nine. Fine!' (OS 1477), and it can be assumed that Dixon with his 'pectoral trauma' has declined to drink anything. For the second round Stephen may actually attempt to order 'Absinthe the lot' (OS 1533), but it is unlikely that anyone is paying attention to him – and several have already left the pub.

The various departures are effected surreptitiously, but none the less with flair: Lenehan is alerted to the presence somewhere in the pub of the drunken Lyons, and takes his time before slinking away to explain that he had dissuaded Lyons from betting on Throwaway (and that Bloom had given Lyons the tip!). To the question, 'Must you go?' Lenehan replies in character, 'All in if he spots me. Come ahome, our Bantam. Horryvar, mong vioo' (OS 1520–2). Bannon plays out the same scenario when he realises that Bloom is Milly's father ('Bloo? Cadges ads. Photo's papli, by all that's gorgeous. Play low, pardner. Slide. *Bonsoir la compagnie*' (OS 1535–6). Bannon's defection tips off one of the company (probably Stephen) that *two* of their number have disappeared: 'Where's the buck and Namby Amby? Skunked?' (OS 1537–8). Stephen may then become the object of Lynch's ironic sympathy, if it is Lynch who knows that Mulligan has absconded with the tower key: 'Kind Kristyann wil yu help yung man hoose frend tuk bungellow kee tu find plais whear tu lay crown of his hed 2 night' (OS 1539–40). Attempting to attribute this 'plea' directly to Stephen must assume that he is capable of both the mocking self-pity and dialectical wordplay, especially since the same intonation is present in the voice that asks for biscuits for Stephen (who would hardly request them himself): 'Item, curate, couple of cookies for this child' (OS 1542). But given the almost universal penchant here for linguistic playfulness, very few of such assumptions of identified speaker can be characterised as certain.

Unlike the studied deployment of characters in 'Circe' (the eight medicals four abreast), the bar at Burke's is a free-for-all that the narrational restrictions of the episode keep invisible – although of course highly audible. How those assembled position themselves (who is in conversation with whom, who is hollering aloud to all) remains shrouded in a darkness that has been stylistically imposed on what must have been a well-lit pub setting. None the less, it becomes apparent that Bloom emerges as a rather important presence among them, a mysterious stranger in their midst, exciting a degree of interest and curiosity, as well as mockery and suspicion. At least one of the party addresses him in mock-Yiddish (probably Mulligan), calling him Isaacs (Mulligan having been responsible for the earlier 'Ikey Moses'), and extending the invitation of 'Yous join uz, dear sir? No hentrusion in life' (OS 1447–8). When Lenehan discloses that Bloom had the tip on Throwaway, a minor replay of the 'Cyclops' confrontation surfaces, and the mock-Yiddish becomes thicker and more sinister: 'Vyfor you no me tell? Vel, I ses, if that ain't a sheeny nachez, vel, I vil get misha mishinnah' (OS 1525–6). While Molly is being verbally undressed at one part of the bar, at another one of the 'medicals' is attempting to shake Bloom's faith in his potato preservative ['I vear thee beest a gert vool' (OS 1481–2), again in mock-Yiddish], and he is also derided for his selection of a non-alcoholic beverage when drinks are being ordered. Bloom is also the centre of attention when 'yon guy in the mackintosh' is spotted and pronounced demented, since he claims to have seen him that morning at the Dignam gravesite: 'Pardon? Seen him today at a runefal? Chum o' yourn passed in his checks?' (OS 1546–54). Whatever Bloom himself had actually said, and what response if any he then made, are inexplicably missing from this otherwise highly vocal enactment of the pub scene, a phenomenon that exists throughout the episode.

Once Bloom has asked for a drink and justified his choice ('Ginger cordial. . . . Stimulate the caloric' – OS 1468–70), he is never heard again in 'Oxen', and even these two phrases can be read as Bloom's words being echoed back at him, the latter perhaps even spoken 'for' him. When the drinkers are ejected at closing time, and the basic nucleus chooses to follow the fire engines south, having voted against visiting Nighttown, Stephen and Lynch depart for the red-light district ('Change here for Bawdyhouse' – OS 1572–3), Bloom alone temporarily lost between the separating groups. His decision to follow in the tracks of Stephen Dedalus becomes known when he appears in 'Circe', but the closing paragraphs of 'Oxen' disclose no trace of Leopold Bloom, tangentially credited by the seekers of 'shady Mary' (OS 1573) as responsible for the darkness: 'who the sooty hell's the johnny in the black duds? Hush! Sinned against the light' (OS 1575–6). The sea of voices has swallowed up Bloom's silence as he hovers at the edge of the boisterous crowd, somewhere on stage but nowhere apparent.

The disintegration of the elegance of language into dialect distortions may well have deprived the proper Bloom of a voice in an area where even Stephen can play the game with lapses into Latin and gypsy cant ['Every cove to his gentry mort' (OS 1493–4) echoes Stephen's thoughts in 'Proteus']. Such indulgences as Black American dialect and mock-Chinese are merely an element of playfulness concomitant with the jocular mood of the drinkers, but the proliferation of Scots dialect owes its origins to the presence of Crotthers, whether spoken by him or by others to him in mocking by-play, and almost every paragraph contains a sentence or phrase to emphasise the presence of the Scot in the social configuration:

> Here, Jock braw Hielentman's your barleybree. Lang may your lum reek and your kailpot boil!   (OS 1489–91)

> We are nae fou. We're nae tha fou.   (OS 1505)

> Hoots, mon, a wee drap to pree.   (OS 1532)

The later repetition of 'We're nae tha fou' (OS 1565) once the drinkers are back out on the street, and one of them is vomiting, elevates the phrase to that of a motif, the constant assertion of stability in chaos, but belied by the condition of the speaker. The phrase stands on its own as Scots for 'We are not that drunk', but is also an odd admixture of Scots and French ('We are not that mad'), when madness ('Trumpery insanity' – OS 1550) is never far below the surface, and with the Scots/French connection, languages in the climactic moments of 'Oxen of the Sun', like the characters themselves, mask each other.

This one contextually validated dialect (Scots) runs like a thread through the sequence as a constant, while previous phrases from the preceding chapters of *Ulysses* serve to keep such major figures as Stephen, Mulligan, Lynch and Lenehan at the forefront, and even Bannon is 'verified' as part of the ongoing narrative by his echoes of the Milly whose voice has been captured in the reading of her letter. By contrast, Leopold Bloom is present primarily as a catalyst, exciting the reactions of others but himself cautious and

reticent of speech, refusing to be drawn in as he had so incautious-
ly been drawn in at Barney Kiernan's. Instead of the narrator of the
tale of his wife's singing tour, as he was in his first pub of the day,
or the defender of humanistic causes, as he was in the second, he is
now presumably committed to his silent watchdog role over
Stephen, and consequently almost unheard from in a narrative
sequence in which only the sound of voices exists to maintain the
narrational flow. Bloom's only vocal contribution may have been to
tell the time when asked ('Ten to' – OS 1471) – and politely utter a
'Don't mention it' (OS 1472) when thanked – wary and watchful,
aware of the time now when he had been unaware of it when
asked by Cissy Caffrey in 'Nausicaa'.

NOTES

1.   Robert Scholes and Richard M. Kain (eds), *The Workshop of Daedalus*
     (Evanston, Ill.: Northwestern University Press, 1965) p. 31.
2.   Clive Hart (ed.), *Conversations with Joyce* (New York: Harper and Row,
     1974) p. 32.
3.   Stuart Gilbert (ed.), *Letters of James Joyce*, vol. 1 (New York: Viking,
     1957) p. 135.

7

Indeterminate Mysteries

The structures that fence in *Ulysses* contain the gaps that keep it open-ended: a day that begins well after sunrise on 16 June and ends in the early hours of the next morning, with certain hours duplicated and others unaccounted for. The remarkable specificities attached to many of the important characterisations are counterbalanced by the extreme marginality of many other characters. Knowing the exact physical measurements of the principal male figure in the novel does not compensate for not even knowing the names of some minor ones, and the single indication that Leopold Bloom's middle name is Paula (It 1855) must provide something of a jolt to the reader who has been acquainted with him for hundreds of pages. (In this case we also have the privilege of putting into question that most unreliable of all 'permanent' texts, the birth certificate, a document of official validity that is none the less subject to the kinds of errors that flesh is heir to.) What excellent capital the reader could make of having access to a name for that expansively developed character, the narrative-perpetrator of 'Cyclops', for whom acknowledged anonymity is guaranteed by his being dubbed '*the Nameless One*' in 'Circe' (Ci 4338–9). Efforts to attach the name Simon Dedalus to him have fallen pitifully short, but attest less to the fallibility of those particular readers than to the frustrating necessity of having to deal with a lack of identifiability for several of the marginal but fascinating characters of the novel.

NOBLEMEN MOST MYSTERIOUS

A casual evening stroller, for example, intrudes upon Bloom's consciousness at the twilight hour along Sandymount strand, and his appearance tempts Bloom to turn this 'encounter' into a work of literature:

Here's this nobleman passed before. Blown in from the bay. Just

went as far as turn back. Always at home at dinnertime. Looks
mangled out: had a good tuck in. Enjoying nature now. Grace
after meals. After supper walk a mile. Sure he has a small bank
balance somewhere, government sit. Walk after him now make
him awkward like those newsboys me today. Still you learn
something. See ourselves as others see us. So long as women
don't mock what matter? That's the way to find out. Ask
yourself who is he now. *The Mystery Man on the Beach*, prize titbit
story by Mr Leopold Bloom.   (Na 1053–60)

Bloom's fictionalisation is as self-reflexive as it is outer-projected: in
'Ithaca' we learn that he himself has a 'small bank balance
somewhere', but of course no 'government sit', nor has he on this
evening been home at dinnertime for a 'good tuck in'. Bloom's
prose piece has an exact title and designated author, and there is
no longer any intention now of sharing authorship with a silent
partner: Molly's temporary defection has presumably eliminated
her from the gratuitous inclusion offered earlier in the day ('Might
manage a sketch. By Mr and Mrs L. M. Bloom' – Ca 518). Bloom's
titular hero, however, goes unnamed, both because Bloom never
gets far enough in his creative impulse to attach a fictional name
and because he does not know the stroller's actual name. (The
'nobleman's' limited and fixed itinerary disqualifies him as an
acceptable Ulysses figure, but the Bloomian narrative strategies
might be as elliptical as the Joycean.)

A relative stranger in the Sandymount area, Bloom has been
sufficiently observant to spot the mystery man/nobleman coming
and going. Gerty MacDowell, a resident of the area, has seen him
before, as has her friend Cissy Caffrey. Although 'rapt in thought'
as he passes, and therefore not quite as observant, Gerty 'scarce
saw or heard' either her companions or 'the gentleman off Sandymount green that Cissy Caffrey called the man that was so like
himself passing along the strand taking a short walk' (Na 304–7),
yet she knows him well enough to know that he is no mystery
man – much less any kind of nobleman. For her Bloom has become
the mysterious nobleman of the moment, and if he could see himself as she sees him, he would discover Gerty's 'dreamhusband'
(Na 431):

She could see at once by his dark eyes and his pale intellectual
face that he was a foreigner, the image of the photo she had of

Martin Harvey, the matinée idol, only for the moustache which she preferred. . . . He was in deep mourning, she could see that, and the story of a haunting sorrow was written on his face. (Na 415–22)

With what ingenuity Gerty writes *The Mystery Man on the Beach*, in lieu of Leopold Bloom, and one suspects that Bloom's 'bourgeois' version of a suburban life would have less chance of publication in *Titbits* than Gerty's 'romantic' version, but Gerty's creativity depends on identifying the actor to play the part. Her choice of Martin Harvey is corroborated by Milly Bloom ('she clapped when the curtain came down because he looked so handsome then we had Martin Harvey for breakfast dinner and supper' – Pe 1054–5), but Milly has only just turned fifteen.

Gerty's life may well be coloured by the fiction that she reads, and the style of narrative presentation in the first half of 'Nausicaa' has become a classic example of parodic superfetation of style and subliminal content, but that fiction serves her for the constant creation of her own fictions, correctives for her prosaic existence. Bloom as dreamhusband is supplemented by the 'nobleman' as dreamfather, replacing the boosing Mr MacDowell. Her submerged thoughts reveal that she knows generally where he lives ('the gentleman off Sandymount green') and that he actually bears a certain resemblance to her own father ('the man that was so like himself'). (The Irishism that identifies 'himself' as the dominant male in the household also doubles as a self-reflexive, emphasising the firm individuality of that anonymous 'gentleman'.) In her comparison with Mr̩ MacDowell, Gerty seems to assume that the mystery man is a sober citizen ('You never saw him any way screwed'), yet her traditional loyalties, reinforced by the moral tone of her apparent reading matter, will not allow her to displace her own father: 'but still and for all that she would not like him for a father because he was too old or something or on account of his face (it was a palpable case of Doctor Fell) or his carbuncly nose with the pimples on it and his sandy moustache a bit white under his nose' (Na 307–11). Gerty's reading material fails her when sordid reality becomes so obtrusive – except of course for the 'literary' Doctor Fell – and she abandons 'fiction' for the obvious ('Poor father!'). But through the back door pre-formulated sentimentality returns as a buffer ('With all his faults she loved him still'

Na 311–12). Gerty proves to be realistically graphic in her descriptions where Bloom had sought to establish social condition and daily habit, as much conditioned by his reading as she is by hers.

The gentleman-nobleman (Gerty apparently does not know his name either) passes by twice observed and then vanishes into hypothesis, only to resurface in the most fictional of fictions as an emanation in 'Circe', one of at least four score of pursuers collectively designated as 'THE HUE AND CRY' (Ci 4362), one of the tailend in the pursuit and as '*the mystery man on the beach*' one of the substantial minority of the unnamed, along with such 'mystery men' as:

> *65 C, 66 C, night watch . . . the Nameless One . . . the Citizen . . . Whodoyoucallhim, Strangeface, Fellowthatsolike, Sawhimbefore, Chapwithawen . . . the Westland Row postmistress . . . friend of Lyons . . . maninthestreet, othermaninthestreet, Footballboots, pugnosed driver, rich protestant lady . . . handsomemarriedwomanrubbedagainstwidebehindinClonskeatram, the bookseller of* Sweets of Sin, *Miss Dubedatandshedidbedad . . . the managing clerk of Drimmie's . . . the constable off Eccles street corner . . . the mystery man on the beach, a retriever, Mrs Miriam Dandrade and all her lovers.* (Ci 4336–61)

The degrees of anonymity and the conditions of marginality almost seem to be unlimited in this catalogue. Mystery 'men' are also women (as well as a dog), and even their individualities are hardly sacrosanct since the numerical indeterminancy exists in the fact that there is no indication of how many lovers Mrs Dandrade had – or has. Some of the unnamed have prior existences in the narrative (and one will have a subsequent existence in 'Ithaca'), while others are only present when tabulated as a corporate part of the Hue and Cry. Any single hypothetical man-in-the-street usually stands alone as the representative of all such, a metaphorical counter, yet the immediate addition of the 'other' man-in-the-street reduces him to the status of anonymous anonymity. On the other hand, the handsome married woman contains within her compound designation a narrative event that can be recuperated in terms of her looks, marital condition, physique, as well as contact with Bloom in a specific location, establishing her momentarily as a character vitally present in a Bloomian fiction.

OF MACKINTOSHES AND MEN

At least two of the unnamed have potent presences in *Ulysses*, those Outis-surrogates of 'Cyclops', the Citizen and the Nameless One, their nameless conditions in these instances hardly connoting marginality. Yet the Hue and Cry is as interesting for its exclusions as it is for those included: no member of the Bloom or Dedalus families, and no Blazes Boylan. And, considering his marginal relationship to Bloom, the absence of that major mystery man, the Man in the Macintosh, proves to be a tantalising mystery in its own right. Bloom had made the immediate association of one mysterious figure with another when he parallels his nobleman with 'that fellow today at the graveside in the brown macintosh' (Na 1061–2). Bloom's interest in the Man in the Macintosh remains minimal compared to the attention given that marginal character by generations of Joyce critics, who have variously identified him in terms of Joyce's previous fiction (the James Duffy of 'A Painful Case'), literally Joyce himself, symbolically as Death and 13 and Christ at the Last Supper, metaphorically as the Irish poet James Clarence Mangan, mystically as the personification of invisibility (akin to Turko the Terrible, '*the boy / That can enjoy / Invisibility*' – Te 260–2), spiritually as the Dear Departed, the Walking Dead. Despite his reappearances in *Ulysses* 'M' (let M stand for the Man in the Macintosh) is never available for a close-up, to be seen with pimples and carbuncles and all. What seems most certain about Mister M'Intosh is that his name is not M'Intosh, although possibly with less certainty than that the name of the boy in 'An Encounter' is not Smith – pseudonyms are assumed in order to disguise one's real name, but the accidental naming of M'Intosh is a matter of superimposition – all names are impostures.

Bloom himself expounds on the mysteriousness of this quintessential mystery man in the first encounter: 'Now who is that lankylooking galoot over there in the macintosh? Now who is he I'd like to know? Now I'd give a trifle to know who he is. Always someone turns up you never dreamt of' (Ha 805–7). Except for his unusual garb M is characterised only by Bloom's choice of descriptive epithets (a 'lankylooking galoot'), and Joe Hynes, the journalist who will finally create the fiction-out-of-facts, does nothing to expand the dossier on M when he asks, 'do you know that fellow in the, fellow was over there in the . . .' (Ha 891–2). By presenting Bloom with a blank space to fill in, Hynes contributes as the author of the obfuscation, the false name of the unnameable. 'Hades' is a repository of vague directions and unrecognised identities, and Hynes's casual 'over there' echoes references to several graves and gravesites: Simon Dedalus was equally unspecific when he referred to his wife's final resting place ('Her grave is over there' – Ha 645), as is Bloom about his own plot ('mine over there towards Finglas, the plot I bought' – Ha 862). Bloom himself is mysteriously unknown to John Henry Mention ('Who is that chap behind with Tom Kernan?' – Ha 690), and he has his own momentary lapse in identifying the brother-in-law of the deceased ('Who is that beside them? Ah, the brother-in-law' – Ha 524). That he does not know Bernard Corrigan's name until he reads it in the newspaper account provides one of the annoying minor mysteries of *Ulysses*. The process of giving identity to the temporarily unidentified (discovering Bernard Corrigan) is a norm in the fictional sequence, as are the less frequent norms of correcting false identifications (Ikey Moses revealed as Leopold Bloom) or of tracking the changes of names for the same identity (for Rudolf Virag read Rudolph Bloom). What Bloom has unwittingly done for M may result in gratituitous obfuscation, but he had already done the same for himself quite calculatingly in providing a covering pseudonym (Henry Flower as mask for Leopold Bloom).

That M stands in proximate relationship to Bloom becomes apparent when Bloom shifts an uncomfortable weight from himself on to the lankylooking galoot: 'Twelve. I'm thirteen. No. The chap in the macintosh is thirteen. Death's number. Where the deuce did he pop out of? He wasn't in the chapel, that I'll swear. Silly superstition that about thirteen' (Ha 825–7). As the thirteenth letter of the alphabet M'Intosh's 'M' will soon show its propensity for disappearance, an act of momentary erasure effected by Bloom himself when presented with the Elijah throwaway in Lestrygonians:

> Bloo.... Me? No.
> Blood of the Lamb.   (Le 8–9)

M's inexplicable appearance, however, is augmented by his equally inexplicable disappearance, as Hynes's '*was* over there' already implied and as Bloom immediately perceives: 'What? Where has he disappeared to? Not a sign. Well of all the. Has anyone here seen? Kay ee double ell. Become invisible. Good Lord, what became of him?' (Ha 899–901). With the absence of Kelly–M'Intosh the mourners at the graveside are reduced to a safe twelve, and Hynes's inflated piece of journalistic invention will expand them to an equally safe fifteen. But in that account Bloom suffers the loss of a letter from his name, 'L', the twelfth letter of the alphabet. And he had been so specific about that letter when providing Hynes with his initial:

> – I am just taking the names, Hynes said below his breath. What is your christian name? I'm not sure.
> – L, Mr Bloom said. Leopold.   (Ha 880–2)

'Leopold' never makes it into the newspaper listing, and Bloom finds himself near the tail end, initialled rather than christian-named, as the depleted 'L. Boom' (Eu 1260) – no 'double ell'. Bloom as 'author' has the function of naming the characters created, real or imaginary, and had already compounded a dual 'L. M. Bloom' (Ca 518) – two Ls and two Ms.

Appearance/disappearance/reappearance: at the end of 'Wandering Rocks' M 'returns' as one more such wanderer in the busy city, not just one of thirteen but one out of the entire male population of the city of Dublin: 'In Lower Mount street a pedestrian in a brown macintosh, eating dry bread, passed swiftly and unscathed across the viceroy's path' (WR 1271–2), defying death. (Only a few streets back the son of the dead Paddy Dignam had saluted the viceregal procession.) Now M's macintosh is described for the first time as 'brown', and although no further description of the man is presented, his behaviour opens the possibilities of his demented state of mind and the depleted state of his finances: the way he feeds himself and his unheeding passage in front of the hooves of the horses identify him as one of life's unfortunates, a poor looney, not unlike the Cashel Boyle O'Connor Fitzmaurice Tisdall Farrell who has also just been within hailing distance of the cavalcade, ignoring it to stare 'through a fierce eyeglass across the carriages' (WR 1261–2). But it also puts M again within proximate relationship to Bloom, who – although solvent and sane – will admit in 'Ithaca' that at the 'Nadir of misery' he sees himself as 'the aged impotent disfranchised ratesupported moribund lunatic pauper' (It 1946–7). M's presence at the grave of someone he may not even have known (unknown to his fellow-morners he hardly can be verified as having a real relationship to the dead Dignam), and his manner of crossing Lower Mount street, suggest a certain aimlessness to his wanderings through Dublin, so that he conveniently falls into the classification of the demented vagabond, a corrolary for Farrell and Denis Breen.

In 'Sirens' Bloom corroborates that M's macintosh was indeed brown when he was seen at the cemetery. He also now seems to be assuming that M was mentally defective, as he mulls over the situation of the Croppy Boy and the British Officer disguised as a priest: 'Breathe a prayer, drop a tear. All the same he must have been a bit of a natural not to see it was a yeoman cap. Muffled up. Wonder who was that chap at the grave in the brown macin' (Si 1248–50). The association with 'Muffled up' and with 'a bit of a natural' seems to lead Bloom's thoughts from 'The Croppy Boy' to M, and yet Bloom himself may have been deficient in his powers of observation at the time, so obsessed with M's powers of apparition and disappearance that he registered no interest at the time about his state of mind or the colour of his coat.

When M makes his third and final appearance – in the flesh – he provokes a lively discussion among the drinkers at Burke's pub, apparently having passed the open door within sight of Bloom and others. The sighting of M is captured in a confusion of conversation (the ten from the lying-in hospital have now mingled with the other customers, and there is no precise way of telling how many of these are actually engaged in the particular talk that surrounds the noticing of a man in a macintosh, or what adjacent conversations intrude):

Golly, whatten tunket's yon guy in the mackintosh? Dusty Rhodes. Peep at his wearables. By mighty! What's he got? Jubilee mutton. Bovril, by James. Wants it real bad. D'ye ken bare socks? Seedy cuss in the Richmond? Rawthere! Thought he had a deposit of lead in his penis. Trumpery insanity. Bartle the Bread we calls him. That, sir, was once a prosperous cit. Man all tattered and torn that married a maiden all forlorn. Slung her hook, she did. Here see lost love. Walking Mackintosh of lonely canyon. Tuck and turn in. Schedule time. Nix for the hornies. Pardon? See him today at a runefal?   (OS 1546–54)

Bloom rather belatedly identifies this particular vagrant as the one he saw at Dignam's funeral, and this is apparently only the second time that he has seen his disappearing mystery figure. Is there sufficient reason to assume that Bloom can be positive in his identification, or does the chance glimpse of a macintosh and the talk of the medical students about a lunatic at the Richmond hospital cause him to draw an approximate – but not necessarily exact – conclusion?

The nature of the cross-purpose conversation(s) is enough for the basic verification of the macintosh, and commentary on his other peculiar clothes, yet neither Bloom nor Hynes in broad daylight had bothered to comment on any other aspect of M's 'wearables'. (Journalist Hynes could not even have registered the existence of a macintosh coat if he allowed himself to 'accept' the name of M'Intosh.) The undernourished look of the tramp elicits comment among the medical students, and if he is indeed a known looney that they have named 'Bartle the Bread', the association with the eater of dry bread in 'Wandering Rocks' seems to have been obliquely confirmed. The medicals, however, seem actually to be talking about someone else that they know from the Richmond for whom this vagabond is only a corrolary. In any case they are confident of their diagnosis: sexual frustrations and grief due to the death (or desertion) of the man's wife, and a consequent decline from once having been a prosperous citizen. An anticipation of this condition can be found in the 'love list' contained in the intrusive narrative commentary in 'Cyclops': 'The man in the brown macintosh loves a lady who is dead' (Cy 1496–7). A particular case history has taken sufficient shape as the medical students piece together their evidence, but the link with Bloom's macintosh-man remains tenuous, and the possibility of two men in macintoshes roaming the streets of Dublin exists as an alternative possibility. As long as the medicals resort to their own naming code (Dusty Rhodes, Bartle the Bread), there is no assurance of the singular existence of a verifiable M.

The major burden of proof is with Bloom, who cannot be relied on to identify accurately someone in a dark doorway after a lapse of almost half a day, when the sole garment of notice is a macintosh, a common enough item in Dublin, although perhaps not on a sunny day in June during a period of drought. Malachi Mulligan and Alex Bannon have had their clothes drenched that evening, since like most sane Dubliners they had brought no protection against rain, while the parallel looney, C. B. O'C. F. T. Farrell, tramps the sunny streets of Dublin with a dustcoat and umbrella.

M's afterlife in *Ulysses* consists of three variations: in 'Circe' he is conjured up as a nemesis for Bloom, appearing suddenly and as suddenly disappearing; in 'Eumaeus' he accompanies L. *Boom* as a newspaper item, *M'Intosh*, in uncomfortable proximity, with only the non-appearing C. P. *M'Coy* interceding (Eu 1260–1); and in 'Ithaca' he persists as a 'selfinvolved enigma' for Bloom, 'Who was M'Intosh?' – at the moment when he is 'gathering' up Molly's 'multicoloured multiform multitudinous garments' (It 2063–6). The shift from the query in 'Sirens' ('Wonder who was that chap at the grave in the brown macin' – Si 1250) to the one in 'Ithaca' ('Who was M'Intosh?') has been occasioned by the appearance in print of the M'Intosh name, which although it has been spoken by Bloom to Hynes had not then registered for Bloom as a proper name rather than a common noun. Bloom knows categorically not to accept the misnomer, yet the power of the fiction, the word in print, the imposing of a name, results in his subliminal acceptance of a 'M'Intosh'. For Bloom, M always exists in the past tense, although he must be aware that M lives on (evidence of the second sighting): his natural habitat is the cemetery where Bloom had first seen him and where he therefore has his fictional locus. In writing the history of M's mysterious moment, as throughout his effort to 'capture' the visit to Glasnevin, Bloom shows himself to be a rather inept author: he does not know all of the characters, lacks the vocabulary for the items of ecclesiastical use, and is even the subject of a conversation that he himself cannot overhear. Whereas he can remain objective about the presumably solvent nobleman on the beach, he harbours ambivalent feelings about the lunatic pauper, distancing him from himself and relegating him into a mystery in the past tense.

The Circean format allows for a wholesale infusion of the past into the activated present, fictional past as potent as any factual past, the improbable displacing the possible, with extended versions of the impossible as well. 'Circe' operates by association with a Murphy's Law (what's in a name?) that anything that *can* go wrong *will* go wrong, while those things that *cannot* go wrong very well *might* (Murphy's Second Law). Miraculously transformed into an exalted and revered Lord Mayor of Dublin, Bloom is suddenly confronted with a voluble detractor who appears quite unexpectedly among the throng of admirers:

(*A man in a brown macintosh springs up through a trapdoor. He points an elongated finger at Bloom.*)

The Man in the Macintosh

Don't you believe a word he says. That man is Leopold M'Intosh, the notorious fireraiser. His real name is Higgins.

Bloom

Shoot him! Dog of a christian! So much for M'Intosh!

(*A cannonshot. The man in the macintosh disappears. . . .*)
(Ci 1558–65)

Most of the associations here are dependent on validated information from within the existing text: Bloom's 'christian' name and his mother's christianised maiden name ('Ellen Higgins' – It 536) work themselves into the pattern with the misnamed M'Intosh (an inadvertent Bloomian invention in the first place). Bloom's tolerant and pacifistic attitudes are violently reversed, and the miraculous appearances and disappearances (rising up from trapdoors and being shot out of cannons) are prosaically explained by the mechanics of the theatre and circus, the known territories of Bloom's interests and experiences, settling the mystery of his emanations. And the self-reflexive aspects of the correspondences in 'Circe' – every face that Bloom confronts returns to him a facet of himself – allow for the transfer of the M'Intosh name back and forth between Bloom and M, but only now that Bloom has seen the funeral account in the *Evening Telegraph*.

Of all the accusations lodged against Bloom in 'Circe', almost all of them somehow seem to adhere as reflected in his own sensations of guilt (the 'facts' in the case). The accusation by M of 'fireraising', however, seems gratuitous (an unnecessary 'fiction'), just one more thing to blame on Bloom. On the face of it, it can be dismissed as the wild words of a lunatic, the 'Trumpery insanity' so blithely pronounced by one of the medical students at Burke's pub. But no sooner was the looney in the macintosh seen outside the pub than time was called and the assembled customers ushered out. Once outside they hear the sound of fire engines roaring by:

Hark! Shut your obstropolos. Pflaap! Pflaap! Blaze on. There she goes. Brigade! Bout ship. Mount street way. Cut up! Pflaap! Tally ho. You not come? Run, skelter, race. Pflaaaap!   (OS 1569–71)

Bloom does not join the fire brigade chasers ('You not come?'), but it is unlikely that it was he who was invited rather than the others who hold back, Stephen and Lynch. He might well have reacted to 'Blaze on' as close to the name that he has resisted saying at any time during the day, but it provides a bridge with the possibility that it is Blazes's house that is ablaze. The subliminal association of M with the fire may be enough to account for the accusation of Bloom as a 'notorious fireraiser', especially since there is also an association existing between M and Mount street ('In Lower Mount street a pedestrian in a brown macintosh'). That Bloom was nowhere near the scene of that incident at that time might disqualify him from the association for a reader who insists on a 'factual' text governed by a controlling narrational presence. For the reader of the fictive text in which conversations take place behind Bloom's back that he is not privy to and certain events are privileged to which he was not a witness, there exists an interplay between what Bloom (or for that matter Stephen) can apprehend in their existences as characters and what defies them by 'appearing' from the confusing realm of the possible. Stephen Dedalus as the potential observer of the totality of possibilities had outlined the process early in the day, not just as he viewed that process but as it might exist:

> Open your eyes now. I will. One moment. Has all vanished since? If I open and am for ever in the black adiaphane. *Basta!* I will see if I can see.
>
> See now. There all the time without you: and ever shall be, world without end.   (Pr 25–8)

The Blazes name that Bloom so assiduously avoids pops up in his thoughts uninvited (as M had popped up at the grave) when the fire recurs at the opening of 'Circe' – following upon its origins at the end of 'Oxen of the Sun', which had to have taken place sufficiently back to allow for Bloom to get to Nighttown. Despite the elision of time Bloom's entrance into Mabbot street is immediately preceded by the 'presence' of the fire he had avoided earlier: '*A glow leaps in the south beyond the seaward reaches of the river*' (Ci 139–40). Bloom prefers to ignore the sign and retreats into Rabaiotti's and Olhousen's shops to buy food. When finally forced to see the glow, he remains tenacious in his determination not to acknowledge its origins. But '*The glow leaps again*' (Ci 165), and at first he

wonders, 'What is that? A flasher? Searchlight', until he apparently
concedes that his explanations are inadequate and probably disingenuous. He tries again – '*Aurora borealis* or a steel foundry?' – until
he must admit what he has probably known all along: 'Ah, the
brigade, of course. South side anyhow. Big blaze. Might be his
house. Beggar's bush. We're safe. (*he hums cheerfully*) London's
burning, London's burning! On fire, on fire!' (Ci 167–72). Having
assured himself by noting the location of the fire that his own
house is safe (that is the house that is his and Molly's), he can delight in the speculation that Boylan's house may be ablaze, mentally slaying the suitor (in relative innocence) but leaving himself
open to the accusation of being himself the 'notorious fireraiser'.

'TELEGRAPHIC LIES'

Although 'Circe' creates far more mysteries than it resolves, at least
for Bloom there is a suspicion that the mystery about M no longer
has anything to do with his ability to appear and disappear at will:
stage machinery has prosaically accounted for 'Where the deuce
did he pop out of' (Ha 826). His identity, however, persists as a
minor mystery for Bloom into the small hours of the morning,
although he is literal in only willing to give a 'trifle' to know (an
example of the Uncle Charles Principle doubling back on itself). To
Hynes, for whom Bloom and M are logically associated, Bloom is 'a
bloody dark horse himself' (Cy 1558), and he certainly is a source of
some speculation to many a Dubliner (Menton, Lenehan, Nosey
Flynn, Davy Byrne, *et al.*): 'Is he a jew or a gentile or a holy Roman
or a swaddler or what the hell is he?' Ned Lambert asks, adding,
'Or who is he?' (Cy 1631–2). Bloom cannot help knowing that the
question exists and that it lingers constantly in the air, but in quite
a different context he remembers his school days, 'Apjohn, myself
and Owen Goldberg up in the trees near Goose green playing the
monkeys. Mackerel they called me' (Le 404–5): is the implication
that his classmates assumed he was Catholic, even though 'To
Master Percy Apjohn at High School in 1880 he had divulged his
disbelief in the tenets of the Irish (protestant) church' (It 1635–6)?
Do his Jewish classmates assume that because he is 'different' that
he is Catholic, or do his Protestant classmates assume because of
that difference that he is Catholic? Bloom's own recollection of the

'slur' is nostalgic rather than painful: in 'Circe' all the High School friends (including Goldberg and Apjohn), collectively known as 'THE HALCYON DAYS', celebrate Master Leopold Bloom by cheering, 'Mackerel! Live us again! Hurray!' (Ci 3330–1).

Bloom is as curious about others as they are about him, yet the identity of a Dublin culprit of some magnitude fails to excite his curiosity – the author of the postcard to Denis Breen. With all of Dublin to choose from, or at least all of the adult male population likely to perpetrate the offence, he quickly narrows down the possibilities to a mere two: 'I'll take my oath that's Alf Bergan or Richie Goulding' (Le 320). Bloom's method of elimination could hardly satisfy a scientific detective like Sherlock Holmes (when scrutinising ablebodied seaman Murphy, Bloom can be quite intensive in 'taking stock of the individual in front of him and Sherlockholmesing him up' – Eu 830–1), but the problem that is of such personal concern to Breen himself is negligible to Bloom, who remains less interested in the pathetic husband than in the all-suffering wife. Those who enjoy the joke of an enraged Breen intent on suing the perpetrator never question the nature of the message (the meaning to them somehow seems agreed and 'fixed') nor do they bother to speculate on the sender – they readily understand the author to be someone very much like themselves, one of their own, while Bloom understands him to be one of the 'others', unlike himself. To Bloom it is not the particular *individual* in this case that concerns him, as much as the *type*, that typical prankster who spends much of his time in pubs and is capable of so trivial a lark. In expansively offering to swear as a witness and even place a bet, the cautious Bloom extends himself (at least metaphorically) in full confidence, yet does not bother to make the choice between Bergan or Goulding for an indictment.

The postcard itself remains an enigma, all the more so since nowhere in *Ulysses* is its message explicated, and no one seems in the least concerned with establishing its 'meaning'. The assumption that those involved (sender, receiver, receiver's wife and all who have been vouchsafed a glimpse of the card or orally presented with its wording) are confident that the letters and the words in their particular semantic construction are universally understood, and that Breen has every reason – even if he were a totally sane person – to be offended (lunatic interpretation parallels logical interpretation, what is insulting to the insane is equally insulting to the sane). Yet only once is the reader present when the card is openly displayed: Mrs Breen shows it to Bloom, whose 'reading' of it produces an interrogative 'U. P.?' (Le 257). The convention of printed texts conceals as much as is revealed, and Mrs Breen's rejoinder to Bloom's question is 'U. p: up, she said' (Le 258). Is her 'up' a supplemental explication or is Bloom's 'U. P.' a condensed form, vocally avoiding the repetition contained in the message? All subsequent versions of the concise 'text' perpetuate the duplication, either because all four letters are actually there on the card or because the formula for reading-cum-explicating expands the two existing letters into four. In a conventional mystery-thriller the text might have provided a facsimile of the original, but Joyce's narrative methods in *Ulysses* subsumes the postcard into the fabric of the verbal intercourse between the characters. All subsequent transmissions in *Ulysses* duplicate Mrs Breen's four-lettered version, with some minor variations (and even the variations in the Joyce manuscripts and the numerous editions of the book are inconsequential), so that the accepted reading seems to be: You Pee Up! The convention determined by Joyce for Molly's night thoughts, innocent of almost all punctuation, causes still another variation in the somewhat simplified 'U p up' (Pe 229), which allows for the same pronunciation and the assumption that Molly acknowledges the urinary allusion, no matter what the culprit 'intended'.

But the 'U p up' of the Gabler-edited text may be merely a 'normalization', a cutting of the Gordian knot, and what exists in most pre-Gabler editions is a far more succinct and overly simplified 'up up', so that we are left to wonder what sort of communication existed between Bloom and Molly when he orally informed her of the contents of the postcard. This 'version' denudes the message of any scurrilous implications, merely repeating the innocent word 'up', and Molly may be underplaying its potent significance because of faulty comprehension. (Perhaps Bloom again failed to tell a story successfully.) There is nothing in Molly's thoughts on the subject of the message sent to Breen that in any way indicates that she even bothers to understand, much less interpret, its import, supporting the contention that the pre-Gabler version is consistent with the narrative context. Molly's thoughts on Breen are all of a consistent development, unchanged by the intrusion of the postcard incident:

I wonder what shes got like now living with that dotty husband of hers ... what was it she told me O yes that sometimes he used to go to bed with his muddy boots on when the maggot takes him just imagine having to get into bed with a thing like that that might murder you any moment what a man well its not the one way everyone goes mad ... and now hes going about in his slippers to look for £10000 for a postcard U p up O sweetheart May wouldnt a thing like that simply bore you stiff to extinction actually too stupid even to take his boots off now what could you make of a man like that.   (Pe 217–31)

Molly may have taken in the significance of the message and chosen to ignore it, maintaining her own perspective on the situation, focusing on the primary condition of the receiver, the dottiness of the husband, as her mind fixes on the absurdity of the muddy boots in bed. What to Breen is an actionable offence, and to his wife a 'great shame' (Le 258), and to Bergan a side-splitting lark, is to Bloom only a minor mystery, and to Molly apparently no mystery at all.

Both Bloom and Stephen display a tendency to create and transmit cryptic messages during the course of 16 June 1904. Stephen's telegram to Mulligan had been sent just after noon as an elliptical indication that he himself would not be joining Mulligan and Haines at half-past twelve to stand them drinks. When Buck catches up with the elusive Stephen, he brandishes the telegram and presents most of the available facts: the message, the signator, the addressee, the address, the source:

He sat on a corner of the unlit desk, reading aloud joyfully:
– *The sentimentalist is he who would enjoy without incurring the immense debtorship for a thing done.* Signed: Dedalus. Where did you launch it from? The kips? No. College Green.... Telegram! Malachi Mulligan, The Ship, lower Abbey street. O, you peerless mummer! O, you priestified Kinchite!   (SC 549–5)

The moment of Stephen's decision to defect, however, remains unspecified, since some time after 11 a.m. he still seems to be intent on keeping the appointment, repeating to himself Mulligan's words ('And after? The Ship, half twelve' – Pr 58–9). Lost somewhere in the gap between 'Proteus' and 'Aeolus', between the realisation that he has not stopped at the house of his Aunt Sara and the piecing together of the Parable of the Plums, occurred the idea of substituting the message for his presence. Whether Mulligan reads the message as an accusation or an apologia, whether the sentimentalist is intended as Mulligan or Stephen himself, remains unknown; whether he recognises the quotation as deriving from George Meredith cannot be determined from any comment he makes in 'Scylla and Charybdis'. Not until 'Oxen of the Sun' does the telegram re-deliver itself, when Buck once again has access to Stephen. In the library Mulligan became carried away with his own rhetoric, as 'Joyfully he thrust message and envelope into a pocket' (SC 556), complaining about being left high and dry – in his parody of Synge's style: 'And we to be there, mavrone, and you to be unbeknownst sending us your conglomerations the way we to have our tongues out a yard long' (SC 564–5). Thereafter, he is busy reading another text, one that was not intended for him, Bloom's calling card. Not until Burke's pub does he turn on Stephen and declare, 'Mummer's wire. Cribbed out of Meredith' (OS 1486). Determining the 'real' signator gives Mulligan his moment of triumph, in effect shearing Stephen of his power, emasculating him ('Jesified orchidised polycimical jesuit!' – OS 1486–7). In the library he immediately accused Stephen of wearing a mask as a mummer, but in the interim he may have learned the source of the quotation and realised the Meredith mask that Stephen had assumed as well, further distancing himself from Buck Mulligan.

Stephen's 'messages' are the most cryptic when entirely internalised, away from the lancet of Mulligan's art, as when he mentally manipulates the vowels of the alphabet, transmitting a silent avowal of his financial debt to George Russell ('A.E.I.O.U.'). The actual amount in 'Nestor' is an unadorned 'Russell, one guinea' (Ne 257), sandwiched in among other debts and debtors, but is unaccountably reduced in 'Scylla and Charybdis' to 'that pound he lent you' (SC 192). Russell is no longer a name on a list but present in the library with Stephen, and it is Russell himself who (unintentionally?) introduces the subject when he dismisses the kind of critical speculation that concerns itself with 'The poet's drinking, the poet's debts' (SC 187–8). Of the five vowels of the alphabet the primary one for Stephen is 'I', the indicator for the first-person singular that designates himself to himself, and he compounds aspects of himself in time into a double set of selves, past and present, child and adult, augmented into a subtle trinity in which the recent self is none the less distanced from the present self:

You owe it.
 Wait. Five months. Molecules all change. I am other I now.
Other I got pound.
 Buzz. Buzz.
 But I, entelechy, form of forms, am I by memory because
under everchanging forms.
 I that sinned and prayed and fasted.
 A child Conmee saved from pandies.
 I, I and I. I.
 A.E.I.O.U. (SC 203–13)

The message of 'AE, I owe you' only works in the typography of
the *Ulysses* text if George Russell's pen name is printed as the
initials A.E., rather than the digraph that is usually transcribed as a
ligature, and the A.E. remains consistently so throughout, conveniently constant because Bloom happens to assume that they are
initials: 'the eminent poet A.E. (Mr Geo. Russell)' (Le 332).
 Stephen had earlier jotted down on the bottom part of a page of
Deasy's letter to the press a quantrain of poetry as he composed it
there on Sandymount strand, another document never displayed
to the reader of *Ulysses* in facsimile, but incorporated instead into
the text of 'Aeolus', where Stephen recalls it (from the missing
portion of Deasy's letter, 'reading' by memory, an absent text, a
blank). His presence on the strand that morning establishes
Stephen also as a Mystery Man on the Beach, and for a brief instant
he leaves his mark in the transitory sands:

He stood suddenly, his feet beginning to sink slowly in the
quaking soil. Turn back.
 Turning, he scanned the shore south, his feet sinking again
slowly in new sockets. (Pr 268–71)

Had those footprints remained extant for any length of time, they
might have stood as a personal message, as in *Robinson Crusoe* or
the Sherlock Holmes stories (in the sixty tales there is only one use
of a fingerprint as a clue, but dozens of footmarks). But the implication in 'Proteus' of the 'quaking soil' leaves little doubt that no
message will survive for the next stroller on the strand to read, nor
does Stephen, who is apprehensive of fixing himself permanently
in Irish soil, dare to allow himself to sink in too deeply. Ten hours
later Leopold Bloom, resting for a while on Sandymount strand, is

totally unaware of any residual presence of the young man who at that place had contemplated 'Signatures of all things I am here to read' (Pr 2). Bloom in his own way also muses on the 'Limits of the diaphane' (Pr 4) as he recalls the mnemonic device of an anagram he had learned at school for the colours of the rainbow: 'Roygbiv Vance taught us: red, orange, yellow, green, blue, indigo, violet' (Na 1075–6) – Bloom's seven colours parallel Stephen's five vowels. The coincidence of Sandymount strand (Stephen in the morning, Bloom in the evening) depends on both of them alone and 'in transit' (Stephen between his awakening in Sandycove and his trek into Dublin, Bloom at the furthest point from his locus in Dublin), pausing to read the landscape and its personal message for them and to record into their own 'writing' what they have read.

The piece that Stephen tore from the Deasy letter has its analogue in a piece of paper that Bloom finds on the beach. Bloom does not anticipate a message, but rather hopes that the paper is a banknote:

What's that? Might be money.
    Mr Bloom stooped and turned over a piece of paper on the strand. He brought it near his eyes and peered. Letter? No. Can't read. . . . Page of an old copybook. All those holes and pebbles. Who could count them? Never know what you find. Bottle with story of a treasure in it, thrown from a wreck. Parcels post. Children always want to throw things in the sea.   (Na 1244–51)

The childhood text that Stephen read in the sand ('child Conmee saved from pandies') has little applicability for Bloom, whose basic concept of self exists in the adult presence, since unlike Stephen he *has* always paid his way, without recourse to borrowing from others, and he carries no list of creditors in his mind.

As the putative author of *The Mystery Man on the Beach* Bloom is still intent on 'writing', and he even contemplates leaving a message for Gerty MacDowell. His letters to Martha Clifford had been written as a lure, but with the intention of avoiding a meeting with her, yet with Gerty that apprehension is no longer there: he has been 'seen' by her and obviously admired, so that he can at least contemplate the possibility of a rendezvous. Toward that end a piece of stick presents itself once he discards the piece of paper:

Will she come here tomorrow? Wait for her somewhere for ever. Must come back. Murderers do. Will I.

Mr Bloom with his stick gently vexed the thick sand at his foot.
Write a message for her. Might remain. What?
I.
Some flatfoot tramp on it in the morning. Useless. Washed
away. Tide comes here. Saw a pool near her foot. Bend, see my
face there, dark mirror, breathe on it, stirs. All these rocks with
lines and scars and letters. O, those transparent! Besides they
don't know. What is the meaning of that other world. I called
you naughty boy because I do not like.
AM. A.
No room. Let it go.
Mr Bloom effaced the letters with his slow boot.   (Na 1253–66)

The incomplete message stands as a paradigm of *Ulysses*, a text of
such intimate revelations delving deep into the thinking processes
of Stephen and Bloom and Molly that none the less leaves some of
their most important thoughts unrecorded. The constant rush of
thoughts that they engender and generate fill numerous crevices,
but leave isolated eddies of possibility untouched. The mysteries of
Ulysses persist in the lacunae created by the confluence of inter-
involved narrative flows.

'I. AM. A.': the shape of the particular lacuna may also be
deceptive, although most readers of *Ulysses* have assumed that a
single noun would be sufficient to supply the quantity to fill
Bloom's gap, the 'A' standing as the indefinite article. The mysterious word left untranscribed in the Sandymount sands, therefore, transmutes the question into an overwhelming one: Bloom
alone under the stars at a transcendental moment should reveal the
essence of his existence, the depths of his soul, the word known to
all men – if they but knew it. Such questions are usually expected
of Stephen rather than Bloom, and during his dalliance at Sandymount he had addressed a hypothetical paramour, asking, 'What
is that word known to all men? I am quiet here alone' (Pr 435), and
in 'Circe' he reiterates the question to the ghost of May Dedalus:
'Tell me the word, mother, if you know now. The word known to
all men' (Ci 4192–3). Although Mrs Dedalus as ghost is effusive
with words, she deflects the interview away from Stephen's
demand of a single word to encompass the mysterious but
monumental concept. One assumes that Bloom knows the particular word that he intends to place in the predicate, yet there is no
evidence that he does; he may have been waiting for an inspiration

when he despaired of ever getting his message recorded. No particular clue, but a tantalising area of possibility, derives for his recollection of a 'wrong' word, that of 'world' for 'word' in Martha's message. Any such lapsus could also affect the transmission of the word presumably known to all men.

Few investigators of the text are content merely to guess at the intended word (the presumed message to Gerty), and extend the possibility to the disclosure of a Bloomian secret of self-identification. Consequently, the sentence is conjecturally completed to *define* Leopold Bloom, in universal terms, or in terms of his masculinity (I am a man/Man), or in terms of his much-overlaid heritage (I am a Jew), or – assuming that the ultimate letter is not the indefinite article but the first letter of the next word – in terms of his state of isolation (I am alone – Stephen had under similar circumstances confessed to being 'quite here alone'). One can even assume that this statement marks his recent humiliation (I am a cuckold) or a confession of guilt (I am ashamed), which returns the considerations to the literal situation: Leopold Bloom addressing Gerty MacDowell. If his intention, at least temporarily, is to leave a message for her that she could read and act upon – a thoroughly ordinary and even practical communication – he might be arranging a future tryst (I am at . . .). But what would he offer as a trysting place: his Westland Row postal address? In which case, the message reads, 'I am anonymous' – a non-message impermanently planted in sand so that not even the flat feet of a Stephen Dedalus could tramp on it in the morning. Bloom has guaranteed, at least for this day, a safe trysting place for Molly and Boylan, and he himself remains displaced, transient, rootless (I am a wanderer).

For a rooted Dubliner Bloom has his Ulyssean analogue in the rootless Dubliner, the mariner encountered in the cabman's shelter. Murphy is intent on establishing his identity through documentation: 'Paid off this afternoon. There's my discharge. See? D. B. Murphy. A. B. S.' (Eu 451–2). That discharge paper should have settled matters, but Murphy is an odd mixture of self-assurance and unease, constantly attempting to prove himself as a fixed identity. In effect he has managed to challenge the identity of Stephen's father, positing a Simon Dedalus who could 'shoot two eggs off two bottles at fifty yards over his shoulder' (Eu 389), hardly the Simon Dedalus that Stephen is expected to recognise as his father. The second document he produces is intended to authenticate his experience with cannibals rather than identify himself, yet

it proves to be self-incriminating as an unreliable text: it is a
postcard and 'The printed matter on it stated: *Choza de Indios. Beni,
Bolivia*' (Eu 474). Bloom applies his 'sherlockholmesing' method as
he 'unostentatiously turned over the card to peruse the partially
obliterated address and postmark. It ran as follows: *Tarjeta Postal,
Señor A Boudin, Galeria Becche, Santiago, Chile*. There was no
message evidently, as he took particular notice' (Eu 487–90).
Bloom's analysis is meticulous for a while, but it soon bogs down
in self-interest, in his own concern with being the Ulysses-mariner
making his own odyssey:

> having detected a discrepancy between his name (assuming he
> was the person he represented himself to be and not sailing
> under false colours after having boxed the compass on the strict
> q.t. somewhere) and the fictitious addressee of the missive
> which made him nourish some suspicions of our friend's *bona
> fides* nevertheless it reminded him of a longcherished plan he
> meant to one day realise some Wednesday or Saturday of
> travelling to London *via* long sea.   (Eu 494–501)

Murphy has produced one piece of documentary evidence too
many, engendering the mystery that his first document was
intended to dispel, but Bloom loses the initiative of unmasking him
by coveting his mask. Yet Bloom has one last test for Murphy
(' – Have you seen the rock of Gibraltar? Mr Bloom inquired'), to
which 'The sailor grimaced, chewing, in a way that might be read
as yes, ay or no' (Eu 611–13). Identifying himself with Murphy
despite his well-developed suspicions, Bloom is eager for 'news' of
Gibraltar, but the seaman is far from forthcoming ('I'm tired of all
the rocks in the sea' – Eu 622), and Bloom loses interest.

In *Ulysses* mysterious messages on occasion answer themselves
(all questions mysteriously 'contain' their own answers: periodical
texts that publish puzzles supply the solutions upside-down in
diminished print on a far-subsequent page). When Buck Mulligan
atop the Martello tower 'gave a long slow whistle of call, then paused
awhile in rapt attention', he is eventually rewarded when 'Two
strong shrill whistles answered through the calm' (Te 24–7) – if he had
not really expected them, he none the less took the coincidental
responses in his stride, but then again he may have calculatedly timed
his own whistle to correspond with the boat whistles at that time of
the morning. (As a 'priest' he can feel confident of responses.)

'STICKS AND STONES'

'Circe', a chapter that recapitulates with a vengeance the Ulyssean day and captures the basic mystique of the developing text, begins mysteriously with its own *'Whistles call and answer'* (Ci 9), and an operative discrepancy has been noted between the cloying sentiment of the call and the sexually unromantic answer, just as a similar difference characterised Mulligan's 'slow' whistle and the 'shrill' replies, Mulligan's status as a priest and the priesthood that he mocks. Implied 'returns' in *Ulysses* are often elliptical, and whereas Bloom once 'marked a florin (2/-) with three notches on the milled edge and tendered it in payment ... for possible, circuitous or direct, return' (It 981–4), he now admits that after six years the coin has not yet come back. Certain mysterious elements in *Ulysses* have their circuitous returns: having abandoned his statement of self in the sand in 'Nausicaa', Bloom 'flung his wooden pen away. The stick fell in silted sand, stuck. Now if you were trying to do that for a week on end you couldn't. Chance.' Immediately after, he concedes, 'We'll never meet again' (Na 1270–2). Inadvertently Bloom may actually have added his 'signature of all things' in the sand, a stick that may be a bit more permanent than his intended words.

The sequence that leads from the wooden pen to the farewell to Gerty ('But it was lovely. Goodbye, dear. Thanks. Made me feel so young' – Na 1272–3) may depend on the image of the upright stick in the sand (although sometimes a stick is just a stick). In the sexually charged 'Nausicaa' chapter the acknowledged climax had occurred coincidentally with the bursting forth in the sky of a Roman candle and Bloom's ejaculation:

> And then a rocket sprang and bang shot blind blank and O! then the Roman candle burst and it was like a sigh of O! and everyone cried O! O! in raptures and it gushed out of it a stream of rain gold hair threads and they shed and ah! they were all greeny dewy stars falling with golden, O so lovely, O, soft, sweet, soft!   (Na 736–40)

The pyrotechnic candle qualifies as a totem of Bloom's sexual potency, which in his subsequent state of detumescence he refers to prosaically as 'My fireworks. Up like a rocket, down like a stick' (Na 894–5). The wooden pen, impotent in that it fails to complete the message, is then flung aside, only to return symbolically to a new tumescence, a cycle beginning with erection and returning to re-surrection.

Were Bloom to read this 'signature of all things', he might assume that sometimes a stick is not just a stick; and Stephen who had walked and read signatures along the strand this morning, his ashplant in hand, seems unlikedly to be in the vicinity tomorrow to read again. Molly, however, might interpret the signs according to her own lights: in her Circean manifestation she reduces symbolic significance to the most mundane level, as she chastises Bloom: 'O Poldy, Poldy, you are a poor old stick in the mud! Go and see life. See the wide world' (Ci 329–30). For Molly once again there is no great mystery to uncover. As mystery-man-on-the-beach Leopold Bloom has had his magnificent moment, but for Molly the 'I am a' blank is easily filled in with a simple 'stick-in-the-mud', which Bloom in 'Eumaeus' distances from himself (somewhat too facilely) when he begins to contemplate that 'long sea' voyage:

> It was a subject of regret and absurd as well on the face of it and no small blame to our vaunted society that the man in the street, when the system really needed toning up, for the matter of a couple of paltry pounds, was debarred from seeing more of the world they lived in instead of being always and ever cooped up since my old stick-in-the-mud took me for a wife.   (Eu 539–44)

Newly 'embarked' on an imaginary voyage (to London presumably), Bloom shifts the perspective to the hypothetical man-in-the-street as being a stay-at-home, himself already at an English Music Hall hearing the usual kind of song about 'the old stick-in-the-mud who took me to wife', yet inadvertently bringing the issue full circle back to Molly and her characterisation of him.

'THE CHANGE FROM MAJOR TO MINOR'

The conventions of the mystery-thriller dictate that not only must the major enigma be satisfactorily (and even logically) resolved, but all minor mysteries as well, the complete timetable filled in, all motives accounted for, all loose ends tied up. These texts frame their characters within a locked room in a snowbound manor house inside a closed universe, what Michael Innes characterised as a mystery taking place in a submerged submarine. Conversely, *Ulysses* posits, in an open universe, a Dublin city and its environs containing thousands and accessible to the outside world. The mysteries of *Ulysses* are those of an ordinary day in an extraordinary universe, and are only mysteries because they contain and present unsolved and unresolved dilemmas and possibilities. The nobleman passes into the eternity of Sandymount strand with his anonymity preserved, and even Gerty's surname remains unavailable to Bloom. The man in the macintosh is slated to appear and reappear at diverse places both as himself and as other men in macintoshes, while a weary traveller, self-professed as a 'landlubber' (Eu 503), although 'at heart a born adventurer' (Eu 502), is in his revery transformed for the nonce from Leopold Bloom to Sinbad the Sailor, to exist as a perfect blank, encapsulated in a large round black dot (It 2332).

The passing of time, the failings of memory, and the human tendency toward self-deception create mysteries even in a novel that presumably occupies fewer than twenty-four hours. Whereas 'Circe' offers an arena in which non-events are more potent than assumed reality, 'Penelope' stages a potent recapitulation of events coloured by time, memory and self-protection. Molly's reactivation of her girlhood in Gibraltar produces a series of remembered and half-remembered names that have almost no previous existence in the text, except for Bloom's awareness of a 'lieutenant Mulvey that kissed her under the Moorish wall beside the gardens' (Na 889–90). All through the narrative Bloom and Stephen have played their various cards, each in the process of 'identifying' someone in some proximate relationship to themselves or of significance to them: now Molly makes her late entry in the field with her deck of cards. She uses her cards to read the future, but they are understandably as vague as Stephen's attempt at augury in reading the flights of birds (*AP*, p. 224). Molly had spread out her deck of cards that morning and now re-reads their significance in terms of the Stephen whom Bloom has only just 'introduced':

wait by God yes wait yes hold on he was on the cards this morning when I laid out the deck union with a young stranger neither dark nor fair you met before I thought it meant him but hes no chicken nor a stranger either besides my face was turned

the other way ... and didnt I dream something too yes there
was something about poetry in it. (Pe 1313–21)

Molly's process of reading parallels the narrational development
within the open universe of predictable and unpredictable possibilities in *Ulysses*: one mystery is solved on the basis of assumption
(Boylan in the cards), then re-solved on the basis of new evidence
(Boylan had masked Stephen), while neither resolution necessarily
is reliable (the stranger posited is a fiction within a suspect fictional
text: the cards of divination). Nor is that text substantial on its own
merits: it can be displaced or corroborated or superimposed upon
by an alternative text: dream divination. Yet there also lurks the
suspicion that Molly, like most readers of any fictional text that
they consider a realistic approximation of their own lives, supplies
a variant text outside the 'given' texts: wish-fulfilment. Stephen as
preferred stranger makes his entrance into Molly's thoughts in the
fictional form that she chooses, just as the strangers of the past
(Gardner and Mulvey and Hester Stanhope) are subject to her
fictionalising memory.

Molly's tendency to arrive at a particular name and fix it
thereafter in place allowed for a Harry Mulvey and a Hester
Stanhope, but the name that remains the most intriguing in
Molly's thoughts is that of her mother. Whatever actually became
of Molly's mother, she seems to have disappeared from the child's
life soon after the birth: Molly offers no recollection of a mother in
her life, but 'remembers' her obliquely and belatedly as she muses
over surnames that she might have had depending on whom she
married: 'my mother whoever she was might have given me a nicer
name the Lord knows after the lovely one she had Lunita Laredo'
(Pe 846–8). The reference is presumably to Señorita Laredo's choice
of Tweedy as her husband, rather than the naming of the baby
Marion, since it is patronymics that Molly is now concerned with
('Bloom ... its better than Breen or Briggs does brig or those awful
names with bottom in them Mrs Ramsbottom or some other kind
of a bottom Mulvey I wouldnt go mad about either or suppose I
divorced him Mrs Boylan' – Pe 842–6). The existence of an
orthodox Jewish Laredo family of long standing in Gibraltar has
been established, but the likelihood of the Laredos ever allowing a
daughter to marry a Christian British Army officer, or anyone
outside the faith, can be discounted, leaving the hypothetical
relationship between Tweedy and his Lunita as dangerously clan-

destine. Equally 'exotic' is the naming of a Laredo daughter Lunita, so that not only the tentative existence but also the tenuous naming of Lunita Laredo becomes highly doubtful. (That Molly has fixed on a mother named Lunita Laredo may indicate either her own predilections or the fictional writing of a name by someone else – most likely her father.) Molly's only other allusion to her shadowy mother is her claim to have inherited physical characteristics: 'Ive my mothers eyes and figure anyhow *he always said*' (Pe 890–2; emphasis added). The credited authority is of course her father, from whom she thinks she got her 'accent' ('all father left me in spite of his stamps' – Pe 889–90), indicative that Molly speaks with her father's voice.

'He always said': various networks of fabrications weave back to Brian Cooper Tweedy, for whom, unlike Lunita Laredo, there are sufficient clues from which to fabricate, if not solve, a complete mystery. Bloom conjectures about his father-in-law that he 'had brains enough to make that corner in stamps' (Ca 64–5), but if that is the case, there should have been proceeds for the daughter to inherit, yet Molly is definite that there was nothing left her 'in spite of his stamps' (Pe 890). Very little about the Tweedy fictions proves to be reliable, even provenance of the Bloom bed, which Bloom seems to have been led to suppose came 'All the way from Gibraltar.... Wonder what her father gave for it. Old style. Ah yes! of course. Bought it at the governor's auction. Got a short knock. Hard as nails at a bargain, old Tweedy' (Ca 60–3). But Molly demythologises the governor's bed and instead muses that 'the lumpy old jingly bed always reminds me of old Cohen I suppose he scratched himself in it often enough', admitting to herself that Bloom has been the object of a deception: 'he thinks father bought it from Lord Napier that I used to admire when I was a young girl because I told him' (Pe 1212–15). Her admission of this particular lie leaves open the possibilities that the various deceptions that have been practised on the naïve Poldy were arranged by either Molly or her father, or both in conjunction.

What Molly must also know about her father, but no one in Dublin necessarily knows, is his Army rank. Whether Bloom really believes that Tweedy was ever a Major ('I rose from the ranks, sir, and I'm proud of it', he recalls Tweedy telling him, in Tweedy's own voice – Ca 63–4) is problematical, but it may simply be a matter of Tweedy imposing that honorific on himself once he reached Dublin, although the drinkers at the Ormond remember something else instead, if they remember anything at all. Simon

Dedalus, Father Cowley and Ben Dollard co-author an indeterminate script as they go along, attesting to the tenuous nature of
Tweedy's identity, as well as Molly's:

– What's this her name was? A buxon lassy. Marion . . . ?
– Tweedy.
– Yes. Is she alive?
– And kicking.
– She was a daughter of . . .
– Daughter of the regiment.
– Yes, begad. I remember the old drummajor.
   Mr Dedalus struck, whizzed, lit, puffed savoury puff after
– Irish? I don't know, faith. Is she, Simon?
   Puff after stiff, a puff, strong, savoury, crackling.
– Buccinator muscle . . . What? . . . Bit rusty . . . O, she is . . . My
Irish Molly, O.
   He puffed a pungent plumy blast
– From the rock of Gibraltar . . . all the way.   (Si 502–15)

The myth of Molly and the Major/drummajor is created out of the
smoke of Si Dedalus's pipe, in brief unconnected puffs, with
lacunae created by ellipses on the printed page and uncertainty
masked as certainty in an area where no one is too meticulous
about accuracy. Truth to them relies on musical invention, on pipe
notes, and such operatic scripts as Donizetti's *The Daughter of the
Regiment*, where the daughter is 'adopted'.

   There is very little reason for Molly herself to lay particular stress
on her father's military career, except to be aware of his 'absence',
when she wants the privacy to read Mulvey's letter (her mode of
reading it was exhaustive, 'to find out by the handwriting or the
language of stamps' – Pe 767). At that important time in her day
'father was up at the drill instructing' (Pe 766–7), evidence that he
was only a sergeant-major and doing the instructing – unless 'drill
instructing' is a compound noun and the major (less likely) was
observing the drill instruction. 'Sergeant major' may be at the
bottom of the hierarchy for Tweedy, and 'major' his own fictionalisation, but in the augmented and fantastic world of 'Circe' a still
more exalted fiction is fabricated by a threatened Bloom attempting
to augment his own credentials:

My wife, I am the daughter of a most distinguished commander, a gallant upstanding gentleman, what do you call him, Major-general Brian Tweedy, one of Britain's fighting men who helped to win our battles. Got his majority for the heroic defence of Rorke's Drift. (Ci 777–81)

Whatever the father told the daughter about her mother and whatever the daughter has been telling herself about her mother, the imaginative fiction of 'Lunita Laredo' has taken shadowy shape, and even Molly knows enough not to dwell on it too frequently for fear of its complete disintegration. Paternity for Stephen may be a legal fiction, but in the mysterious case of Lunita Laredo (an unlikely name to begin with), maternity may be a fiction as well – and not necessarily a legal one. The stigma of her mother, however, had been a factor in the marriage to Leopold Bloom: 'he hadnt an idea about my mother till we were engaged otherwise hed never have got me so cheap as he did', she muses (Pe 282–4). She also credits her Jewish heritage as a factor in attracting Bloom, recalling the evening when they first met and their mutual interest in each other: 'we stood staring at one another for about 10 minutes as if we met somewhere I suppose on account of my being jewess looking after my mother' (Pe 1183–5).

But if Molly assumes that her Poldy is particularly fascinated by her Jewish beauty, she may be missing the significance that Spanish beauty has in attracting him. In 'Lotus Eaters' he delights in 'the darkness of her eyes. Looking at me, the sheet up to her eyes, Spanish' (Lo 494–5); in 'Sirens' he again considers her 'Big spanishy eyes' (Si 808); and in 'Nausicaa' he dozes off to images and essences of 'perfume your wife black hair heave under embon *señorita* young eyes' (Na 1281–2). In 'Eumaeus' Bloom shows Stephen a photograph of Molly, asking specifically, 'Do you consider, by the by, he said, thoughtfully selecting a faded photo which he laid on the table, that a Spanish type?' (Eu 1425–6), and there seems to be little doubt that he himself does. (He had further exoticised Molly when he contended, 'That's where Molly can knock spots off them. It's the blood of the south. Moorish' – Na 968–9.) But Molly's is not the only Spanishy photo that Bloom carries with him, since there is also an erotic photo of 'buccal coition between nude señorita (rere presentation, superior position) and nude torero (fore presentation, inferior position' – It 1809–11), which Molly is fully aware of and admits that she resembles: 'Im a little like that dirty bitch in that Spanish photo he has' (Pe 563–4). The Molly of the past (the picture she shows to Stephen) and the erotic señorita retain their significance as surrogates for the present Molly, and Bloom retains his fascination with her Spanishy beauty. What Molly assumes is Jewish may for Bloom be Spanish, and between them they maintain those private fictions of their own that seem to approximate each other without actually completing each other.

A *Ulysses* Bookshelf

This list includes resource works at present available for research on James Joyce's *Ulysses*:

Benstock, Shari and Benstock, Bernard, *Who's He When He's at Home: A James Joyce Directory* (Champaign: University of Illinois Press, 1980).

Bauerle, Ruth, *The James Joyce Songbook* (New York: Garland, 1982).

Bowen, Zack, *Musical Allusions in the Works of James Joyce: Early Poetry through Ulysses* (Albany: State University of New York Press, 1974).

Deming, Robert H., *Bibliography of James Joyce Studies* (Lawrence: University of Kansas Libraries, 1964; 2nd edn: Boston, Mass.: G. K. Hall, 1977).

Deming, Robert H., *James Joyce: The Critical Heritage*, 2 vols (New York: Routledge and Kegan Paul, 1970).

Ellmann, Richard, *Letters of James Joyce*, vols 2 and 3 (New York: Viking, 1966).

Ellmann, Richard, *Selected Letters of James Joyce* (New York: Viking, 1975).

Gabler, Hans Walter, *Ulysses: A Critical and Synoptic Edition*, 3 vols (New York: Garland, 1984).

Gifford, Don with Seidman, Robert J., *Notes for Joyce: An Annotation of James Joyce's Ulysses* (New York: E. P. Dutton, 1974); revised and expanded as *Ulysses Annotated* (Berkeley, Calif.: University of California Press, 1989).

Gilbert, Stuart, *Letters of James Joyce*, vol. 1 (New York: Viking, 1957).

Groden, Michael *et al.*, *The James Joyce Archive*, 16 vols on *Ulysses* (New York: Garland, 1977–80).

Groden, Michael, *James Joyce's Manuscripts: An Index to the James Joyce Archive* (New York: Garland, 1980).

Gunn, Ian and McCleery, Alistair, *The Ulysses Pagefinder* (Edinburgh: Split Pea Press, 1988).

Hanley, Miles L., *Word Index to James Joyce's Ulysses* (Madison: University of Wisconsin Press, 1937).

Hart, Clive and Knuth, Leo, *A Topographical Guide to James Joyce's Ulysses* (Colchester: A Wake Newslitter Press, 1975).

Hodgart, Matthew J. C. and Worthington, Mabel, *Song in the Works of James Joyce* (New York: Columbia University Press, 1959).

Macaré, Helen H., *A 'Ulysses' Phrasebook* (Portola Valley, Calif.: Woodside Priory, 1981).

Rice, Thomas Jackson, *James Joyce: A Guide to Research* (New York: Garland, 1982).

Staley, Thomas F., *An Annotated Critical Bibliography of James Joyce* (New York: St Martin's Press, 1989).

Steppe, Wolfhard, *A Handlist to James Joyce's 'Ulysses'* (New York: Garland, 1986).

Thornton, Weldon, *Allusions in Ulysses* (Chapel Hill: University of North Carolina Press, 1968).

Index